PRAISE FOR # PASTORS OF PROMISE

When Jack Hayford speaks, sensible people listen and learn. I include
myself in that group! Jack is a giant and doesn't know it; furthermore
he doesn't need it. His head has not been turned from success and
high visibility. His love for the Lord is contagious!

JOE C. ALDRICH
President, Multnomah College and Biblical Seminary, Portland, Oregon

Most Bible books are named after men because we need examples to
show us God's way. Jack Hayford's name could be the title as well as the
author of this book because he is a pastor of promise. A generation of
pastors around the world knows and honors him as a man of integrity
and a pastor who writes what he lives.

LEITH ANDERSON
Pastor, Wooddale Church, Eden Prairie, Minnesota

I listen to Jack Hayford because of who he is, and that is
why you need to read this book, spun out of a huge pastor's
heart of love and integrity.

NEIL ANDERSON
Founder and President, Freedom in Christ Ministries, La Habra, California

I consider it an honor to know Jack Hayford; he is my friend and co-laborer.
Jack is a pastor of pastors, a true leader. Throughout the years I have
admired his honesty and openness concerning ministry. His leadership
principles are a true portrayal of a biblical discipler of leaders.

SONNY ARGUINZONI
Pastor, Founder of Victory Outreach Ministries International
La Puente, California

Few pastors can speak to the pastor's lofty role with more authority
and credibility than Dr. Jack Hayford. He really "walks the walk,"
therefore, he can "talk the talk." His success as a pastor and world-
renowned church leader, coupled with his moral and spiritual
authenticity, clearly enable him to perform the valuable service
provided by *Pastors of Promise*. Read this book and be blessed.

BISHOP CHARLES E. BLAKE
Senior Pastor, West Angeles Church of God in Christ, Los Angeles, California

PRAISE FOR PASTORS OF PROMISE

in any pastor's life, whether that conversation is in person or through his excellent writings. Jack Hayford is must reading.

STEPHEN GREEN
Senior Pastor, First Church of the Nazarene of Pasadena, Pasadena, California

Jack Hayford has earned the right to be heard. He has been successfully pastoring people for 40 years. His children are now grown and they love and respect their father. His wife adores him and his long-term friendships are too numerous to count. He honors the integrity of the Scriptures and enjoys the life of the Spirit. He is trustworthy, joyful, strong, yet sensitive and, of vital importance to me, he is neither cynical nor weary. Instead, he provides for us a model of successful longevity. I highly recommend this book.

TED HAGGARD
Pastor, New Life Church, Colorado Springs, Colorado

Pastor Jack Hayford brings to the pastoral office an unusual brilliance of mind, exceptional talent, remarkable skills, a righteous character and an abundance of spiritual gifts. He has become a model for tens of thousands of pastors and church leaders in this country and around the world. Very few leaders execute the office of pastor with such balance and dynamic life, but we all can benefit from his skillful pen and anointed ministry.

DR. JOHN HOLLAND
President, International Church of the Foursquare Gospel, Los Angeles, California

I commend to you this book, as it confronts us with our responsibility to be generative in our biblical discipling of men to be the husbands, the fathers and the servant-leaders after God's own heart.

DR. JOHN A. HUFFMAN, JR.
Senior Minister, St. Andrew's Presbyterian Church, Newport Beach, California

Pastors of Promise is a timely word from a godly man with a desperately needed message of hope for all of us.

BILL HYBELS
Senior Pastor, Willow Creek Community Church, South Barrington, Illinois

Pastor Jack Hayford is known for the many qualities that form his reputation as a spiritual leader. In the forefront of these is personal integrity. He is

immensely qualified to address this and other matters of importance, as he shares
from his heart, to the spiritual leaders of today. I thank God for him.

GREG LAURIE

Pastor, Harvest Christian Fellowship, Riverside, California

Jack Hayford is a model of diligence, faithfulness to the Lord and enduring
loyalty to a local church. It's the long haul that manifests integrity and proven
character. Many have fallen in the battle. Hayford is still standing—
a tribute to God's marvelous grace.

JOHN MacARTHUR

Pastor-Teacher, Grace Community Church, Sun Valley, California

Whenever a pastor asks me, "John, who has been your mentor?" I give two names:
my dad and Jack Hayford. For years, I have sat at the feet of great church leaders
so I can learn and grow. No one has taught me more through words and walk than
Jack Hayford. When I am with him, I feel close to God.

JOHN C. MAXWELL

Founder, Injoy, San Diego, California

Pastors of Promise is long overdue. The challenge for integrity, faithfulness,
purity and effectiveness for God is presented in a phenomenal way.
This is important reading for every pastor.

BOB MOOREHEAD

Senior Pastor, Overlake Christian Church, Kirkland, Washington

Pastors of Promise is a road map for avoiding the obstacles of ministry, helping
pastors navigate a healthy course through them. Jack's integrity and leadership
skills have resulted in his great success in ministry, and I encourage any pastor to
take advantage of the hard-earned knowledge presented in *Pastors of Promise*. I only
wish I'd had the benefit of these insights when I was starting out 27 years ago.

DOUG MURREN

Pastor, Eastside Foursquare Church, Kirkland, Washington

Jack Hayford, one of the truly great pastors in America, is also a very effective
pastors' pastor as he shares the secrets of dynamic, supernatural preaching and
leadership in the Church today.

DR. LLOYD JOHN OGILVIE

Chaplain, United States Senate, Washington, D.C.

PRAISE FOR PASTORS OF PROMISE

Jack Hayford writes from the rich tradition of a proven ministry
and from the depths of personal integrity to inspire all God's leaders to
press on in our high and holy calling. As you read *Pastors of Promise*,
you will discover that the Lord has given him the tongue of the
learned that he might know how to speak a timely and stirring word
to pastors in this day of great promise.

JAMES RYLE

Pastor, Boulder Valley Vineyard, Longmont, Colorado

In the church of today, the need of the hour is for pastors to step up their call.
Jack Hayford is one who has done that for years, and has been used by God to
mentor pastors around the world. Now he offers to those who have not been
privileged to meet with him personally the result of a lifetime of biblical
and practical insights about pastoring. In *Pastors of Promise*, Jack's passion
is for pastors to step up and into their call in these days of God's
imminent grace in the Church. With a possible revival of the
Church on the horizon, *Pastors of Promise* is just what
pastors need to prepare for this eventuality.

DALE SCHLAFER

Vice President/Renewal and Revival, Promise Keepers, Denver, Colorado

Of all the pastors I have known, admired and learned from, no one has
commanded more profound respect, affection and esteem than Jack Hayford.
He is my spiritual and professional hero. Now he has written one of the
most important books for our time.

DR. ROBERT SCHULLER

The Crystal Cathedral, Garden Grove, California

Jack Hayford personifies the very best definition of the word "Pastor."
His tone is sincere and his words believable. I thank God for the input of
Jack Hayford into my personal life.

DR. MORRIS SHEATS

Senior Pastor, Hillcrest Church, Dallas, Texas

Christians in America recognize Jack Hayford as not only a pastor to
fellow pastors, but also as a national pastor to the entire Body of Christ.
No other pastor on the Christian scene is more in demand, is more acceptable
to more churches and denominations, and speaks more directly to the present state

PRAISE FOR PASTORS OF PROMISE

of the Church than Jack Hayford. His new book *Pastors of Promise* should be on the shelf of every Christian leader, both clerical and lay, in America.

VINSON SYNAN
Dean, School of Divinity, Regent University, Virginia Beach, Virginia

I know of no other pastor in America who has had a greater impact upon other pastors than Dr. Jack Hayford. He has done a masterful job of communicating his pastor's heart to other men and women in pastoral ministry. With his keen insights, his remarkable transparency and his impeccable integrity, he has influenced the lives of thousands of church leaders.

B. E. UNDERWOOD
Pastor, The Pentecostal Holiness Church, Oklahoma City, Oklahoma

In his book *Pastors of Promise*, Jack Hayford draws from his rich background of ministry in every phase of church life. Utilizing keen insights from his own experience as one of the nation's leading pastors and as a man whose life and ministry have touched literally thousands of pastors, Pastor Jack provides an inspired methodology for pastoral leaders to make the most of this hour of destiny to motivate, model and mentor others in the kingdom of God. This is one of those books that will be a *must* for every pastor and church leader interested in a renewed anointing of the Holy Spirit.

DR. PAUL WALKER
Pastor, Mount Paran Church of God, Atlanta, Georgia

Jack Hayford has been a friend, colleague and mentor to me for nearly 20 years. I am sure he doesn't know how grateful I am for his leadership in this area in that most of the above has come through the modeling he has exhibited, as well as the teachings, both in print and on tape. Every leader will benefit by reading this book.

JOHN WIMBER
International Director, Association of Vineyard Churches, Anaheim, California

Jack Hayford does a phenomenal job defining the pastor's role in today's society. He also offers practical guidelines for building and developing biblical leadership in men.

ED YOUNG
Pastor, Fellowship of Las Colinas, Irving, Texas

THE HAYFORD PASTORS SERIES

Jack Hayford

PASTORS
OF
PROMISE

POINTING TO CHARACTER AND HOPE AS
THE KEYS TO FRUITFUL SHEPHERDING

Regal

A Division of Gospel Light
Ventura, California, U.S.A.

Published by Regal Books
A Division of Gospel Light
Ventura, California, U.S.A.
Printed in U.S.A.

Regal Books is a ministry of Gospel Light, an evangelical Christian publisher dedicated to serving the local church. We believe God's vision for Gospel Light is to provide church leaders with biblical, user-friendly materials that will help them evangelize, disciple and minister to children, youth and families.

It is our prayer that this Regal book will help you discover biblical truth for your own life and help you meet the needs of others. May God richly bless you.

For a free catalog of resources from Regal Books/Gospel Light please contact your Christian supplier or call 1-800-4-GOSPEL.

Library of Congress Cataloging-in-Publication Data
Hayford, Jack W.
     Pastors of promise / Jack Hayford.
        p. cm.
     Includes bibliographical references.
     ISBN 0-8307-1747-1 (hardcover)
     1. Pastoral theology. 2. Church work with men. I. Title.
BV4011.H348 1997   96-50192
259'.081—dc21   CIP

1 2 3 4 5 6 7 8 9 10 11 12 13 14 15 16 17 18 / 04 03 02 01 00 99 98 97

Rights for publishing this book in other languages are contracted by Gospel Literature International (GLINT). GLINT also provides technical help for the adaptation, translation and publishing of Bible study resources and books in scores of languages worldwide. For further information, contact GLINT, P.O. Box 4060, Ontario, CA 91761-1003, U.S.A., or the publisher.

CONTENTS

PART II

  - Perspective on the pastoral potential in motivating men to a local program of growth through dynamic gatherings.
  - Pointers on program content and scheduling help toward a practical formation of a "men's growth" gathering.
  - Proven curricular focus is provided, the outlined material sampling the *10 concepts* essential to men's growth in Christ.

ACKNOWLEDGMENTS

After having written 30 books, one would think the task would become a little easier, smoother in delivery and more prompt in arrival. This book is, in terms of my experience, the ultimate contradiction of that proposition. Accordingly, I want to accept every blame for the fact it has been nationally "announced" for months before I was even finished, with orders being placed by dear and faithful Christian booksellers.

They had been advised of a "release" date by my oh-so-patient publisher at Regal Books, only to discover I was still "in labor" at the "book maternity ward."

In any case, the "child" has arrived, and I only hope the reader will approve and say, "What a marvelous addition to the family!" I also hope you will know it is more than platitudinous that I express my deep thanks to key people who attended the "birth."

To Bill Greig Jr., Bill Greig III and Kyle Duncan—your understanding, patience, support and brotherly kindness always overwhelm me. (Thank your dear wives for patience with any frustration about my lateness with this book, which may have indirectly reduced your ability to relate at a breakfast or dinner table, but which unrelatedness you so kindly suppressed whenever you were with me! You are incredible gentlemen!) A deep thank you also to your staff and editors, especially Kim Bangs and Virginia Woodard.

To my dear daughter and son-in-law, Christa and Doug Andersen— my "Very-Proud-Of-You" thanks! To this couple goes a special tribute for the excellent work that has afforded the bulk of Part II in this book. The challenge of distilling representative teachings I have used with the men of our congregation—illustrating the 10 curricular concepts we use—was met and mastered by Christa and Doug. Their achievement of this task, amid the business of their own duties as pastors (and while sojourning a pregnancy as well as the remodeling of their newly-moved-into house), gives all the reason in the world for a multiple salute!

Our pastoral team at The Church On The Way is a large part of the reason for much of what I have learned; I hardly know how to honor them adequately. To all of you brothers and sisters, and your spouses and children—*THANK YOU! Pastors of Promise* could be written with credibility only because you model its principles constantly and faithfully among and before our assembly. If I am a fruitful pastor at all, you are the preponderance of the reason!

Anna, you are all through this book, as you are throughout the fullness and the details of my life. I love you and thank you, for the fact that you always serve beside me as "one also called." Among our congregation, everybody knows you are "the key" to anything I am. I praise our Lord Jesus for you daily—He is "The Key" that opened the door to our life together, and who has locked us for a lifetime in such a happy union. *Your* promise, faithfully, lovingly and supportively kept, is without question the reason I have become a "pastor of promise."

Jack Hayford

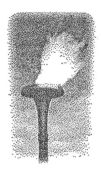

PLEASE READ THIS, FIRST!

Dear "Fellow" Pastor,

This opening letter is to clarify three things: (1) *Who* I am writing this book to, (2) *Why* I have written it the way I have and (3) *What* I hope you will find in it.

First, this book is written to men who pastor.

Although some pastors who read these words may disagree, I personally am deeply convicted that the Bible *does* include the possibility of a *pastoral* ministry in the list of those a woman may serve. I have, however, not written this book in neuter or multiple gender.

I have written to *men* who pastor because I am more confident that I may be on target with them. A woman pastor faces a variety of challenges a man does not encounter, and I believe only a woman can effectively address those. As for the many areas where a man's and a woman's call and concerns parallel (and they are in the majority, in pastoral terms), a woman may find reading this book useful. I have a particular passion in this (first) volume, however, and it is focused on *the pastor as a man;* on how a man *thinks* about his pastoral task—and especially about other men. Which leads to—

Second, this book is about "fathering" men.

A distinct mission that is within the privileged call of a pastor is the call to "father" other men. It is a *high promise*—not unlike that which Abraham received. I want to talk about this because God is *very earnestly reaching to men today*—and the pastor is a "key" in this process.

Third, you will only find part *of the pastoral office addressed here—the* beginning *part.*

This book is intended to achieve only *one-third* of my task in seeking to outline my view and approach to pastoral ministry. Two books will follow this one—each one year after the other—1998 and 1999.

My objective in this book is to focus on the *foundations of fruitfulness,* to offer a mind-set and a *pathway.* I believe this is a right way to *think* about pastoral leadership, and thinking that way will bring stability and trustworthiness to a pastor's style—and he will *endure.*

I also believe that such a clearheaded approach will result in a clear-eyed integrity—in his own *heart,* in his *home,* in his *marriage,* in his *study,* in his *walk with God,* in his *congregation,* in his *private counsel,* in his *public leadership,* in his *dealings with men and women,* in his *relationships with staff and laity,* in his *approach to the community*—in his *life.*

So please sit down with me.

In another book beyond this one I will focus on the pastor's *passion,* and after that I will address the pastor's *purpose.* Here, let me discuss your *promise*—and best of all, the Father's promise to us both.

I am honored to have this time with you.

A fellow shepherd,
Jack Hayford

PART I

CHAPTER ONE HIGHLIGHTS:

- Nothing is so distinct as the sense of "call." It is the one reason for being in ministry—and the one most attacked.
- Six unforgettable calls, kept in focus with the Holy Spirit's help, assist my maintaining a holy sensitivity to issues within my larger "call."
- This book is offered for reasons of passion, compassion and promise.

*But what things were gain to me,
these I have counted loss for
Christ...that I may gain Christ...
[and] press toward the goal for
the prize of the upward call.*

PHILIPPIANS 3:7,8,14

WHEN GOD CALLS A SHEPHERD

Jackie Vernon's name is among the least likely to provide the opening words for a book to spiritual leaders in the Church of our Lord Jesus Christ. He was a comedian—a laugh-getter of a generation ago—whose deadpan, expressionless face opened routines with the words that declared his gratitude for having any work at all. He would explain: "See, there isn't much call for people in my line of work. I'm a shepherd."

The audience howled, because the comedian made his crack in the urbane setting of a twentieth-century television studio or a Las Vegas showroom. Shepherds were as out of place and unnecessary to the situation as a blacksmith's anvil to a jet-engine mechanic, and shepherding as irrelevant in the minds of the crowd being entertained as the same smithy's hammer to a computer repairman.

I laughed, too. The line was too funny for even a shepherd not to enjoy the humor. Yet I never heard the words without reflecting that they were laden with potential *double entendre* as far as I was concerned. Because I *was* a shepherd, and still am—having just stepped into my fortieth year of pastoral service to our Lord's Church—I thought to myself even then: *I wonder if my vocation is laughable in the world's eyes.* That thought tempted me to feel a kind of embarrassment at my own laughter.

This was not because I believed the comic had any snide or evil intent in his line, nor did I really suspect the crowd was actually laughing at pastors. I still felt a vulnerability, however, to the world's tendency to see spiritual values—and leaders—as irrelevant. I was neither gripped by para-noid suspicions, nor feeling my calling as a shepherd of souls was inferior or irrelevant to any other vocation. The words of Paul, however, came to mind; words that expressed his perspective about the attitudes some have toward spiritual leaders. The very nature of our calling as shepherds puts us at the mercy of these same judgments today.

> *I think that God has displayed us, the apostles, last, as men con-demned to death; for we have been made a spectacle to the world, both to angels and to men. We are fools for Christ's sake, but you are wise in Christ! We are weak, but you are strong! You are dis-tinguished, but we are dishonored!* (1 Cor. 4:9,10).

Though the reference was meant for an ancient apostle, it may equally well be said of the contemporary pastor, for the role of "shepherds" is too rarely valued. During the 40-year span of my min-istry, a radically dimin-ished view of the social significance of "the min-istry" has evolved. I remember how in mid-twentieth century North America some books

A PASTOR POURING OUT HIS LIFE TO SERVE SIN-SICK SOULS, USU-ALLY RECEIVING SMALL MATERIAL REWARD, IS COMMONLY SLURRED AS "IN IT FOR THE MONEY."

about pastoral work warned the reader against the temptation of entering the ministry for the sake of the social prestige the position could provide.

Today, such a remark would be seen as a joke. Yet multitudes are not laughing. They are the shepherds into whom God, at some moment in the past, *breathed the promise wrapped in a call*—a call to serve Him in a role of spiritual leadership.

THEY ARE THE CALLED

Three years ago, I invited pastors across the nation to write to me and describe as well as they could, "The reason I'm in the ministry." Unsurprisingly, yet a very telling fact, almost to the person the answer was the same: "I was called by God."

Anticipating that kind of answer, I had asked for a brief elaboration of the response. The testimonies ran the gamut from childhood experiences to miraculous deliverances, from inner impressions or "the Voice of the Lord" to circumstantial guidance confirmed by trusted friends or other pastors.

People do not really become pastors for other reasons. In a generation now distant, pastors were held in esteem. In the pre-1960s era, "a man of the cloth" was valued in secular society and invited into the corridors of community influence along with educators, physicians, civic leaders, judges and successful business people. However, we are living in another time.

Today's church leader lives in America's so-called "post-Christian" era, in the cynical post-fallen-TV-evangelist setting. This era has shrouded ministry with a cloud of public doubt that has brought the once-designated *highest* calling to often be regarded as less than the lowest. Perhaps it is a commentary about both our society and its times that a prostitute working her latest "trick" is virtually dignified as "a member of the world's oldest profession," but a pastor pouring out his life to serve sin-sick souls, usually receiving small material reward, is commonly slurred as "in it for the money."

Still, the primary explanation for the fact that in the United States alone more than a half million such dedicated servants labor tirelessly, serving humanity in the name of God for one reason, can be described in two words: *"I'm called."*

Critics may attribute it to "guilt motivation," but pastors describe their mission as born of "a love for God and man." Skeptics sneer in smirking ignorance, suggesting that the pastoral vocation is only born of a desire to control the vulnerable or manipulate the gullible. Cynics spit their disdain at *all* clergymen, on the empty proposition that the evidence of moral pollution or financial corruption among a handful of exceptions justifies their judgment on all. While a society echoes the barbed commentary of mockers, not a day goes by that society is not being reached and rescued at a hundred thousand places by the silent, relentless, untiring and unselfish service of its unsung shepherds of souls. The reason: They answered "a call."

Called from "Beyond"

No humanly conspired or psychologically generated source or power can explain this phenomenon. It is more than a mysterious human motivation; it is a mighty and a heavenly one—"a call from the 'beyond' by the One above all!" Nothing else could cause capable, intelligent men and women to leave or refrain from more profitable or more socially accepted enterprises.

Of course, some quacks, kooks and crazies claim the same "call" we do, and some sensible, dedicated people in other professions have a deep sense of mission. Beyond all these, however, an almost unfathomably deep and broad reality looms—large and strong. It is the throb and pulse of "the call of God," and we know it.

It extends deeper, wider and higher than any other sense of vocation, however valid, transcending even the inner urges of people who have lofty goals—those of scientists, writers, athletes, explorers and teachers. For, as shepherds who have been "called of God," we have answered an inescapably insistent summons; we are committed to serve a cause that pursues values earth can't quantify, and offers hope unto an era when earth will have vaporized.

SIX CALLS I CAN'T FORGET

A recent alert to my own soul as a shepherd brought me to a confrontation with six "calls" I need to keep in focus, as the Holy Spirit helps me maintain a holy sensitivity to foundational issues within my larger "call" as an under-shepherd of the Great Shepherd. The following six "calls within my call" can too easily become subordinated to other "things." I need to hear, then find the way today:

1. To define and focus my personal call.

The information explosion that summons my attention to a thousand matters of miscellany, and the social pressures that seek to redefine pastoral mission, require my review of "who and what am I—*really!*" Paul's words to Timothy, "Stir up *your* gift" need to be heard afresh.

2. To remember (and pursue) my primary call—prayer.

Every pastor faces a calendar of demands, from meetings to administrative duties to answering "counseling" expectations by parishioners. These are not unimportant, but they are secondary. I must never forget the apostle's words, "We will give ourselves to prayer and ministry of the Word."

3. To walk in mindfulness of my Savior's call.

A recurrent weariness, depression or sense of staleness tends to overtake the souls of leaders. That is why I need regularly to hear Jesus say—to ME, "I am the vine," and let a fresh surge of the vital life of *Himself* flow through me (John 15:5); or keep mindful that His "Come unto Me" is as directed to me in my present setting as it is to the blindest lost soul (Matt. 11).

4. To join in praise with the call to worship.

Preoccupations with the multitudinous things that clog the pastor's mind when a service is in motion make heartfelt worship a difficult pursuit at the moment. No judgment to pass here. However, the Holy Spirit's "worship awakening" necessitates my own pastoral heart preparation *earlier*, so I have indeed *led* the sheep to "Enter into His gates with thanksgiving, and into His courts with praise" (Ps. 100).

5. To sustain a passion for extending the gospel call.

I must never forget the partnership I have with the Holy Spirit in issuing an invitation to eternal souls to come to the eternal Savior: "And the Spirit and the bride say, 'Come!' And let him who hears say, 'Come!'" (Rev. 22:17). This is not a matter of evangelical ritual; it is a matter of biblical wisdom and obedience.

6. To grow a people sensitive to the final call.

A mix of substance and superficiality abound in today's Church, around the subject of prophecy and the Second Coming of our Lord Jesus Christ. However impatient the superficial may cause me to become, I am still responsible under Christ to be certain my flock is ever mindful of His words, *"Surely I come quickly."*

HOW DO YOU DESCRIBE A CALL?

"A call" cannot be described in any one way, but those who have "heard" it recognize the constraint it contains, and cannot do anything else. God's "call" is a composite—a magnificent combination of factors that can be found in opening the pages of Scripture, and seeing the responses to His voice calling the ancients. To read their responses to His words is to feel the same heartbeat that resonates in the minds and souls of those He calls today.

- They have answered the summons of the Savior, like Peter, James, John and Andrew, hearing Him say to *them*—"Follow me, and I will make you fishers of men."
- They have chosen to follow in Abraham's footsteps, "Going out, not knowing where," because they hold in their hearts his same hope for a place and a people.
- They have experienced Isaiah's sense of personal inadequacy in the presence of God's holiness, but have received His cleansing and responded with their own, "Here am I, send me."
- They have overcome Jonah's fears, resisted Balaam's deceit and refused Simon's greediness, seeking to minister Barnabas's comfort, John's love, Elijah's miracles and Solomon's wisdom.
- They have felt Jeremiah's inescapable assignment as being preordained to ministry before birth, and known Elijah's doubts of personal significance, wondering if anyone else cares anymore.

Whatever their circumstances—beyond last Sunday's low ebb, beyond today's discouragement, beyond a society's scorn, tempted to feelings of worthlessness, a consummate conviction remains—an inner compulsion that brings a reannouncement of Paul's cry: *"The love of Christ constrains me...and, woe is me if I preach not the gospel!"*

Yes, today, some people still attest to the value of a spiritual shepherd, and both perceive and honor our mission. Wherever people are wise enough to recognize their need as sheep, godly leaders are appreciated, and whatever value society may or may not place on shepherds, God has made His opinion clear:

The Almighty holds shepherds in very high regard, and His Word reveals sheep tending as a high-level office in heaven's books. It shows the role of *shepherding* as being filled with significance—to be defined and rewarded on the highest terms.

- *Leadership is key to its definition*; seeing God has assigned the term "shepherds" to those in the highest offices of human responsibility, calling kings, judges, political officials and teachers, as are priests and prophets (see Jer. 25; Ezek. 34; Nah. 3).
- *Love is the reward for its effective exercise;* seeing that among the most endearing terms both the Old and New Testaments apply to the Lord Himself is the title "Shepherd"; a love expressed by those who have found Him faithful (see Ps. 23; John 10).
- *Life-giving truth is entrusted to those serving this role;* seeing that shepherds were the first of humankind to receive the announcement that the Savior had been born, and thereby were first to spread the best news this world has ever heard (see Luke 2).

The combined elements inherent in those facts not only demonstrate God's validation of the role of the shepherd, but they also evidence the reason the pastoral office holds such promised possibilities—and *requirements*. The call to shepherding is:

1. Charged with divinely assigned high responsibility to lead, to model and to govern in His kingdom, and thereby our task is one of great accountability before God;
2. Granted the profound privilege of rescuing and serving deep need, and thereby we often are recipients of great affection from those to whom we have ministered the love of God; and
3. Endowed with the highest trust—the eternal gospel placed upon our lips, thereby putting us at the pivotal point of relaying and multiplying the spread of heaven's message to mankind.

Our call is by no means a "leftover" assignment. By God's definition, it is contemporarily relevant and eternally significant—and *always marvelously filled with promise.* Four decades of shepherding have proven to me that, contrary to the comedian's line, a greater need than ever exists for people "in this line of work."

ENCOURAGING PASTORS

During the past three weeks, while breaking away for a change of pace at one of Anna's and my favorite hideaways, I had the opportunity (and her permission!) to accept a couple of pulpit invitations. Both were at pastorates served by dedicated couples who were discipled for pastoral ministry because of our influence. Of course, a great deal more than formal professional interest attended our visits, both with the couples in private and their congregations in public, but I had this book on my mind, too, as I had begun writing it.

One of these couples is in the middle of watching burgeoning growth take place in a new congregation they planted: the bright, young congregation, the new subdivision community, and the refreshing creativity of the imaginative pastoral team—all provide an air of excitement.

The second couple is forging a comeback path. The couple accepted the call to a congregation ripped apart in the pain and shame of the aftermath of the preceding pastor's moral failure and financial irresponsibility. A small but growing number of years are accumulating now, but the people and the community that has been watching closely are coming to renew trust. The church has not only recovered, but is also growing—and genuine joy and spiritual health is flowing there.

I could relate other stories—such as a congregation located *near* a burgeoning church, whose pastor is discouraged, unable to understand why his flock does not grow too. As I write these words, somewhere a hundred *faithful* shepherd-husbands are wrestling with demons of deception that are luring them toward compromise. They have not surrendered yet, but spirits of fear and confusion have swirled a dust cloud of blindness that is setting up a "fall"—unless a breakthrough of divine grace born of power prayer, by people who care for their pastors, strikes down the darkness.

THREE REASONS FOR WRITING THIS BOOK

All the previous information flavors my thought and motive as I set forward. Here I am—invited to the task *and privilege* of writing to pastors. Frankly, no one is adequate to pursue such an enterprise. Given today's multifaceted expectations of men and women in pastoral work, an encyclopedia would not suffice. Further, scores of recently published books to pastors, joined to thousands surviving from preceding decades, could be enough to stop me in my tracks.

So why *am* I writing this book?! The answer can be summed up in three words: *passion, compassion and promise.*

My *passion* is born of a constraint. I do not believe myself to be wiser than any others who have already written to pastors, but my circumstance and exposure of years have given me a passion for pastors. For 20 years, I have spoken to an annual average of more than 20,000 pastors, usually in conferences, but also in other media, because I love being with and caring for these "called ones." Pastors and other spiritual leaders top my priority list for time and personal investment, only being second in importance to the charge of my own pastorate's duties.

I also feel a deep *compassion for pastors.* I know full well how the grandeur of the call itself, and how the richness of promise and significance of purpose that summons us to pastoring, can set us up for disappointment. The shepherd's task is pursued in a hot box of personal pressures that can squeeze out his life. They include battlefields of spiritual warfare in which calculated satanic attacks are designed to break his spirit, and the uncharted terrain of challenges containing potential pitfalls waiting to destroy his ministry. The grandest of our God-given opportunities seem always to be met by the greatest of the adversary's strategies. So I have a heart of concern, desiring to stand with those who struggle, warn those in jeopardy and encourage those en route to victory.

Above passion and compassion, is the PROMISE! More than anything I feel today, is the gripping sense that a divinely ordained, high season of *promise* is coming upon the Church. As I look at our "hour" in history, and its awaiting mixture of blessing and adversity, I am possessed by one overarching conviction: The season opening right now is unmatched by any time the people of God have ever known for offering promise and possibilities!

God-ordained open doors are beckoning us to enter a thousand arenas with hope. Human sin and failure have worked their worst, and hell's darkness is thicker than ever on the collective mind of humankind. Still, to be a pastor today is to hold heaven's highest hope—and to extend its power in the face of our world's darkest hour.

Here is the promise supporting that hope:

Where sin abounds, grace much more abounds!

All that keeps it from being "an incredible promise" (Rom. 4:20) is our Father's absolute credibility when He gives a promise, and when He issues a "call." He *has* called—He has called *you,* or you would not be reading this. He has called me too, along with you, and neither of us can honestly deny it, even during those dark hours when the liar is having one of his heydays of shepherd bashing at our expense. "The call" still persists, and to answer it at this promising moment in history calls us to a new, discerning level of pastoral leadership. None of us—neither the pastor nor the people—want to miss the realization of all the promise our God-intend-ed hour of destiny holds.

PASTORS HAVE A CALL *TO SEED*, *TO FEED* AND *TO LEAD*—AND IN ALL, *TO SUCCEED!*

Thus, I have set my hand to write to you, fel-low-servant; to write to spiritual leaders about the shepherding office—about pastors. In a quest to sharpen focus, I have recognized the need to write three books, not one. I plan to write of the pastor's PROMISE, PASSION and PURPOSE—of our call *to seed, to feed and to lead*—and in all, *to succeed!*

THE SHEPHERD AS A MAN

As I have already mentioned, *Pastors of Promise* is the first of these three books, and it focuses on issues I felt I had to start with—for several reasons.

First, because above all our gifts and any of our skills as shepherds, pastoring is essentially a "replicating" procedure. More than anything else, whatever we may *do*, we each reproduce exactly what we *are*. Therefore, I see the shepherding task as a call to "multiply manhood"—*to seed LIFE*, and to realize the promise (or the problem) of *"multiplying 'in kind.'"* We will each reproduce the kind of people we are ourselves; the people we influ-ence become "like Christ" to be sure, but in the likeness of Him they see in and receive from us.

By "manhood," I mean to refer to the male role in the process of beget-ting life rather than necessarily to any gender specification. Still, as lead-ers called to *"seed life,"* there *is* a special significance in what we multiply through the *men* we lead—and even more *that* we do. I believe that God's promise of life-begetting fruitfulness has been written in the spiritual genes of our calling, but I also believe a clear vision is needed on the path to healthy multiplication.

This pathway points to the promise of multiplying fully redeemed *humans:* people born of *promise*, not robots manufactured by programmed religion. So it is that what I am as a man determines what my offspring "in Christ" will become, and it drives me to recognize I have no real option but to grow myself, through a commitment to love and integrity in love and relationships. No mantle for pastoral anointing allows for bypassing or neglecting our true humanity, and lasting effectiveness in a leader's min-istry will only be proportionate to his effectiveness in learning to live.

I begin with this "human" aspect of spiritual leadership for two reasons:

1. It is the most foundational.

The real beginning place of ministry is not in cultivating my talents as a pastor, but in understanding my role as a person. I will inevitably multiply *through* my life what is true *of* my life, thus the starting place is where I am as a "becoming-in-Christ" man.

2. It answers to the most fundamental.

Beginning with the "human" side is consistent with what I see the Spirit of God doing on earth today. God is working on men today— an "awakening" verifies

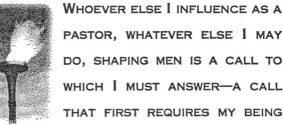

WHOEVER ELSE I INFLUENCE AS A PASTOR, WHATEVER ELSE I MAY DO, SHAPING MEN IS A CALL TO WHICH I MUST ANSWER—A CALL THAT FIRST REQUIRES MY BEING SHAPED MYSELF—*AS A MAN.*

His priorities. Whoever else I influence as a pastor, whatever else I may do, shaping men is a call to which I must answer—a call that first requires my being shaped myself—*as a man.*

So as we step into the following pages, I would gently ask for the gift of two things from you, fellow-servant.

First, your fellowship in communication. You will find as you read, and as you have probably already discovered, my approach on these pages is very subjective. I am seeking to talk with *you,* writing in a personal way as I discuss "you and me," as a pair of people who are equally serious about pursuing spiritual leadership. As I write, I see us as partners in service, and as joint participants in God's present blessing, tough times of tribulation and a future of promised triumph.

Second, I want to invite your periodic review of the Pastor-Leader's Personal Declaration that follows. As you progress through this book, frame the habit of speaking this declaration aloud—as a *pastor of promise.* To a degree, the Declaration is nearly an outline of what follows, but more than that, it is a faith-filled statement of God's promised potential in each of us who have been called to shepherd. So let me encourage you to "speak" the promise of God's *call,* and to expect the fulfillment of His promise, believing "He who calls you is faithful, who also will do it" (1 Thess. 5:24).

PASTOR-LEADER'S PERSONAL DECLARATION

1. I am *called* by God my Creator, to *minister with promise* in declaring the gospel of my Lord Jesus Christ.
2. I am given my Father's promise of His unshakable faithfulness, and my Savior's *promise* of my *fruitfulness.*

3. As a son of the Father, I am a *bearer of the promise* that His grace shall *reproduce "sons"* through me.
4. As a husband of one wife, I am a *keeper of my promise* to *love her* as Christ loves the Church.
5. As a child born of God and filled with His Spirit, I am *promised growth* in Christ's character as I guard my *heart with integrity.*
6. As a spiritual leader, I am *promised spiritual authority* as I joyfully choose to live an ordered *life of submission.*
7. As a man of God, I welcome the *Holy Spirit's promised power,* flowing daily from my *personal communion* with Jesus.
8. As a servant of the Most High, I hold the *promise of an increasing stewardship* as I *live accountably* before God and man.
9. As a warrior of the King, *His promised presence* and victory assure my *conquest over the adversary*'s lies and tactics.
10. As a *pastor of promise* I live in the hope of *God's fulfilled purpose* in me, the men I lead, and those we influence together.
   Amen and Amen!

LET'S PRAY TOGETHER

In the light of *His* commitment, I always feel better about *mine!* Before I knew Him, He not only knew me—but He also knew He would call me. So as we start, let's pray together for an increase of what has been *His purpose from the beginning;* and let's believe for our Master's *mastery* to evidence itself as we are open to His grace—grace to assist us together toward becoming *Pastors of Promise.*

Dear Lord Jesus,

We come to You—who have saved us and called us with Your holy calling, both as saints, and as shepherds.

I pray, dear Savior, that You will not only bless our hearts with Your presence as we walk through these pages, but that You will also bond our hearts more closely to Yours.

We acknowledge first and foremost that before we ever became shepherds, we were lost sheep. And we admit that however proficient we ever become at shepherding, we must never forget we are still very sheeplike, and so very needful of You.

We would keep mindful that in Your humility, before You became "that Great Shepherd of the sheep," you first became "the Lamb of God." So we forbid ourselves any pretension, readily and humbly confessing, Lord, we can only learn Your way of shepherding by being "lamblike"—by forsaking any air of professional presupposition, and commit-

ting to seek a teachable and childlike spirit.

So we come with this prayer, for humility to hear and for grace to learn of You. Bless us, we ask, unto the increase of Your character, wisdom and power in our lives and ministries—as we fellowship in Your Word and Spirit.

Two shepherds, under Your watchcare, Amen.

Now, come and meet me on the first day of my formal involvement in ministry; the day Anna sat beside me as we drove eastward to find the possibilities in our "promise" as pastors.

REFLECTION QUESTIONS

1. Review how you experienced your "call" to be a pastor. What was the time, the circumstances and your feelings at that time?
2. Have you ever been taunted because you are "in this line of work"?
3. Can you identify with any of the six "calls within my call"? Explain how.
4. Have you ever been helped by, or helped other pastor couples in their times of need? Remember when and how.
5. Recall your first pastorate. As it was a time of learning, recall any humorous moments, serious moments, frustrating moments and satisfying moments that launched your shepherding experience.

CHAPTER TWO HIGHLIGHTS

- Abraham's response to God's call upon his life can mold a template for today's pastors.
- God delights to use our ordinariness to work His will in extraordinary ways.
- Pastors, do not surrender your dreams or let them become the ashes of past hope-filled memories. Learn from biblical dreamers such as Joseph, Daniel and Peter.
- Settle on this conviction: God's placement of my life is *His* idea in *His* providence, and not the mere result of my or another's doing.

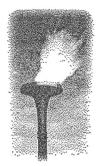

To Timothy, my true
son in the faith.
1 TIMOTHY 1:2

THE PROMISE OF A FATHER-TO-BE

I was humming to myself as the lyrics strummed through my mind: "Goin' out without knowin', followin' the way that He's showin'." High clouds slightly shrouded the sky as the sun began its upward journey, glinting a mix of silver and gold from far south and appearing low on the winter horizon. The two of us exchanged glances—it was genuinely exciting. At last, years of study and in-service training behind us, and a short 18 months of youthful marriage on our track record, we were actually on our way.

Anna's smile indicated her sense of our shared adventure as she glanced a kind of "knowing happiness" look from her seat beside me. Through the rearview mirror, I could barely see the landscape behind us, peeking back from above the carefully packed backseat stacked to the legal limit. Our old blue '51 Chevy, which we had loaded the day before, economizing on every inch to be able to fit in everything we owned in this world, was now chugging through the pass above San Bernardino, California. We were headed eastward for the six-state region designated in our denomination as the Great Lakes District. Most importantly, we were at long last truly "entering the ministry."

Though we had no certain place to land, we did have the assurance of a bishop's promise, and we also had a temporary assignment guaranteeing our having something immediate to do upon our arrival in Iowa. Dr. Vincent Bird had said, "Come on and let's get started together. Until a permanent pastorate opens up, I've got an idea I think you'll like and that will provide good experience and fulfilling ministry." His enthusiasm, joined to his encouraging interest in us, prompted our acceptance of a temporary itinerary—conducting youth revival services for a three-month period.

We had accepted the good bishop's proposition, although our primary vision was to have our own pastorate, however humble or obscure. So now, though we had no actual place to unload our car for the next 3 months, we were indeed "on the way." The culmination of college studies, and a more recent 10 months of planning, was packed in our hearts and in our little car. Now it was all being expressed in a "go for it" faith that was taking us two-thirds of the way across the continent. We were moving, "lock, stock and barrel," to a part of the nation neither of us knew much about, to serve in a circle of pastors and leaders who were mostly unknown to us. The happiness in our hearts was tangible, however, because now it all was really happening. We were "Goin' out"!

Those words were on our minds and lips because of something that had touched my heart during my devotions only a few mornings earlier. Reading in the book of Hebrews, my attention had been caught by the words of chapter 11, verse 8. They seemed to perfectly describe Anna's and my situation on the eve of our departure into the work of the Lord:

> *By faith Abraham obeyed when he was called to go out to the place which he would afterward receive as an inheritance. And he went out, not knowing where he was going.*

I had been both stirred and amused by the Bible's forthright and unapologetic candor, evident in the frank remark: "He went...not knowing where he was going." Later, at breakfast, I shared the text and my thoughts with Anna: "We're not alone, Honey. In fact, we're in good company when it comes to heading out without a sure landing place!"

Seeing Abraham's readiness to obey God's call, though he was virtually without any knowledge of where that call would lead him, was a comforting confirmation. Our situation was parallel, and the simple facts required the same admission, "I don't know where I'm going." We were not so presumptuous as to feel any Abrahamic sense of history about ourselves, but we did feel a certain confidence in direction, notwithstanding our uncertainty of destination.

"No," Anna had said in return, "we don't know where we're going. But just as surely as Abraham did, we *do* know who we're going with!"

She had been as heartwarmed as I had by the inspiration we had found in the Word. She had responded in her own consistently agreeable way, for she shared a sense of "God's call" with me. I had a partner who was as fully convinced of our mission as I was, though at that early point in my own understanding, I had yet to appreciate how enormous a gift to me from God her partnering faith in our call really was. Nor did I yet have the maturity in life to begin to grasp the unique emotional requirement such a call places upon a woman's "nesting" instincts. It would be years until I would appreciate the depth of the devotion to both the Lord and her husband that allowed my wife—or that causes any leader's wife—to lay aside all claim to a settled life with a secure home and income, to pursue without complaint the promise of a life as a pastor's wife.

But right now, my folksy, syncopated melody was filling the car:

Goin' out without knowin', followin' the way that He's showin'.
Goin' out now to serve the Lord, and I know He'll see me through.

Anna picked up the strain with me, and we sang the little ditty as the Mojave Desert broke onto our view and the shadowy forms of giant Joshua trees whizzed by on either side. Although my self-composed lyrics were born from the life of  IF HIS WILL IS FOLLOWED, IN GOD'S TIME, HIS BLESSING AND FULFILLMENT ARE CERTAIN.

Abraham, and based in the Word of God, at that moment I had only a small idea of how fully and thoroughly they reflect the promise of God to those who answer His call to ministry.

THE ABRAHAM TEMPLATE

Today, however, having 40 years of public and pastoral ministry behind us, the concept has become a conviction. What I saw so simply put in the words about Abraham, and with equal simplicity took as a personal encouragement, I now see as a pointer to a pathway of assured promise for every leader who will receive it. I now deeply believe that the whole passage, describing Abraham's answer to God's call upon his life and its mission, was long ago established by Father God as a *pattern* for a promise of "fatherhood." I have come to see how near precisely the same promises are meant for men and women who answer God's call with a willingness to allow Him to extend His life and purpose through them.

Today, I am persuaded that we are intended to see—and to receive—Abraham's experience as more than simply a historic testimony. I believe it's also a prophetic template—a grid of hope over which any "called" person can hang the future; a point of beginning a walk with Him, assured by the promise that if His will is followed, in God's time, His blessing and fulfillment are certain. Here, in the person of Abraham, the man later called "the father of us all" (Rom. 4:16), God's Word sets forth a paradigm of promise; a picture of the very thing that any spiritual leader can expect— from the tests through the trials, to the transcendent moments and triumphant events. Through the whole of his life and pursuit of God's will, Abraham provides a template for leaders today—a picture of the pathway to *"fathering"* under *the Father's* counsel and purpose.

Such a view appears to be consistent with the intent of our Lord for all who seek to obey His call to spiritual leadership. The Abraham Template may be revealed in the Old Testament, but when I read Paul's words to Timothy in the New Testament, I can't help but gather he may well have said such things to him. As surely as the apostle had called him "my son," he most certainly had engendered the same expectation in that young pastor: "You therefore, my son, be strong in the grace that is in Christ Jesus. And the things that you have heard from me among many witnesses, commit these to faithful men who will be able to teach others also" (2 Tim. 2:1,2).

It seems certain that as surely as Paul would write in the Roman Epistle of the "fathering" concepts that unfold from the life of Abraham, he would surely have taught Timothy the same. He would have relayed a life principle rooted in the ways of God, that occasion an understanding about life transmission. Paul was not calling Timothy "my son" by using paternalistic condescendence nor an air of intimidating authority. If anything, the accompanying words carry the same order of hope that God spoke to Abraham: "You'll be a father—I promise you." And there is abundant reason for each of us who pastor to pursue our ministries with the prospect of fruitfulness and fulfilling relationships—of becoming a "father" to others. It is the heaven-given promise of "a father-to-be"; one of the appropriate hopes of a pastor or spiritual leader called of God Almighty, the Father of us all.

I have no question that any of the principles that distill from a study of Abraham's life are equally applicable in their own way for any believer. God's promises have their practical points of "working" in life-begetting ways with all who are willing to appropriate their possibilities. Unlimited potentialities are inherent in a faith-walk because the living God who calls each of us to His own high purpose for our lives is unlimited in His ability to bring fruit and fulfillment to all who follow His ways. Right now, however, I am particularly interested in the way God's call to Abraham as "a father-to-be" projects a picture of the pastoral mission—how He prototypes our "fathering" possibilities as leaders today.

The use of the *title* "Father," common in much of historic church tradition, has generally been separated from the *truth* in the term. Of course, in most Protestant circles, the idea of the congregation's spiritual leader being called "Father" is something generally met with objection. The grounds for protest are usually offered in Jesus' words: "Do not call anyone on earth your father; for One is your Father, He who is in heaven" (Matt. 23:9). The spirit of the immediate context of His prohibition seems to separate a title from a truth.

Jesus was confronting the Pharisees, as He so often was forced to do by reason of either their spiritual shallowness, stubbornness or sightlessness. In Matthew 23, He pointedly attacks the religious pride in these leaders who paraded themselves as rulers called "fathers in Israel." Yet for all their claims of the title, they did nothing to live out the truth of fatherhood, which was to serve the interests of those they led. Jesus was seeking to dissociate the minds of the people from false models, and the context revealing this intent modifies His prohibitional remark.

Joined to the rest of the Savior's own teaching, as well as to the apostles', a fuller view of how the term "father" was used in a spiritual context is provided. The New Testament not only clears the way for an appropriate mention of "spiritual fatherhood" among godly leaders, but it in fact also demonstrates the meaning and desirability for such a role. It unfolds a "fathering" lifestyle that did not require the formalities of title, but in which the hope and the health in the truth of spiritual fatherhood was realized and served.

SPIRITUAL FATHERHOOD

For example, Paul freely designates Abraham as "the father of us all" (Rom. 4:16) in affirming the patriarch's pioneer role in the "faith-walk" under God's call and leading. This terminology is obviously used for more significant reasons than mere respect. Abraham is called a "father" because he is being acknowledged as one whose way of life and faith sired the same in others.

This understandable and acceptable usage allows Paul to unpretentiously proceed in using the figure of fatherhood to describe himself. Writing to the Corinthians, he refers to his own ministry as their founding pastor, and says, "For though you might have ten thousand instructors in Christ, yet you do not have many fathers" (1 Cor. 4:15). He emphasizes that he has no claimed right or desire to dominate them, for his sole longing is to see their lives advanced in God's grace and goodness (see 2 Cor. 1:24). In seeking to remind them of his role in the birthing of their spiritual journey, however, he is unhesitant to use "father," not to demand a title but to declare a truth.

The apostle Paul also frequently uses the term "my son" in acknowledging his God-given privilege in influencing men. By reason of his role in having won and discipled such men as Timothy and Titus—now young pastors—he calls them "sons." He does the same in the case of Onesimus, a recent convert whose early growth in Christ was under Paul's influence while they were both in jail (see 1 Cor.  **THAT A LEADER SERVES AND SHAPES PEOPLE IN CHRIST CLEARLY ESTABLISHES THAT A PATERNAL ORDER OF LIFE-TO-LIFE TRANSMISSION HAS OCCURRED.**

4:17; Phil. 2:22; 1 Tim. 1:2,18; 2 Tim. 1:2; 2:1; Titus 1:4). In this bevy of texts where the idea appears, it becomes obvious that having "brought a soul to Christ" is not the only qualification for explaining spiritual fatherhood. Rather, that a leader serves and shapes people in Christ clearly establishes that a paternal order of life-to-life transmission has occurred and may be so designated. Moreover, the truth transcends gender, as Paul uses the figure of a mother's travail to describe the pain of spiritual parenting (see Gal. 4:19).

Further insight into this biblical idea is gained in John's first Epistle, where we are presented with the concept of "fatherhood" in the life of the Church nearer the end of the first century. Throughout this letter, he repeatedly refers affectionately to his readers as "my little children." He does not claim this term for himself alone, however, as though it were confined to apostolic authority. Twice, in a clear reference to those seasoned in Christ by years and service, he says, "I write to you, fathers" (see 1 John 2:13,14). It seems evident in God's Word that the idea of spiritual "fatherhood" acknowledged spiritual maturity and designated leadership. It was applicable because these were men through whom others were being brought into, cared for and built up in the life of faith in Christ and unto growth in the truths of the kingdom of God.

In short, the idea of "fathering" as expressive of church leadership is not only established in the Word, but its intent is also obvious. It is not so much a title that is to be employed as it is a truth that may be experienced. Its use is not intended as a conferral of an honorary title, but as a referral to fulfilling a humble task. It becomes the reward of a self-sacrificing leader who has served a person or group in the spirit of a loving parent, rather than the right of a manipulative manager, demanding tyrant or exploitive overlord. We are describing a life-infusing, trust-winning, growth-begetting role in other lives, and when such is served, the "hope" of spiritual fatherhood may well become a proper promise to be expected by any of us. It becomes perfectly applicable to the ministry of a pastor who "fathers" in that:

1. He is assigned a local oversight, and under God serves there as a *representative* of the heavenly Father, always accountable to Him for the care of that small portion of His "whole family in heaven and earth" (Eph. 3:15); and
2. He is charged as a spiritual steward, as a parent with children, appointed by God with the *responsibility* to lovingly and faithfully provide the spiritual care and management of the "household," as having "devoted themselves to the ministry of the saints" (1 Cor. 16:15).

Along with a pastor's "fathering" role in representation and responsibility, a biblical picture of multiplying and replicating the role of a father is also presented. In the deepest spiritual terms, a pastor's ongoing ministry is "seeded by God," equipped with the promise of a "father-to-be." The composite deposit of God's Word on our lips and His Spirit in our hearts provides a dual life source for both—multiplication and replication. The Word of God we minister and the life of Christ we model through the indwelling of His Spirit are given to shepherds in a unique way, or the qualifications for leadership ministry would not be expressed as they are. Although every believer is given the Word and the Spirit as resources for his or her own ministry and multiplication, a distinct responsibility is incumbent upon us who lead in Christ's Body.

The simplest reading of 1 Timothy 3:1-13 pointedly reveals the character and qualifications expected of the local pastor, and the carefulness and dutifulness with which he is to model life and minister the Word. We hold a unique place in the divine order, and I believe it is as important to see the privilege it allows as the responsibility it assigns. The precepts of responsibility are demanding because the potential for multiplication is so great. The fact is that "fathering" is going to take place: a multiplying of either life or death, truth or error, love or fear, wisdom or folly. Make no mistake about it—we who pastor will multiply *something*; it is inherent within our calls. My point is not only to note with sobriety the greatness of our responsibilities in passing on the seeds of life we have received in Christ, but I also want to highlight their promises.

I want to awaken a sense of holy expectancy, of certainty that because God has put His call upon you and His seed in you, a guaranteed rich potential is already present of your ministry being mightily multiplied. Be it our Abrahamlike call or our Timothylike youthfulness or timidity, the fact is that as "sons" we are created anew as "fathers-to-be." Incorporated in the very figure of fatherhood is the promise of fruitfulness—of the life and power of God being multiplied through the otherwise frail human agency of people like you and me.

We are not to perceive ourselves in any other way, however impotent we may feel. Though we know ourselves to be mere men, we have nonetheless been called and capacitated to transmit the life-begetting, life-shaping grace and power of the eternal Father. Thus the Bible reveals how that which God has declared to be the potential of each believer offers those of us in the pastoral offices a distinctly profound and promised possibility. As ones who in answering God's call to "go out...not knowing where," we have a share in the hope of "Abraham's seed, [to become]...heirs according to the promise" (Gal. 3:29). That means *us*, you and me, whose call is to provide leadership among the flock of the living God.

So, dear fellow servant, in beginning this book of conversations with pastors, I want to engage *you*. I most want to convey the *promise* of pastoral ministry in a way that points to practical pathways of pastoral pursuit that will bring the realization of your "fatherhood" to new dimensions of *fruitfulness*. That God's Word offers this prospect and promise is unquestionable, and I am not suggesting that such fruitfulness has in certain ways already begun in and through you; it doubtless has. Rather, I am writing to encourage still greater hopes and higher expectations, for our Lord Jesus has called us each to a full lifetime of *promised increase*—from glory to glory and from faith to faith. *The Father's* seed is alive in us, assuring a multiplying seed through our ministries, thus the promise of continual and fulfilling growth and increase of fruit is more than merely possible—it is impending!

PASTORS OF PROMISE

The Abraham Template is a sound biblical source of promise inviting each pastor, with ready faith, to engage the model he manifests. It is a paradigm of promise that reveals God's complete ability and utter faithfulness to bring *life and blessing* through a spiritual leader:

> To enable "fathering in faith,"
> To guarantee "bearing increasing fruit,"
> To assure "begetting spiritual offspring."

God's promises to Abraham are timelessly transferable concepts, and I do invite you to look at the personal significance present for your own ministry in the promise he received and the possibilities he realized. But before we probe the promise, I want to anticipate—and dismantle—a practical, virtually ever-present problem. I do not want to risk even one reader supposing I am so captivated by the joyousness of promised fruitfulness that I am blinded to the present weariness of someone whose faith is lagging. I do not want to run ahead yet with what I am confident of, seeming uncaring of ones for whom I feel compassion. I have learned full well for my own part that becoming bold to receive God's promises often first requires a great need for receiving the comfort of God's Spirit. Let me explain.

Years of serving beside and ministering to hosts of fellow shepherds have taught me how vulnerable we all are to feelings of fruitlessness and failure. A dual vulnerability exists here: Along with our normal human propensities to doubt, our spiritual callings as pastors also make us especially chosen targets of the adversary. Satan's

WHAT HE DID IN ABRAHAM'S LIFE, HE WILL DO IN YOURS, TOO!

strategic plans and tireless efforts against the Church unquestionably center on the proposition that if the shepherds can be smitten, the sheep can be scattered, or at the very least weakened. Thus, any call to shepherds—to "pastors of promise"—necessitates a realistic acknowledgment of and dealing with doubts or discouragement. Take a few minutes to think with me, and let's try to identify feelings or thoughts that so easily can preempt hope and block the appropriation of life-multiplying faith.

Enemies of Hope

For example, when it comes to God's assurance that "fruitful fathering" is a possibility, are you ever distracted by the glaring presence of places in your life or ministry where outright barrenness prevails? I daresay you are the same as I am. Our compulsion to a tough honesty about little or no fruit makes any exercise in self-assessment a defeat. I can read of or listen to God's promise and be stirred. Soon, however, haunting evidence of my ineffectiveness peculiarly has a way of making an enemy of the hope the Father wants to become my friend.

To illustrate, Abraham's promise of fatherhood took a quarter century in *beginning* to be realized. The seed of the promise had a long season to wait until its fruit appeared. Further, the natural world reveals that not only do various plants vary in the waiting term until they become fruit-bearing, but also that years vary in their relative fruitfulness. Both biblical revelation and natural creation teach us that present *apparent* barrenness is not a conclusive assessment. However truthful or logical these facts may be, they seem to offer little comfort when tough or barren times appear to prevail in our ministries. Joined to that, the lying whispers of the devil tease tirelessly, confirming every personal sense we have of our own inadequacies.

Further, another suspicion claws at our souls and seeks to dominate us: "Who do you think you are anyway?"

However faithful we may be to teach others, "'God is no respecter of persons'" (Acts 10:34, *KJV*). What He did in Abraham's life (or any other Bible character's life), He will do in yours too! We preach it, and believe it, but when it comes to our own pastoral circumstances, the argument does not seem to refer to us. Arguments to the contrary are too abundant, making it clear, "There may be some Abrahams around, but I am sure not one!"

We all get the same journals, and we all read the success stories of other pastors and churches. The blessing of materials intended to inspire and instruct turns into a barrage that batters our confidence, so often serving only to amplify any feelings of comparative unworth. We read of those pastors whose works unfold models of growth and effectiveness, and as we contrast them with our own efforts, they become more than humbling— often they are crushing. This is not so simple a matter to confront as though the problem was the sin of having succumbed to jealousy. Most pastors I know do not feel unkindly toward brethren being blessed, so the struggle is not a small-souledness toward others or a regret about their fruits. It is simply a matter of wondering, *When, if ever, will there come the season of my full fruitfulness?*

I remember our first pastorate, how after two years of slow and unimpressive growth, a former schoolmate two years behind me, who had just graduated and entered ministry, took a pastorate in a nearby town. His work flourished! His congregation zipped upward in six months to a size more than double ours. Naturally, he never pointed this out when we met (though our church's district newspaper gave plenty of space reporting his achievements; commentary that was not intended to demean anyone's work, but that seemed to shout to me: "You don't know what you're doing!"). I can honestly say I did not yield to bitterness or jealousy, but I felt buried by my own limited fruitfulness. Clearly, I either did not "have it," or was somehow being judged by God (for any of the number of reasons that easily come to mind when a spirit of condemnation or unworthiness assails us). How can we address such times in our ministries? What is the answer to such moments when a pastor faces them?

It is always found at the same place: on "promised" ground.

I believe the secret to vanquishing the collective enterprises of satanic spirits of doubt, condemnation, futility or unworthiness is in our *seizing* the sword of God's promises, *striking* down those lying demons and *stepping* into an abiding place those promises intended us to enjoy. So step with me onto the sure terrain of God's Word—a place where you and I can once and for all lay hold of a tangible certainty. Please see it as such because it is true:

God has declared His irrevocable
purposes in us—in *you,* and in *me.*

That unshakable conviction leads me to begin with Abraham, for as I
noted earlier, God helped me begin there. Eventually I came to see how
Abraham's experience not only provided a biblical confirmation of Anna's
and my first steps—"Goin' out without knowin'," but I also gained a far
deeper perspective. I came to see what a gift Abraham's promise is to all of
us who are to lead in faith's pathway. I also saw how God's promises to
Abraham are ours; a prophetic revelation of His will and way to enable
"fathering" and fruitfulness in each leader who answers His call. Look
with me at the biblical basis for this conviction, and let's see how careful
study verifies its validity.

> ············· **DON'T FORGET TO DREAM**
>
> Pastoral vision is intended to be kept warm and alive by
> our insistent requirement of ourselves that we *not* surren-
> der our dreams to the ashes of past hope-filled memories.
> Keep your dream in view; it is the will of God that we do!
> (See Acts 2:17,18.) Let's take lessons from biblical
> "dreamers."
>
> - Joseph—A *rejected* dreamer who refused to deny
>   his dream (see Gen. 50:15-21). LEARN: Don't let
>   your spirit sour, let it soar!
> - Daniel—A *prophetic* dreamer who influenced world
>   shapers (see Dan. 2). LEARN: Don't let the
>   world's image shape *you,* shape *it!*
> - Joseph—A *paternal* dreamer whose sensitivity
>   saved the life of his family (see Matt. 2:13-15).
>   LEARN: Don't pace yourself by the world's clock
>   or style, but place "haste" in obedience to God's
>   Spirit.
> - Peter—An *adjustable* dreamer who kept teachable
>   even though his was a "leading" role (see Acts 10:9-
>   23). LEARN: Don't bog down in your own limited
>   view of things.
> - John—A *persecuted* dreamer whose optimism could
>   not be quenched by trial (see Rev. 1:9-18).
>   LEARN: Don't lose confidence in tomorrow
>   because of what you face today.

Pastor, hold your dreams in hands of faith, kept open before the living Lord who alone is the fulfiller of dreams. (Examples: dreams of accomplishment [goals]; of growth [fruitfulness]; of fulfillment [purpose]; of freedom [spiritual victory]).

- Receive your dream—*Talk* in a way that does not dissipate it.
- Pursue your dream—*Walk* in a way that does not violate it.

I can be sure my dream comes from God, when its birth is begotten by the Holy Spirit, and when its fulfillment will glorify Jesus Christ's purpose. In contrast, I can identify a fantasy, for it inevitably panders to pride, lust, sensuality or covetousness, and thereby betrays its hellish or carnal source.

A *dream* is conceived of the beautiful, righteous and profitable, and is rooted in *truth* and fulfilled through obedience and discipline.

A *fantasy* is conjured of the self-serving and self-righteous, and deludes with notions of unrequired discipline and quick fulfillment.

A TRANSMITTABLE PROMISE

When the Lord first called Abraham to learn the life and pathway of faith in the living God, He made a commitment to him. He promised not only to bless Abraham, but to multiply him as well. I would like to invite you to see this commitment as a transmittable promise—as a commitment intended for us to see being as relevant to us today as it was to Abraham. Begin with me by reading of God's call to him in its entirety:

> *Now the Lord had said to Abram: "Get out of your country, from your kindred and from your father's house, to a land that I will show you. I will make you a great nation; I will bless you and make your name great; and you shall be a blessing. I will bless those who bless you, and I will curse him who curses you; and in you all the families of the earth shall be blessed"* (Gen. 12:1-3).

At least seven facets of promise are given here: (1) a place of promised possession; (2) an offspring, in time unto sizable numbers; (3) a degree of blessing that would bring personal affirmation by others; (4) a presence of blessing that would touch those around him; (5) a God-granted favor on people who were favorable toward him; (6) a God-assured protection from those who would oppose him; and (7) a multiplying of blessing through him, eventually touching the whole world.

The profoundly simple and beautiful but often overlooked fact is that the New Testament broadens the implications of God's promises to Abraham, applying them in a redemptive sense to all believers.

And if you are Christ's, then you are Abraham's seed, and heirs according to the promise (Gal. 3:29).

As we shall see, it is not an exaggeration of the spirit of this truth as revealed in the whole New Testament to imply that elements of God's promises to Abraham are ours to enjoy. That each believer's life may realize these to a different degree as well as in a different personal context does not diminish either the essence or the substance of the commitment God makes to "Abraham's seed." The only "diminishing" possible, given the whole scope of the promise revealed, is to deny the Holy Spirit's intent for us to see the inheritance Abraham's promise contains for us all. In this study, it is not my purpose to explore the way each of the previously listed seven features of blessing apply to Abraham's children through faith. But in affirming that as his "seed" Abraham's promise is ours to adopt, let me illustrate biblical and practical points of its application.

For example, a "great" name does not solely imply global fame, but may be realized in the observations made by those who behold God's miracles, character or influence on or through our lives (see Ps. 71:20,21; 126:2,3). God's promise to defend us from evil calculated against us is a divine curse against all that would seek to destroy you or me (see Ps. 23:4,5; Isa. 54:17). The blessing of the gospel transmitted through our witnesses (see Acts 1:8), as well as the impact of our intercessions shaking nations (see Ps. 2:8,9; 149:5-9), are both means of God's fulfilling His Abrahamic promise to "bless the nations" through His seed. This promise, of course, is most fully realized in the person of Jesus, and the salvation He has provided for humankind.

The reality and applicability of God's promise to Abraham is supremely relevant in many ways, and is intended for every one of the redeemed. My primary objective here, however, is to underscore the way I believe each pastor deserves to see the implications of this promise.

The unique and distinct applicability of Abraham's promise to spiritual leaders is in our roles as pathmakers—people who step out into the way of faith, and who lead others by teaching and example to do the same. In this regard, Abraham realized his role as a "father," and his fulfillment of that aspect of promise is expounded in Romans 4 in a way that presents a dual truth—only half of which is usually noted.

Most New Testament students are aware of how the book of Romans develops, so that the purpose of mentioning Abraham in the fourth chapter is understood. Here, Abraham's faith in God's promised purpose in his life is used to demonstrate how "justification by faith" has always been apart from works. In other words, "His faith was accounted unto him for righteousness" even before the physical act (or work) of circumcision was made a "law" for his household. But the matter of justification by faith is only the *first* aspect of a dual truth developed in this text, showing the *saving* power of faith.

The *second* aspect is a companioning concept that occasions the frequently referenced fact of Abraham's "father" role. This facet of promise elaborates the *multiplying* power of faith. In contrast to "justification by faith" (*which begins promise in us*; Rom. 4:3), we discount "fatherhood in the faith" (*which multiplies promise through us*; v. 18). This is stated in the words, "Contrary to hope, in hope [Abraham] believed, so that he became the father of many nations, according to what was spoken, 'So shall your descendants be'" (v. 18).

This two-tiered promise to Abraham deserves to be embraced by every believer. It moves faith beyond the joy of being positionally secured in Christ, to the promise of becoming practically fruitful in Him. Just as surely as the promise of "the righteousness of faith" (Rom. 4:13) was assured to his spiritual offspring, so the spirit of Paul's whole exposition breathes with an ever-broadened hope.

JUST AS SURELY AS WE CAN RECEIVE A SALVATION WE COULD NEVER EARN, SO JOYOUSLY MAY WE HOPE TO REALIZE A MINISTRY WE COULD NEVER ACHIEVE!

As I have already said, I believe the message extends further; it holds forth a special promise to spiritual leaders—to those of us called, as Abraham was, to lead in the path of faith. This passage beautifully elaborates the hope that we who are charged to walk as leaders who follow in Abraham's footsteps (see Rom. 4:12) may experience the grace of a multiplying seed as did this "father." That is, as surely as our salvation is secured by faith alone, so surely may we expect fruitfulness—the increase of a spiritual leader's spiritual offspring, and the fulfillment of our realizing God's purpose in His call.

In so many words, the same power that saves and secures a soul in the righteousness of God is promised to extend its operative power to produce through us the fruitfulness of God—spiritual fatherhood. The dimension of the promise is there—wonderfully! Just as surely as we can receive a salvation we could never earn, so joyously may we hope to realize a ministry we could never achieve!

> *Therefore it [the promise] is of faith that it might be according to grace, so that the promise might be sure to all the seed...who are of the...faith of Abraham, who is the father of us all...[through] God, who gives life to the dead and calls those things which do not exist as though they did* (Rom. 4:16,17).

Did you see how dynamic the guarantees are in this text? It shows *hope* where things are as dead or barren as Abraham's late-in-life impotency or Sarah's change-of-life womb. It shows *promise* where "things do not exist" that you and I may see as impossibilities. Whatever lifelessness or unfruitfulness may taunt your or my sense of mission, whether personally, domestically or professionally, we are nonetheless God's *called ones*, and our calls contain a God-ordained Abrahamic order of promise.

The clarity and call of this truth recommends we pursue it in its practical, pastoral implications. Let me urge you to begin laying hold of this realm of promise by glimpsing at specific points of promise and hope for those of us who are called to spiritual leadership. Consider the two most basic aspects of Abraham's promise: (1) the promise of a *people* and (2) the promise of a *place*.

A PLACE OF PROMISE

I did not know it when we began our ministry, but I am certain of it today: To every person God calls into pastoral ministry, Abraham's promises with parallel certainties are offered. It begins with a place of promise. It means that wherever your present location may be, whether settled for years or as uncertain as Anna's and mine was as our little car navigated eastward that day, God has made a divine commitment to bring you to a place in His will where His promise will be fulfilled. Perhaps this promise needs our first and foremost embrace because of our oh-too-human tendencies.

Probably nothing is more challenging to any pastor's faith than the recurring temptation to move. Though it has now been more than 27 years since I came to my present assignment, my ability to relate to this point of emotional vulnerability is unhindered. How readily my own soul has been unsettled: "Flee as a bird to your mountain" (Ps. 11:1). Whatever the thrill of promise present upon arrival at a new place of ministry, disquieting circumstances seem like a hawk chasing the dove in our souls that brought us to our places of the Holy Spirit's appointment.

Too well do I remember the ache, the sense of agonizing failure that hung like a summerlong cloud over my soul years ago. To climax a springtime of attendance records in our new church plant, we went into a tailspin that nearly crashed our hopes completely. We were losing members hand over fist. People left because it was summer, a convenient time to disappear after having discovered they did not really want to pay the price of being a part of a fledgling congregation. People left because they were moving, as summer seems the most common season for relocating to other job opportunities. People left because they went to another church, and honestly expressed their sense of God's call to do as much. Other people left— get ready for this!—simply because people were leaving! (Talk about "the straw that breaks"!) Thus, what was a small congregation to begin with almost became a nonexistent one.

It was the second Sunday morning in August, and an oppressively humid day as I remember it. After attempting to sustain some degree of enthusiasm while preaching to 6 adults instead of 40, I shook hands with the last to leave, and turned back to walk down the aisle of the empty sanctuary, having one idea in mind. I was ready to get into the car and leave— that afternoon! Anna, notwithstanding the fact that she usually was "up" when I was "down," and vice versa, was as depressed as I was. I will tell about it later, but only a solid encounter with God that evening brought me face up to the conviction that our *being in that place* was His idea. That meeting renewed my hope as He literally "rekindled" my sense of "promise" concerning that place.

Such "rekindlings" have been essential for me, even in settings in which the outside observer would presume otherwise. How many would presume a megachurch pastor could grow beyond discouragement? As recently as five months ago, I wrestled with nagging feelings of self-doubt. No subtle campaign, rumor or substance in any way supported these ideas, but my soul was being constantly pressed with doubts about my effectiveness and questions of future promise. It was a heyday for satanically spawned lies, spoken by no one but the devil and to no one but me: "You're through. You're just in the way here." Or, "What has been a season of fruitfulness is over—not only past, but things are headed for a diminishing. Get out now!"

Has that happened to you lately? What is a pastor of promise to do?

Of course, no final rule states a "right amount of time" in serving a pastorate. It probably should be noted that "as a rule," most of us pastors are regularly in jeopardy of too readily leaving our places of God's promised purpose before the seeds of promise have come to fruition. Escape tempts us all, and often. Credibility, trust and spiritual dominion all take time to establish, and Abraham's promise of "a land" calls for my commitment to "lay down my life." My "place" of ministry needs always to remain a "non-negotiable" in the face of circumstances that scream, "Get out!" Our point of retreat when battered by such an assault needs to rest in the answer to one question: *Did I believe it was God's call when I came to this place?* Honesty with that answer will settle my commitment to wait on His promise here until He calls me elsewhere.

Although the land seems barren and the season fruitless, if I know I am at His place for me, I can wait—confident in the promise that God has not appointed me to terminal frustration at a place apart from His presence, or His purpose. His laws are "seedtime and harvest" (Gen. 8:22). His promise is that however soul-wrenching or presently wearying the labor, as His servant I will inevitably reap the reward of this land's harvests, and the seasonal rejoicing His Word promises:

> *Those who sow in tears shall reap in joy. He who continually goes forth weeping, bearing seed for sowing, shall doubtless come again with rejoicing, bringing his sheaves with him* (Ps. 126:5,6).

THE PROMISE OF A PEOPLE

Abraham's seed is also given the promise of a "people." In his day, the birth of children was interpreted as the direct equivalent of a person's being blessed by God. Nothing has changed much in that regard either. As spiritual leaders, you and I serve in roles where we are sorely pressed to measure our worth in attendance figures, budget dollars or total membership. More central to our mission is the feeling of very limited fulfillment unless people are being brought to life in Christ—again, it's a matter of "numbers," however spiritual the issue. Whether we like to admit it or not, we not only suffer from internal feelings of inadequacy when the "people-figure" does not meet expectations, but we also suffer from a sense of judgment being passed by others—however silent their observations.

What is your response to small numbers, or to the passage of weeks without seeing a person truly "born again" by the power of the Holy Spirit? If you are, as I have been on occasion, in need of a reminder that the promise of "people" is as certain as any God gives His servants, take hope from Abraham again. His long-term bewilderment about his and Sarah's incapacity to bear children is permanently inscribed in the Scriptures; and remember, this is the man God chose to describe as the "father" of living faith! Listen to him virtually "charge" the Lord with his complaint: "Look, You have given me no offspring" (Gen. 15:2,3). Read

those words, then join me in never forgetting: Abraham's fear of fruitlessness did not remove him from God's circle of blessing!

If fears of past apparent ineffectiveness try to corner you, remember
that night in Corinth on the day after Paul had been kicked out of his place
of ministry by folks who wanted nothing to do with him. The words of the
Lord to him make clear that all he could think of was his last three ministry stops, where pain and rejection attended his way. Then, the same
Savior who called him drew near to assure him, whispering: "Do not be
afraid,...I have many people in this city" (see Acts 18:1-10).

Listen, dear fellow shepherd, you and I are possessors of Abraham's
promise of a people. Just as surely as God gave that promise to a beloea-
guered apostle, His promise is sure to you and me today: "Son, don't be
driven by doubts or fears of fruitlessness: I have a people for you—and
they're nearer than you think!"

OUR PROMISE FOR TODAY

This promise of God to Abraham, and the assertion He made to Paul, are
both at the root of the hope I want us to pursue together. Strikingly, they
were separated in history from each other by about the same amount of
time that separates us from the most recent of these two "called ones"—
about 2,000 years. Abraham's venture westward from Ur is set at somewhere near 2200 B.C.; Paul's ministry in Greece occurred approximately
A.D. 50. As we stand at the threshold of the third millennium, the promises of God and His power to fulfill them in servants who "go out without
knowing" are still the same. The promise of a place and a people—of a site
where a fruitful pursuit of God's will may be realized, and where a family
of faith may be grown—is still unchanged.

We may think the landscape of human need looks radically different
from what we might believe to be the view in Abraham's time, or even
Paul's. When the magnitude of our local or global circumstances taunt any
one of us with a sense of futility—by reason of its vexing glut of moral filth,
its abounding pain and violence or the ever-present smirk of pagan pride
that so often meet our claims to faith—remember that Canaan and Rome
both set records for human degradation, too. The promises given to those
who model faith in ministry were not offering fruitfulness in a greenhouse
of privileged environment, but on the searing desert where hell seemed to
be having its own way. "Everything's different but nothing's changed. And
everything's changed, but nothing's different."

Notwithstanding the fact that modern media may bring daily news of
the agonizing presence and proliferation of evil into our living rooms by
means and with an efficiency unknown to Abraham or Paul, the Almighty

One who calls us foresaw this moment. Nothing has changed with Him either. He is still saying: "I have a place for you"; and everywhere in our villages, cities or counties, the living God is also still speaking—seeking leaders who will hear His word and believe His promise: "I have many people right here—where you are right now!"

PARADIGMS OF UN-PROMISE

Studying the Abraham Template reveals other parallels besides the elements of promise. Some episodes teach us by contrast, as we watch him deal with circumstances in ways un-promised. For example, we might learn from Abraham's response to the promise of offspring that, as we know, came neither readily nor easily. After more than two decades of hoping, his and Sarah's long-term wait for children became so deep a point of emotional stress and difficulty for them that it eventually resulted in dissension between them. Their experience presents an all-too-familiar tale. The analogy has so often become true to pastoral experience that it presents a paradigm of how tactical confusion takes over when we are hoping for "fatherhood" while barrenness prevails.

In how many places, even this moment as we speak together, is mutual frustration breeding a division between a pastor and his congregation—or a pastor and his spouse? How often is blame registered, or are desperate and counterproductive plans laid with the takeover of a frustration born of apparent fruitlessness, or feelings of futility at not being able to realize progress, growth or fulfilling relationships? Although each believes he or she has done the best that is possible, it still seems dreams are unfulfilled and goals are unrealized. Eventually, such irritation often presses toward actions introducing unforeseen complexities that become a further irritant. It happens again, as with Abraham: Human desperation hoping to gain the promise of "fatherhood" produces "Hagar plans with Ishmael results." Genesis 16 provides a study in the more-than-frustrating fruit of our strivings with frustration, and we birth "less-than-promised-plans" that add to our problems.

The hope for "a people" is dulled if not lost at such times, and during some long nights in a leader's soul, it is hard to remember that beyond Abraham's and Sarah's barren season would come the day they would laugh for joy—and name their child "Laughter"! As a pastor of promise, I need to let my heart embrace this template of truth.

I will "father" a people!

You and I need to see that certainty of fruitfulness as having been placed in the spiritual loins of everyone of us who walk in Abraham's footsteps. The nagging doubts—*Will fruitfulness never come?*—grind at all our souls. Paul would also express his own frustration about his recurring experiences of the soul's travail involved in this order of "birthing" as he labored over the slow-to-reverse responses of the Galatians (see Gal. 4:19).

Another paradigm of "un-promise" is seen in Abraham's temporary flight to Egypt, and his puzzling program of self-protection that compromised his and Sarah's relationship. In Genesis 12:7, after he answered God's call and left Ur and then Haran in obedient pursuit of His will, the Lord appeared to him and said, "I will give [you] this land." "This land" was fully occupied by the Canaanites, and apparently this unpromising fact, joined to a drought, moves Abraham completely apart from God's direction to journey southward to Egypt. His actions there transcend cultural justification as he puts his wife "up for grabs" by the local king to spare his own neck (see vv. 11-15). Through God's mercy, he is not only delivered from his dilemma, but also returned to his intended place in God's will with overwhelming lovingkindness attending his recovery.

As a contemporary Abraham who sets out "not knowing where," have you found the "land" inhabited by disinterested residents? "Canaanites" seem to still constitute the environment in which God calls pastors of promise to find a place and a people. (They sometimes form the new pastor's welcoming committee!) How many people in your town seem convinced or even interested in the possibility that God has given you His call and promise and sent you into their midst?

The neighborhood in which God's promise lives has not changed much in 4,000 years, but there is no better place to live! At the time God called Anna and me to the San Fernando Valley in California, people counseled against it: "Get your kids out of Los Angeles!" When the church began to grow, people said, "Get out into the suburbs where there's space and better opportunity!" But God said, "Stay here. I have a plan." Today, all four of our kids have grown up, whole, healthy and holy, and our congregation is positioned to be a redemptive instrument in an increasingly urban setting.

To be sure, the setting at the earth-scene level is more often flavored by problems than promises, as humans see it. But, pastor-friend, we share a promise from a "Higher Source." So make a declaration with me, please: Say, "YES! Yes, Lord, I am of Abraham's seed, and Your call still carries within it the same seeds of certainty!"

Today's promise is still the same to pastors like you and me. God will give us spiritual offspring in a special place! Thus, He will give a people—a people through whom God will cause His blessing to flow to the world around them! The promise happens through men of "Abraham's seed" who will answer the Father's call to a pastoral role of "fathering." How can I begin?

REFLECTION QUESTIONS

1. Paul designates Abraham as "the father of us all." How do you see this relating to you in your role as a pastor.
2. Paul's use of the term "my son" acknowledges a God-given privilege in influencing men. How have or how would you desire to influence men in your ministry?
3. Describe some of your feelings of fruitlessness and failure. Openly discuss them—at least with God.
4. Describe some of your feelings of fruitfulness and fulfillment. Openly praise God for them.
5. The sidebar in this chapter highlights biblical examples of dreamers. How are you pursuing receiving your dream?

CHAPTER THREE HIGHLIGHTS

- Each pastor-leader needs and deserves to be gripped by a glimpse of the "imminent" present. *We are on the brink of a sweeping move of God's Spirit—everywhere!*
- A dramatic, if not overwhelmingly dynamic, move of God is apparent in what He is doing with men. *A mighty, Holy Spirit-begotten men's awakening is spreading everywhere!*
- The focus of God on men today is clearly beyond stadiums. Each of us is called to rise "as a man of God...a man of spiritual integrity," and to answer his call at home, as a man of Christ and His Church.
- An undeniable reality is present: God *initiates* through men. But contrary to secular or carnal ideas, that never gives men private privilege or a higher hand of power.

The things that you have heard...
commit these to faithful men.
2 TIMOTHY 2:2

CHAPTER THREE

A TIME TO BEGET SONS

However dark the scene on the human horizon, the Church stands today at its grandest moment of destiny. Notwithstanding society's plethora of problems or the media's ceaseless reports of human strife, stress and sickliness, far more than a mere "ray of hope" can be seen on the horizon. All of us who are called to leadership in the Body of Christ today have come to an incredibly bright hour of promise.

This is not a wild-eyed claim born of dreamy-eyed optimism or hyperenthused euphoria. Neither am I less aware than anyone else of the pronouncements of "irrelevance" and "loss of influence" that are made by cynical social observers and even some religious analysts. The drumbeat of the secular world is not only constant with its dark spirit of antichrist sentiment and hostility, but its rhythm is also born of a musical score written in ignorance of the greatest stories of this era. Hear it! The Church of Jesus Christ is alive and advancing!

As a spiritual leader, my only defense against the emotionally paralyzing and spiritually deteriorative effects of the pounding cadence of dismay is to tune into another than the world's wavelength. Just as James described the "wisdom" of this world as "earthly, sensual, demonic" (Jas. 3:15), so its evaluations of God's ways will derive from a blinded or corrupt perspective, and reports of His works will be either negative or neglected entirely. Whatever the latest word on the evening news or in the morning paper may say to the contrary, the dynamics of God's grace and power are immanently manifest today.

IMMANENCE AND IMMINENCE

"Immanently" is a carefully chosen word, which is as appropriate to describe the Holy Spirit's international workings today as it is to name one of the most basic traits of God's person. That He is "immanent" is to affirm He is "everywhere present"—pervading the universe, not merely as a cosmic presence, but as Creation's active and personal caretaker. To see above the minutia of our own private world, as well as beyond the trivia deemed important by newscasts and journals, is to find God at work in an unprecedented way today.

To lay hold of the sense of "promise" I believe each pastor-leader needs and deserves to be gripped by, a glimpse of the "imminent" present in the "immanent" needs to be captured. By this I mean, you and I need to see the broad dimensions of the Holy Spirit's pres-

YOU AND I ARE AT THE MOST PROMISING POINT IN THE HISTORY OF THE CHURCH!

ent mighty workings, because the convergence of so many great things seems to forecast an even greater fact: *We are on the brink of a sweeping move of God's Spirit—everywhere!*

Let me invite you to lift your eyes with mine—to look at what is happening, as a foretaste to even more I believe we have reason to expect soon—imminently. Do not expect to find much of the following report on the front page of your local paper, or the top story on any network news, but the capsulized summary here is only a "brief on blessing." It only hints at the abounding evidence present today of a fact I urge you to accept and respond to with me: *You and I are at the most promising point in the history of the Church!*

SIGNS OF IMMINENT GRACE

As pastors of promise on the brink of a new century, more than a freshness of calendar is at hand. The Holy Spirit is renewing wineskins everywhere He can find hearts open and available to the flowing of His graces. Notable among His works are the following:

- *Revitalizing signs of worship and praise are sweeping into every sector of the Church.* Freedom and joy once seen as the province of only a few sects or ethnic groups, are now filling houses of worship in every denomination. What is occurring is more than simply increased warmth and enthusiasm in services. A new under-

standing of worship and its practice and place in the life of the
local congregation is being seen for what it is: the fountainhead
of evangelism! The health in this aspect of God's present working is seen in a growing balance that both respects the values of
ancient worship traditions, while still being open to new creative workings of the Holy Spirit. He is resurrecting and applying the simplicity of biblical patterns of praise, and adding the
freshness of new song and new forms to ignite worship in
human hearts in the language of a new generation.

- *Practical steps of reconciling action are being taken by leaders in congregations and denominations.* Where insensitivity toward ethnic
pain and racial division have been historically characteristic,
repentance and servant-spirited partnership are now being initiated. In an hour when societal polarization and ethnic strife
and separatism appear to be removing any long-term hope of
true communal or national unity, God is at work to make a
statement. The Holy Spirit's action in the Church may well be
about to demonstrate to the world the one way human harmo-
ny can exist: in the circle of the true love of God. This is more
than an exercise in "political correctness gone to church." What
God is doing is beginning to raise up models of "Kingdom correctness"—the original and divine order that transcends
human hate and fear.

- *Revival signs in mass evangelism are increasing, and irrefutable signs
and wonders are appearing in many places.* As many as 33,000 decisions for Christ were recently recorded in one community;
Billy Graham's globally televised crusade in Puerto Rico was
beamed into more than 100 nations at one time; the harvest in
former Iron Curtain countries is so rapidly expanding that the
greatest challenge is to train leaders to shepherd flocks of new-
born. The proliferation of credible, specialized ministries
through multiple media are garnering a harvest in every corner
of society. People who have not visited church—yet!—are
coming to Christ in the secret corners of their own needs.
Manifest miracles of supernatural grace are restoring everything from broken marriages to broken bodies, and bringing
deliverance from every order of addiction or bondage.

- *Righteous signs of a growing unity in the Body of Christ are seen in
citywide concerts of prayer, a new passion for fasting, intercession and
sound-minded spiritual warfare.* Regional prayer summits among
groups of community pastors are bringing a breakthrough in
relationships, the transcending of denominational prejudice,

judgmentalism and bigotry, and a new unleashing of the power of the living Church on its knees is being discovered. This climate of prayer is opening the door to a new and true biblical and trustworthy order of ecumenism. Tens of thousands of pastors—along with their congregations—are coming to terms with Bible-based  **SMALL-MINDED SECTARIANISM IS BEING REVEALED AS AN UNWORTHY RELIC OF THE PAST TO BE DISCARDED.** honesty that reveals a spiritual unity amid our vast diversity as believers in Christ. Small-minded sectarianism is being revealed as an unworthy relic of the past to be discarded.

Such signs of high promise are occurring in profusion today across North America and in much of Europe. In the United States, the vitality many thoughtful observers see in this move of the Holy Spirit is causing some to use such terms as "a second Great Awakening." This reference to the profound spiritual shake-up that took place in the middle 1700s in colonial New England gives us a sense of the substance in these "signs of imminent grace." By any description, evidences of expanding blessing and a ripening harvest are abounding, and there are reasons for extraordinary hope.

RIGHT WHERE WE LIVE

Considering all the signs of promise—and the spiritual blessing beginning to break through on many fronts—perhaps the most significant sign of imminent concern for local pastors is one that is touching nearly every one of us right where we live. It is inescapably evident that a dramatic, if not overwhelmingly dynamic, move of God is apparent in what He is doing with men. *A mighty, Holy Spirit-begotten men's awakening is spreading everywhere!*

Suddenly, in a way that no man or movement could have generated, God is capturing the attention of men in the Church. It seems as though an inner trumpet has sounded within the souls of multitudes of men, just as the shofars openly resounded in Israel long ago to gather the men in Jerusalem each year. Stadiums across the nation are being packed to the brim—sellout crowds of 60,000 to 70,000 are common. To the bewilderment of the press, praises to the almighty God are thundering above the loudest cheers ever attending the sports events those venues have witnessed.

This movement is not the product of human promotion. Although the secular and religious press may *report* it, no human means or media has

manufactured it. The Holy Spirit's move among men is a creation of God—
a work of the Almighty. It signals to those of us who pastor that *here* is as
significant a place for our response as any at hand. Why?

First, because the present move of the Holy Spirit among men is not
focused on stadium events. Although the most visible evidence of God's hand
at work in this regard is in stadiums being filled, the most dynamic evidence
is elsewhere. The focus of the Promise Keepers ministry—the primary voice
to date in this movement—is clearly beyond stadiums. The directions given,
as each man is called to rise "as a man of God...a man of spiritual integrity,"
is to answer this call at home, as a man of Christ and His Church.

The center of gravity for this movement is not the stadium, but the
sanctuary; not to rally around a renowned speaker, but to stand with the
local pastor. Equally in focus is a man's learning to live as a servant to his
family and his community; to be a good husband and father, and to be a
reconciling, healing agent in his town or city. Although massive stadia may
provide a distant point of convergence for an annual weekend of challenge,
the focus of today's awakening of men is at that one central and continuing place of God's timeless workings—the local church!

Thus, it would seem obvious: At this hour, probably nothing is more
pivotal or strategic to my pastoral role than focusing on men. "Pastors of
promise" indeed! Here you and I stand, called of God to serve in a moment
when an entire generation of men are in need of "spiritual fathers." As a
shepherd, I have been placed by the Master to serve the men of His flock
at a season of history when men are at once the most needy and the most
ready! A confluence of three forces has influenced this need:

1. An entire generation has known few trustworthy leaders or
   heroes who have character;
2. We have experienced a complete generation during which societal forces have emasculated the role of males;
3. God is awakening a generation of men to reopen their hearts and
   souls to find the divine answer to their quest for true manhood.

ANSWER TO AN AWAKENING

In this spiritual and cultural environment, our pastoral call is clear: *Answer
to an awakening!* It is not a matter of simply seizing an opportunity, as though
one's pastoral mission was to be alert to moments that might be manipulated for promotional gain. Absolutely not! Pastoral effectiveness is not the
fruit of clever opportunism, but of hearing the call of the Spirit of God and
responding to His priorities in His ways. Jesus Christ, the builder of the
Church, is at work in men today. As a colaborer with Him (see 1 Cor. 3:9),

we each need to tune in to the voice of the Holy Spirit, and to His manifest works as they summon our partnership in pastoral mission.

Let me urge you, fellow shepherd—passionately! Begin at this point of imminent grace: *begin with men.* I know of no more strategic place to set my sights for future fruitfulness than to answer to this "sign of imminent grace"—this awakening among men. To start here is to start right, because a double dimension of fruitfulness is certain to be forthcoming.

First, to focus on building men is to charge myself with assuring my own growth as a model of godly manhood: *I* will grow. Second, to build men is to align myself with biblical patterns and priorities that lay the foundation for fruitful church life: the *church* will grow.

Exhorter and Example

Thus, here is that aspect of "God-at-work-today" that not only deserves my attention, but that will also summon my own growth as a man as well as a shepherd. As Christ's appointed overseer of my local flock, whether I recognize it or not, I am already the central point of spiritual reference in an awakening. Whether one man or a hundred answers the "stadium call" to commit to return and support his pastor and congregation, the pastor has been made the pivotal point in two ways: as *exhorter* and as *example*.

In the first role, my exhortation—my bold-but-brotherly encouragement—is essential in affirming and releasing the men in my congregation. They need the assurance that this awakening is valid, having their pastor's "go for it" as they seek to answer the Holy Spirit's call to them today.

The second role, my example, is the more significant and most demanding the sensitive pastor-leader has been given in this awakening. The role of "example" is not self-appointed, but is at the heart of all pastoral mission. As His undershepherds, Jesus has placed you and me as His "stand-ins"—as men who by lifestyle and servant-spiritedness will model biblical manhood.

This is an awakening of men to be matured and discipled—men newly ready to follow Christ the Lord. They have heard a heavenly trumpet call and know it is their hour in God's purpose. They are still "sheep needing a shepherd," and the Holy Spirit has called them home—to church, and to us who have been given the responsibility by God to lead.

> As the Holy Spirit is moving among men, a new thunder is filling stadiums: Praise to God—proclamation of His purpose! Early in the sequence of my being privileged to speak at some of the Promise Keeper men's gatherings, my hymn-writing instincts were captivated. I experienced a sense of *need*—at least *my* sense of a need—for a tower-

ing anthem that would proclaim what a man is about and what God wants to do in him. One day, the classic melody "Finlandia" came to mind (the same melody to which the hymn "Be Still My Soul" has been set).

When I listened to a gathering of 300 pastors sing the song at a conference in which I introduced the following, "I Am a Man," I felt God had confirmed my heart's sense of need and answered it. Since then, I have led hundreds of thousands of men in singing the following song, as the Holy Spirit is using every media possible to awaken them to His purposes today.

I AM A MAN
SUNG TO TUNE OF "FINLANDIA"

I am a man created in God's image,
Of Adam's race, now marred by pride and sin.
But thru' God's Son, Lord Jesus Christ, my
    Savior,
I am a man who's now restored to Him.
The Mighty God who made me has redeemed
    me,
Now I'm His man, for Jesus reigns within.

I am a man reborn to serve my Father.
"Your will be done in me," my spirit cries.
My life has found its dignity and purpose,
I'm not a creature of brute chance or lies.
To Christ my King I yield my whole existence,
Now as His man, I'm destined for the skies.

I am a man appointed by my Savior
To show His love in all I do and say.
His Holy Spirit is my source of power.
To live in light and point to Christ the Way.
Lord fill me now and help me seize the
    moment,
That as Your man, I'll serve Your cause today.

I'll be a man who walks with God in worship;
I'll be a man who walks with men as friend.

I'll be a man who loves and serves his family;
I'll be a man on whom God can depend.
Lord Jesus Christ, my King and my
        Commander.
I'll be Your man, until my life shall end.

Jack W. Hayford

This is not to minimize the place God is given by hosts of key laymen who are already providing stimulus and leadership in the Church or among men. Nor is it an insistence on an outdated hierarchical sense of self-importance, as though nothing can or should take place without you or me being "number one." Rather, the call of God to *men* is a call to each man to take his place—his role in God's intended purpose and order. For the local pastor, the call involves the unique privilege as well

SITTING IN THE MIDDLE OF A SHRIVELED VINEYARD, OR CRIPPLED AMID ONE'S OWN COMPROMISED INNER INTEGRITY, TAKES THE WIND OUT OF THE SOUL'S SAILS.

as assignment to motivate, model and mentor. Not because this is our *claim*, but because this is fundamental to our *call.* Well beyond privilege, we are looking at a holy responsibility.

Somewhere, I hear some pastor's heart whispering an uneasy, if not fear-ridden response—saying, "Not me, Jack." It may not be you, dear brother reader, but somewhere, reading these words right now, a fellow-shepherd of ours is wincing at these words. That whisper of doubt comes as a sign of heaviness from one whose own personal failure or pastoral fruitlessness block the path to his full reception of the promise this hour holds. Sitting in the middle of a shriveled vineyard, or crippled amid one's own compromised inner integrity, takes the wind out of the soul's sails. Breezes of revival and awakening may indeed be present, but collapsing a shepherd's soul is the adversary's most effective means for halting a local congregation's "catching the wind." If that shepherd is you, dear friend, I want to help you "take heart" not to lose it.

With everything that is in me, I urge you to hear Jesus' words: "Fear not! Doubt not!" Keep walking with me—forward. I want to beg of you, right here, right now, to suspend any preliminary judgment you might be tempted to make on your own possibilities as a pastor of promise. Even if you are reading this book and your life is confused or miserably disordered—stay with me. Or perhaps your flock is so small or spiritually impoverished that not even one faithful man is regularly present, or any men who seem at all spiritually responsive—there is still great promise. How so?

Because God is awakening men today, you have the highest reason to expect He's not going to pass you by! Because He is working with men, He is ready to work with you—and *through* you! He will give you men—one, two or many to serve—because He is at work seeking to do something among His sons in particular. Furthermore, He is ready to reshape or restore *anything* within your life or mine that is less than worthy as a model of manhood or of good shepherdlike behavior. So move forward with me. Move beyond any of your faith-restricting facts of frustrating or fruitless circumstance, and look at the promising facts that beckon to us as pastors.

TWO FACTS—A STARTING PLACE

Two facts provide a clear starting place for today's "pastor of promise":

1. God is calling men to discover their places in His purpose; and the center point to which they are being directed is to their local congregations, to partner with their pastors.
2. God has called you/me as a man of His—appointed to a place where He has given me reason to expect a people, and where I might live out His commission to expect to "father" sons of His.

The most significant thing about these dual facts is that they *both* apply to you and me, for we are each both—a man and a pastor. In short, (a) the Holy Spirit is calling me to let Him shape and firm (or recover and rebuild) anything of my own manhood that needs to be reconditioned after the order of the Father's intent. Then, (b) He is ready to fulfill His promise—endow me with grace to serve this hour by enabling me to answer it as a God-ordained "father" to the men of my local church family.

Thus, as the Holy Spirit is moving to redeem a generation of men whose minds and manners have been muddled by the disintegration of the world's order, He is pointing to pastors, placing us in view first of all. He is summoning us to recover the New Testament order for building men, and with it He is also placing a personal claim upon our own modeling role as true men ourselves.

The truth is, however, that the same emasculating forces that have diminished the perspective of most men on what biblical manhood involves has been pressing upon us as well. None of us who lead can possibly have remained completely uninfluenced by our culture's ideas and habits. Nor dare we suppose we have remained unmarked by the effect of the invisible spiritual forces that seek to refashion the base of Father God's character and ways in us.

Because He is committed to "fathering sons" through you and me, it is understandable that He will want to work on us first. Pastors of promise are not only the focus of a Holy Spirit awakening, but we will also become the focus of the Father's first workings. He will first and foremost want to purify us—to refine our spiritual genetics. If Christ's work in us constitutes the "strain" He intends to be transmitted through us as "fathers," we are wise to be open to His refinement at every point of our lives and thoughts. Whatever is deficient or distorted will become manifest in the men we lead, and thus God is calling us not only to lead in an awakening, but also to be reworked ourselves—humbled before Him with a readiness for renewal in our own souls.

GOD IS CALLING US NOT ONLY TO LEAD IN AN AWAKENING, BUT ALSO TO BE REWORKED OURSELVES—HUMBLED BEFORE HIM WITH A READINESS FOR RENEWAL IN OUR OWN SOULS.

You and I are not only being called to a new pastoral mind-set that will prioritize how we develop men, but also to a new place of manly honesty before God. We are not only being called to shepherd a generation of men toward biblical manhood, but also to let the Father shape us as men ourselves—as sons of His who, upon "fathering" other men, will have a godly, purified spiritual genetic secured in us. Only thereby will the fruit of our lives poured into other men replicate God's order of man, not our own.

PRIORITIZING WITHOUT MINIMIZING

Yes, God is at work in doing two things simultaneously—*reviving* the Church and *restoring* men. These are separate works, yet dynamically related, for if the Church is to move to its maximum potential, there is a need for men to find their places in God's economy for it. Yet to accomplish this, there is a fundamental need to discern and define; a need to recognize how easily a focus on men can be misinterpreted by society at large or the women in our congregations. There is an equal need to describe exactly what this emphasis on men does and does not mean.

Whatever may have happened at anytime or anyplace in its history, the Church was never intended to become an institution that tolerates or justifies an agenda of male chauvinism, either intentionally or unwittingly. At the same time, its history is clear—the Church has only risen to serve its fullest purposes when men rise to serve theirs. Only when men have answered to and accepted their responsibilities to lead the way—on God's terms—are the deepest furrows made and the richest harvests

GOD HAS NEVER RELEGATED WOMEN TO AN INFERIOR OR A SECOND PLACE; HE SIMPLY HAS GIVEN EACH GENDER A *DISTINCT* PLACE!

garnered. God has never relegated women to an inferior or a second place; He simply has given each gender a *distinct* place! His divine will in achieving this has obviously been distorted at times, but wherever His terms are applied, a woman's place, worth or potential will *never* be reduced. Indeed, it will be maximized, and the fruit will be the release of each woman to her highest possibilities—in life, and in Christ.

Putting the First Last and the Last First

Addressing this balance is crucial at the outset. Defining the pastor's call as a "father," and his prioritizing ministry to men in answer to an awakening, can easily be misunderstood. Still, the undeniable reality—both historically and presently—is present with us: God *initiates* through men, but contrary to secular or carnal ideas about that assignment, it never gives men private privilege or a higher hand of power. The sum of our Lord Jesus Christ's entire teaching about leadership or a leading role is that it puts the first last and the last first.

The call to prioritize ministry to men is a call to lead each man to a place of humility, responsibility and servanthood. The task is not easily achieved, given the thrust of the world mind, and its ability to imprint our own as leaders and as men. We are appointed, however, to "father" a new generation of "sons" who see, understand and will live out the truth of true manhood. Answering that appointment requires our being gripped by a conviction, and being willing to serve it with a tender sensitivity to the balance it demands. Yes, it is true, the fullest realization of either gender—and of the society as well as the Church itself—will only be possible when men are awakened to and responsible to serve their roles. So in the present awakening, pastors of promise are needed to lead men into a divinely ordered alignment.

By "alignment," I am referring to our need to line up with the details as well as the basics of God's divine order. I mean that each man—myself and those I serve as pastor—needs to be assisted to find his place in God's purpose and grow in it. To do that, each man needs to be helped to discover and find partnership in being discipled in the elements of the Father's plan for and pathway to true manhood. Most men—even those fairly regular in church attendance—have too little instruction in, or understanding of, what true biblical manhood entails. This is not so much for want of either intent or intelligence, for most believing men would probably like to know how to "make life work" on God's terms, and most certainly have the brains to learn it. The fact is that few pastors have been trained to prioritize discipling men.

Worse yet, given the mood of the world mind today, we are all so pressured to "equalize" the place of women and men that the place of a man in the divine order becomes confused and thereby has become *minimized*. Thus, our pastoral challenge is to find God's way to "father"—to develop a breed of holy offspring who know His ways. We need to become humbly "man enough" to pursue this task beyond the pulpit—however valuable that discipling tool of objective instruction. We need to "father" by touch as well as by truth— through the subjective infusion of life-to-life, pouring ourselves into men as we open our hearts to share our own struggles in growth. Such shaping of men, by "pastors of promise" who learn to "father" according to that promise, returns to the foundational plan for the Church, its life and its health.

FINDING THE ORIGINAL PATTERN

The New Testament way to realize such promise was set forth in the life of the Church long ago. Though contemporary pastoring has too often become defined by a score of other assignments, the original pattern can still be found and applied. At the Church's beginning, the foundational pastoral task was essentially wrapped in two phrases: (1) Pour yourself out, as pastor-to-men, and (2) teach those men to do the same, as man-to-man. This dual assignment is encapsulated in Paul's injunction to Timothy:

> *You therefore, my son, be strong in the grace that is in Christ Jesus. And the things that you have heard from me among many witnesses, commit these to faithful men who will be able to teach others also* (2 Tim. 2:1,2).

Notice closely how the opening words establish the nature of the apostle's influence on this young pastor: "You therefore, *my son*." The words carry a combination of authority mixed with affection. The young man is both commanded and comforted in the same breath—"You are to *lead*, but I've shown you how and I know you can do it!"

I can't read those words without sensing what Timothy must have felt—a surge of a rising personal assurance, born of Paul's confidence in him. I want to urge you to join me in hearing the Holy Spirit's whisper to us in those same words, for He did not record them to simply report a fact from history. Nor are they only recorded there as though intended to provide mere poetic beauty, as though to say, "What a paternal graciousness Paul models to his young charge!" Rather, as surely as Timothy most certainly received comfort in Paul's assuring kindness, I believe you and I are to find the same. They contain both a promise as well as a mandate.

Listen closely with me to the words, "You therefore, my son." For the God who called us—the ultimate Father Himself—is calling again, and assuring adequacy. He is charging us with the same pattern for pursuit in ministry, according to His original plan for multiplying fruitfulness in the Church. Further, in calling us "sons," He is making a designation not only laden with grace and affection, but also filled with the promise of an adequate genetic dynamic for the "fathering" task we are being assigned.

For us who provide pastoral ministry today, a clear mandate is set forward here. It is a priority that could easily be overlooked. For example, how wisely might we pause to study the context, and be reminded of our pastoral need for the same Holy Spirit-filled dynamic (see 2 Tim. 2:6,7) or for faithfulness in studying God's Word (see v. 15). A holy anointing of the Spirit and a divine enablement in the Word are essential to pastoral ministry. How often have we prayed for power as pastoral leaders, and labored in our studies about messages faithfully preached, and still unwittingly overlooked the fathering/discipling priority we have been given?

Today, however, the Holy Spirit is working to restore focus on our fundamental call to beget "sons," and in returning that to appropriate priority, we can expect new power in the Spirit and a new quickening as we minister the Word. When the original order is in place, all the benefits of the full divine order begin to flow together unto mightiness! At the same time, however, let us remember the opposite is equally true: A fullness of God's power and truth, without a focus on God's priorities in ministry, will inevitably result in a dissipation of holy energy and eventual frustration is certain to follow.

A SIMPLE-BUT-PROFOUND PATTERN

Look at the basic, original and simple-but-profound pattern for pursuing a pastoral mission with biblical promise. The second part of 2 Timothy 2:2 sets forth a two-step process:

1. Timothy is charged with "committing" the things of God to believing men—men openly committed to growing in Christ: *pastor-to-men.*

2. Then, these are shaped to shape others, at an increasing depth of relationship and breadth of fellowship: *man-to-man*.

This sense of pastoral mission—being awakened to the priority and promise God has given us about building and developing men—was not clear to me until I had been in ministry for more than 15 years. It came about through a distinct encounter with the Lord at entirely another season in the Church. No massive "awakening of men" was occurring, and materials were hardly to be found that pointed to the pathway of discipling men. What was I to do, and how was I to approach it?

In the fifth chapter, I ask to tell you the story, to relate the process by which the Holy Spirit helped me begin to "father sons," and thereby to gain a thousand "brothers." Because I am not sure all the means and methods available today necessarily result in such joyous fruit—such unity of family, or dynamic community. However beneficial the present profusion of discipling resources may be, I see an underlying deficiency. A vast resource of excellent materials for men is available right now, but to my perception there is almost a void of what I see as essential conceptual underpinnings. *It is my conviction that to (1) gain a man's conviction of his place, and then to (2) grow a man's consistency in serving it, requires a process of dismantling and deliverance as well as a pattern of dedication and discipleship.*

I see as necessary, to secure long-term transforming renewal and leadership development in a man, an answer to two foundational questions:

1. Why are men prioritized by God as they are (the answer to this question brings us to a woman's place in God's order)?
2. Why are men so reticent to respond to their places in God's plan (but women much more readily respond to spiritual promptings with sensitivity and service)?

To respond to these questions is not only to answer to significant issues that block men's growth, but also to confront essential points of bondage that bind men's souls.

Of course, founding a program that "begets sons" *will require* (a) establishing a pattern and program of discipleship for men: (b) bringing a biblical focus on husbanding and fatherhood; and (c) guiding men into service and ministry where human need and holy purposes direct. The wealth of resources available today most commonly focus on these matters. The fruit of such a teaching program *will result* in a pastor's fulfilling a "fathering" role in a practical way.

By reason of my "encounter" story to follow, I was brought to a sense of each man's need for an inner perspective on the complications Adam's

Fall has welded into the male psyche. In answering my call to prioritize shaping men, I have become convinced that too often we are tempted to build on a foundation that has not gone back to bedrock.

Pastors of promise are ones who will experience *both*—Abraham's and Paul's mission fulfilled: the "land" will be gained, the "nations" blessed, and "much people in this city" reached because of "sons" being multiplied. If, as we have said, we need to prioritize men in our pastoral mission to realize such promise, I believe we will be most certainly and effectively advanced on our way when we clearly know and can teach the answer to one question: Why do men have so primary and foundational a place in God's order and workings?

REFLECTION QUESTIONS

1. How have you responded to the new Christian men's movement, and what does it mean to you and the men of your congregation?
2. How have you been an exhorter and an example in building men?
3. The text says that the "call" involves the unique privilege as well as assignment to motivate, model and mentor. How has this been accomplished in your life?
4. If you pastor a small church, and not many men attend regularly, how do you envision changing that circumstance as a result of reading this chapter?
5. How can pastors discern and define how the focus on men can be misinterpreted by society at large or the women in our congregations? Describe what this emphasis on men does and does not mean.

CHAPTER FOUR HIGHLIGHTS

- Men in all cultures tend toward a *machismo* attitude—a kind of "masculinity" that exposes itself in a need to establish "turf."
- Those seeking to minister to men face the same thing a missionary does when ministering in a distinct culture. A men's gathering *is* a distinctive culture of its own—often called "a man thing" in today's slang.
- Pastors need a forthright willingness to solve the potential problem of alienating women and/or tolerating residual male chauvinism that lurks in the Church.
- A study of 1 Timothy 2:8—3:8 reveals important issues about understanding the roles of men and women, and the original order of God's creation.

I desire therefore that the men pray everywhere, lifting up holy hands, without wrath and doubting.

1 TIMOTHY 2:8

THE MYSTERY OF MEN IN GOD'S DIVINE ORDER

Few things are more likely to stir debate or conflict than to assert that men are "first" in God's human order. It is a puzzling proposition, although the Bible is clear that it is to be so. The range of attitudes this fact stirs runs from dogmatic, thumping agreement to infuriated, vociferous rejection. Is this a storm God wanted to cause, and if not, why this apparently mysterious start to things?

I see two "mysteries" in this regard: First, "why" is this so; and second, "how" are men and women to respond to it? A surprise encounter, years ago, evolved in the realization that truly effective ministry among the whole congregation depended upon my solving these dilemmas.

As a result of answers I gradually gained, not only has a strong men's ministry been built, but also incredibly great blessing and profit have come to women, children and whole families. As well, the effect was dramatic—and continues to be—on our entire congregation's life, and an ever-broadening influence is seen in our community for Christ. This fulfilled "promise" in pastoring began at a specific moment, on an icy cold, bitingly crisp winter morning. What happened that day eventually prodded me to find workable, biblical answers to these mysteries, and to the mystery of the male psyche and the responses it generates in men.

"BEGIN TO GATHER MEN"

It was February in Illinois, and the sun was still too low in the sky to affect the early morning's bitter cold. The whole area was frozen, and the snow was literally snapping under my feet with each step as I was walking near the banks of the Mississippi. I was thinking about the series of meetings I was conducting at a church there. As I trudged through the snowdrifts, mixing exercise with a time of prayer, I sensed a whisper in my soul: *Begin to gather men and to train them, and as you do, I will raise up strong leadership for the future.*

That prompting came during the early seasons of a visitation of divine grace that first brought unusual growth to our small Southern California congregation. Looking back, I am still amazed. In no way could I ever have dreamed of the grace that has since followed. But that winter day, I did sense the wisdom of the Lord's word to my soul. I recognized the practical wisdom and sound mindedness of cultivating men of commitment—guys who have a sensible kind of spirituality, and who would show a servant-minded availability.

Six weeks later, I sent my first letter to about three dozen men in our church. I personally invited each of them to meet me on a Saturday morning. I said I wanted to share my heart with them about the men of our congregation. At the same time, I placed an open announcement in the church bulletin, but I was counting on "striking fire" with a key group for starters. For having no precedent, the gatherings made a reasonably good start: Guys were responsive, and though the group was not large, neither was our church at that time.

Early on in those meetings I first recognized a "trait" of men when they gather; a phenomenon that, since then, I have noticed almost everywhere guys get together. Eventually I processed this issue, and made a half dozen discoveries along the way. At the beginning, though, I did not do much—just moved slowly, learning as we went. As a young pastor, I was into doing things I had never been taught, for "men's ministries" had not been a forté in any pastoral models I had seen nor included in any curriculum my formal training had provided.

"Thinking Through" the Meetings

This men's "trait" was hard to put my finger on at first. I did not recognize its source or have a clear definition how to describe it. At times, I wondered if it was just a feeling of mine—was it only something significant to *my* perspective? Although I entertained suspicions about my feelings, I carried the concern in prayerful thought.

As my times together with our guys approached each month, I formed the habit of "thinking through" the meeting—picturing it in my mind—imagining the various men and how they had responded (or had not) in previous meetings. More than simply preparing my teaching materials, in prayer I would envision the unique qualities or observable weaknesses I sensed in guys who were more or less representative of our men in the church. As I did, the Holy Spirit helped me begin to dissect the "feel" of our meetings, and discernment came regarding a certain "man mood," which had virtually become a pattern response at our "men only" meetings.

The "mood"—maybe you have seen it too—is a kind of brusque, manly, glad-handed sort of "shine on" that guys seem to affect when they get together. To some degree, I was happy about the "camaraderie" aspect of it, that "Hey, buddy!" sort of good-naturedness that is generally present when guys get together for good times. Within this otherwise inoffensive way of relating, however, I detected another "spirit," then and now, in man-to-man settings and relationships. Although this "something" is usually submerged in an upbeat mood, I am convinced it needs to be identified and addressed; to neglect to do so will eventually become self-defeating in bringing guys to genuine self-discovery as men.

"Spiritualized Machismo"

When it is in a setting of believing men, I call this "spirit" "spiritualized machismo." *Machismo*, of course, is that exaggerated, if not artificial, "masculinity" that muscles itself into any scene in which a man feels the need to establish "turf." It appears often in the 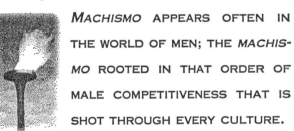 **MACHISMO APPEARS OFTEN IN THE WORLD OF MEN; THE *MACHISMO* ROOTED IN THAT ORDER OF MALE COMPETITIVENESS THAT IS SHOT THROUGH EVERY CULTURE.** world of men; the *machismo* rooted in that order of male competitiveness that is shot through every culture. Although *machismo* is a word coined in the Latin community, its traits are not limited to any group. It can surface in everything from the crude and the lewd, having its own set of cheap terms for manliness; the sensual and sexual, garnering conquests to verify "studsmanship"; tied to achievement, power, money or their manifest signs, or to a strutting style or street smarts.

All or any combination of these are used in humanized efforts at verifying manliness. At their least harmful expression, these "man traits" are only generated by the *human* spirit, but if left unidentified and unchecked they will give place to something more; to a "man pride" energy that is *entirely* of the spirit of the world. Reflection of the world-man's *machismo* will eventually deceive, and project a "man-ish strength" that can become a deceptive substitute for a deep and true spiritual penetration of a man's life.

At the time, though, I was just starting to recognize this trait.

A Kind of Death Syndrome

I was wrestling with the question: Why do I feel uncomfortable with the mood of the men's gatherings, especially because most of the guys are so upbeat and positive—laughter, slaps on the back, jibes, good humor, "praise-the-Lords" and all?

In my observation, one of the greatest challenges in the settings of today's stadium-size men's events is to find the way past the "look-how-successful-and-grand-we-all-are-here" mood, and to cut to the gut of the individual man's soul with reality. It does not require a stadium-size crowd to generate that superficial front that can blockade genuine, long-term transformation through spiritual encounter. It can happen in a breakfast booth with 5 guys, in a chapel with 25 or in a fellowship hall with 50.

I now see this as a kind of death syndrome, potentially sure to kill the possibility of men "going deep." As a pastor, I was wondering, *What has produced this strain of carnal independence and self-sufficiency that runs through the male psyche?* I knew I was as vulnerable to it as any guy—I even felt it when among other pastors. It is that "I'm as good a man as you are, any day" need to be on top, to win, to establish turf or to vindicate self. However polished it appears—even if shouting the challenge, *"I love Jesus, yes I do! How about you!?"*—it is tinctured with male pride. Unconfronted, it will keep any man from actually coming face-to-face with God in true humility, and with other men in genuine honesty.

A CULTURE OF THEIR OWN

During the time I was seeking the Lord for discernment and wisdom, I suddenly saw something: In seeking to minister to men, I was facing the same thing a missionary does when ministering in a distinct culture. It became clear: A men's gathering *is* a distinctive culture of its own—often called "a man thing" in today's slang. Recognizing this, I thought of the problem of "syncretism"; the creeping tendency to compromise the full truth of God's Word when ministering cross-culturally.

We are all familiar with cases of spiritual disasters resulting from syncretism, when a culture's tastes or preferences are preferred above spiritual truth or disciplines. Such compromises are a sad matter of history, when a watered-down "christianity" is offered by a misguided zeal to hasten a society's acceptance of the gospel. By allowing the assimilation of cultural traits that betray true conversion into the life of believers, the syncretist fails to discern between "culture" and "error." Such strategic failure has introduced confusion around the globe, and resulted in putting a Christian cosmetic on everything from idolatry to animism.

Now I recognized my challenge. My pastoral pursuit of a ministry to men was a call to a "distinct culture," and I was put on guard against my capacity for "syncretism"—right here in my own congregation.

I knew I needed to take decisive steps. I was committed to contend for an atmosphere where real disciples would be developed; for building men who would become uncontrolled by the world spirit, including the subtlest deceptive traits of a world-minded "male culture."

That False Bravado

My mandate was clear: *Confront anything that tends to tolerate or nourish however slight a surrender to the world spirit, including that false bravado men virtually always reveal around other men.* That "have-to-prove-myself" pressure almost every man feels when he is with other guys may manifest itself with a more polished style in a spiritual setting, but it is still a man's "cultural" thing. To fail to discern and confront it will stunt the eventual potential of the men we seek to disciple. This "man thing" is no holier when transferred to a men's worship or study setting than it is in a bar or at a football game.

THIS "MAN THING" IS NO HOLIER WHEN TRANSFERRED TO A MEN'S WORSHIP OR STUDY SETTING THAN IT IS IN A BAR OR AT A FOOTBALL GAME.

First, I knew that the excitement the guys felt was not bad in itself. I did not feel obligated to "kill" exuberance, however temporal, because there is a value in the emotion of brotherly camaraderie, *esprit-de-corps* or brotherly good cheer. We all know that excitement alone, however genuine, has its limits, but I believed the upbeat tempo in our gatherings could be retained, and a penetrating, transforming approach to discipleship be realized. I felt I had an assignment from the Holy Spirit: *Find a way inside every facade the world breeds in men.*

Here was a call to learn how to keep the best of the "winning locker-room" mood, but to move the men further—to bring them into the "throne room of heaven." So we do, even today, bring the men there with a *readi-*

ness for and a *realization of* genuine worship before the living God. I believe that such an encounter paves the way for each man to become honest with himself, transparent with other guys and move into an openness to deep dimensions of discipleship.

A BEVY OF LESSONS

This quest for substance beyond exuberance, and frequent prayerful times of thought it birthed, helped me toward what, for me, were profound pathways that led to something more than a quick answer or a tricky technique. It was as though a whole "theology for men's ministry" was born; and a bevy of lessons began to distill in my mind, bringing focus and understanding. For example:

1. I was helped to see, at least to my perspective, why we pastors tend to gain only a limited numerical response from men when we try to establish "men's meetings."
2. I seemed to find a key to "breaking through" to a deeper dimension with men, overcoming the masculine reserve toward acknowledging a warm, continuing interest in spiritual things.
3. I discovered something of my own "fears," surprised to actually face a peculiar intimidation when I went to lead a "men only" meeting.
4. I uncovered a secret in communication, which opened the way to gain the trust of the men I was hoping to disciple.
5. I was brought face-to-face with a hitherto unrecognized (by me) "male chauvinism," which had never been defined as such in my understanding, but which was nonetheless a sanctified fixture in the mind-set of most in the Church.
6. I was helped by the Holy Spirit to "sort out" what I now see as the "gender-difference-solution" to the issue of clear biblical priority placed upon men—to lead.

(Rather than outlining these specifics as I proceed, I think you will find each of the previous items unfold as I relate the turning point that opened my understanding. The groundwork for an effective ministry among the men of my congregation was laid on a layer-by-layer basis, as God's Word for "manliness" came clearer to me.)

UNVEILING A KEY PASSAGE

Central to my growing list of discoveries was an "unveiling" of a key passage in 1 Timothy. From God's heart, and the pen of Paul—who was effective in developing men for leadership—a cluster of concepts distilled that answered other things I was noticing in those early men's meetings.

For example, it bothered me that some guys did not see the difference in a disciplelike "gettin' it on with growth," and a macholike "gonna really 'wear the pants'" cockiness. Too easily, some guys saw our resurgence of a focus on men as something of an antifeminist counterattack, having an undercurrent tantamount to the proposal of a gay-bashing crusade. No, nobody spoke this way "out loud," but the rumble existed beneath the surface then, and it still does. Men who have been demeaned and redefined for a generation are frustrated.

Still, whatever teaching or ministry may be needed to withstand or neutralize the world's confusion about men and their roles, more is needed than anger or protest. I knew we needed a conceptual base for our men's ministry that was more than something merely founded on an antisocietal or propolitical agenda. This is why my encounter with 1 Timothy meant so much.

To open the way for discussing the whole cluster of "men's issues" that emerge here, let's first read the extended passage of the oft-quoted verse that began to reveal the text to me.

1 TIMOTHY 2:8—3:8

I desire therefore that the men pray everywhere, lifting up holy hands, without wrath and doubting;

in like manner also, that the women adorn themselves in modest apparel, with propriety and moderation, not with braided hair or gold or pearls or costly clothing,

but, which is proper for women professing godliness, with good works.

Let a woman learn in silence with all submission.

And I do not permit a woman to teach or to have authority over a man, but to be in silence.

For Adam was formed first, then Eve.

And Adam was not deceived, but the woman being deceived, fell into transgression.

Nevertheless she will be saved in childbearing if they continue in faith, love, and holiness, with self-control.

This is a faithful saying: If a man desires the position of a bishop, he desires a good work.

A bishop then must be blameless, the husband of one wife, temperate, sober-minded, of good behavior, hospitable, able to teach;

not given to wine, not violent, not greedy for money, but gentle, not quarrelsome, not covetous;

one who rules his own house well, having his children in submission with all reverence

(for if a man does not know how to rule his own house, how will he take care of the church of God?);

not a novice, lest being puffed up with pride he fall into the same condemnation as the devil.

Moreover he must have a good testimony among those who are outside, lest he fall into reproach and the snare of the devil.

Likewise deacons must be reverent, not double-tongued.

APOSTOLIC APPEAL OR "HOT POTATO"?

My first discovery came one day as I noted the full context of 1 Timothy 2:8. I was preparing for a men's meeting, and while reading "I desire that all men everywhere lift up holy hands," was suddenly struck by the adjacent words. Right there, side by side with this grand apostolic appeal calling men to prayer and worship, was one of the real "hot potato" passages of the New Testament.

I was puzzled at how the neighboring verses seem to "take a shot" at women, and because I pastor amid our culture's muddled mind-set, I felt challenged to answer the questions these passages present. Let me elaborate before pursuing the text.

Resisting Error, Balancing Truth

During the past 30 years, the rise of the vocal, often rabid, feminist movement has presented a very real liability to sensitive pastors. How can we resist the arrogant, rebellious spirit often seen in militant feminism, and not appear to deny the fact that women have suffered certain injustices in our culture? How can we present the truth in balance, showing a man's call to lead, without appearing to diminish the high significance of a woman's place or potential?

For my part, the challenge is not in answering the question, "Where do men and women each fit in God's order?" It is knowing how to relate that truth sensitively to a Bible-impoverished, spiritually blinded society. It is hard sometimes even to "get through" to believers! The loaded rhetoric, mutual suspicion and gender hostility met at every turn today have created a climate of opposition that is tough to navigate. Screams of "male exploitation" are sometimes justified, and not *all* demands for "women's rights" are unreasonable (though the militancy mind-set and methods are often less sensitive than the insensitivities that are being protested!).

In this milieu, how can a pastor find a way to describe the benevolent, redemptive and dignifying objective the Father has intended for women? He *has* placed men "first," but how can I communicate this to a culturally begotten "silent shriek" if a woman's mind deafens her to hearing what the Bible so beautifully and redemptively intends?

Men do not hear well either, for once the subject of "the man's role in God's plan" is on the table, too many guys presume they already understand it: *"We're number one!"* The nuances within the "men first" truth—above all, the self-sacrificing cost to a man if he commits to fulfilling that role—roll off the soul like rain off a skylight. Heaven is shining in, but the Spirit can too seldom find a ready heart, so even in the Church today, the status quo of cultural confusion is difficult to overcome. A host of Bible-believing men and women continue to either overreact to feminist claims, or are unduly shaped by them.

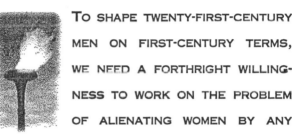

TO SHAPE TWENTY-FIRST-CENTURY MEN ON FIRST-CENTURY TERMS, WE NEED A FORTHRIGHT WILLINGNESS TO WORK ON THE PROBLEM OF ALIENATING WOMEN BY ANY RESIDUAL MALE CHAUVINISM THAT MAY LURK IN THE CHURCH.

As pastors with the heartfelt promise of a call to shape men to find their highest and best, however, we need to be equipped with an approach to the Scriptures that unveils what God has locked in His Word to unlock in people's lives! To shape twenty-first-century men on first-century terms, we need a forthright willingness to work on the problem of alienating women by any residual male chauvinism that may lurk in the Church. It is hardly acknowledged, but it is there—and it needs to be addressed with balance rarely shown until recently.

Enough belligerency and misinterpretation of Scriptures has been spread for years by the loveless and legalistic rantings to warrant the scorn of some protest. Enough "angry Christian" responses, and a long enough history of ecclesiastical justifying of chauvinistic habits, have occurred to verify the views of some worldlings who fault Christians as narrow-minded and indifferent to either social grace or good sense.

Because of all this, men need and deserve more than a parroting of the "male-centrist" posturing often presented as "biblical." Discipling men today calls each pastor of promise to do more than merely enunciate a man's "role-call" to leadership. We need to also help them understand God's evenhanded treatment of the sexes in His Word, and thankfully, 1 Timothy 2 opens the doorway to a deeper understanding that is intended to set *both* genders free!

"Charting the Course"

Before I ask you to walk through verses 9 to 15, let me describe where I plan to go. I have shared what follows with pastors from a variety of backgrounds and for many years. Whenever I have, a special grace has always seemed to attend those settings; one I want to invoke now, praying, "Father, help us see into Your Word and past the human thought habits that bind and confuse—in Jesus' name." With that prayer, let me "chart the course"—that is, overview some key issues—and then we will go back and "study the map" more closely.

ADVANCING THE REFORMATION

First Timothy 2:8-15 reminds me of words from my book *Worship His Majesty:*

> Nearly a half-millennium ago the Church was shaken to its roots—dragged by the nape of the neck to confront the reality of God's Word, and forced to face the fact that its forms had chained its people rather than freed them. The dual truths of "justification by faith" and "the priesthood of the believer" were trumpeted forth and the true "church"—the people of God—was released through a recovery of the revelation of God's Word.[1]

The Church *has* experienced a revival of worship—a global renewal of vital life—as the biblical priority and the spiritual warmth and passion for worship have "advanced" the Reformation in our times. A fundamental starting point for every spiritual leader should be the mightiness of the Holy Spirit's work in "reforming the Church." Bringing it beyond its medieval blindness and dearth was not completed in one century of theological reawakening. Just as a recovery of *sound doctrine* occurred in the time of Luther, Calvin, Zwingli, Huss and Knox, so a renewal occurred in *practical holiness* in Wesley's time, a stirring to *world missions* in Carey's and an awakening of passionate *evangelism* in Finney's and Moody's.

Further, the twentieth century has seen a refreshing of the living Church through a return to a first-century *dependence upon the Holy Spirit*. Besides a resurgence of *life in wor-*

ship, the global Body of Christ has experienced a renewed understanding and availability of the *Spirit's gifts*, so that an entire generation of Christians is realizing new dimensions of effective *"every member" ministry* and Body life.

As waves of wonder are sweeping the Church today, as God brings a men's awakening across the earth, we might well expect a "de-cobwebbing" of ideas about men's and women's roles. Each wave of the Holy Spirit's work of ongoing Reformation carries a companion phenomenon: He continually unveils long-buried simplicity and vitality that was *always* in the Word, but that human tradition buried. Bear witness to the present plethora of books about men as another stage of our Lord's advancing the Reformation, joining an awareness of His Word with an awakening of His Spirit.

Although opening the windows of heaven to fresh air is not always a welcome action, for many medieval pre-Reformation traditions run deep, a fresh breeze still is blowing through the Church today. As the Spirit of all true Reformation is at work (His name is "Holy"!), He is showing BOTH—the *grounds* for acknowledging God's policy of "men first," and also its *goal*! It is neither to secure a "christianized chauvinism" or a "sanctified feminism."

I am about to relate what I have proven to be a biblical pathway for communicating the truth of *"men first"* as a God-ordained redemptive means for achieving an eventual full and equal partnership between husbands and wives. My approach refuses to cower to the world spirit in the militant feminist movement. *Although I want to affirm the Bible's revelation regarding the woman's original (and ultimately proper) place, I want to remove the idea she was ever to be "second"!* My approach

GOD'S "ROLE" ORDER FOR EACH GENDER DID NOT INTEND A SUPERIOR ROLE PLACEMENT OR A PREFERENTIAL, PREDESTINED PRIVILEGE GIVEN MEN TO BE INSINUATED UPON HUMANITY'S WOMANKIND BY AN ARBITRARY CREATOR.

insists that God has indeed positioned the redeemed man "first" in reference to the believing woman, *but we will see this revealed as a redemptive role—not as a privilege, a permanent position or a "right" to primacy, but to servanthood.*

To "raise" a man to this role, I believe the truth of *"men first"* must be separated from confused ideas of "male superiority." God's "role" order for each gender did not intend a superior role placement or a preferential, predestined privilege given men to be insinuated upon humanity's womankind by an arbitrary Creator. Contrary to the angry presumption of the feminist, and miles apart from the dogmatism of traditionalized Bible interpretations, God's *"men first"* agenda has a deeply redemptive purpose. Further, His decree regarding the man's and woman's role, though practical to be desired for all humanity, is actually only incumbent upon believers in Christ. To attempt imposition on the worldling is to invite confusion, for only in Christ and by His power can the faith and dynamic for these biblical roles be lived to their fullest.

THE STARTING POINT FOR UNDERSTANDING

Foundationally, we need to see that God's *"men first"* decision was not one He made as Creator, but among His first actions as Redeemer. I am persuaded that this role for the man is as basic in the redemptive scheme as it was when God said "the seed of the woman" was essential to crush the serpent's evil work. It is complementary in His strategy to bring full restoration to mankind; it is a part of His means to implement *a redemptive remedy aimed at recovering the earlier, pre-Fall equality of man and wife.*

God's prescription of roles after the Fall points the way to something wonderful, to a restorative means by those who are restored to Him through the salvation provided through "the seed of the woman." Just as our "new birth" brings back our relationship with God, so I believe a "renewed understanding" can bring back God's original intent for relationships between men and women in general, and husbands and wives in particular. It hinges on each man's understanding and acceptance of his role.

So it is that this text will target men who know Christ to get "on track" in understanding themselves and their call as men:

1. To learn the true meaning of manhood with all its implications for cutting free of carnal and false religious ideas of "manhood";
2. To accept the call to a divinely appointed "redemptive mission," as a recoverer of possibilities that sin has removed.

Whenever I have taught these two things, more and more guys begin to take their place of leadership, and their wives a place of godly submission. The man's motivation, however, is not tainted with the subtle pride a traditionalized *"men first"* agenda can easily breed, nor is the woman cast as a demure, Pollyanna-ishly sweet thing who passively submits. Instead, an *active* submission is born in women whose responses differ because of the *servant-spirit* of men who understand the God-ordained goals of their leadership roles.

Let's see how *God's target in calling men to lead is to release a redemptive dynamic that, once set in motion, not only fulfills His Word, but also frees and elevates women and enriches and enhances marriages. In addition, when men accept their "leading" roles, **everything** finds its maximum release and realization and brings the fullest fulfillment to women, families, churches, businesses and the community at large.*

MAPPING THE PATH TO UNDERSTANDING

First Timothy 2 provides answers to tough, practical questions. Its exposition gives solid foundations for a man's self-understanding, and thereby his responsible movement forward into true manhood. *It unravels a tangle of problems:* (1) from the reason men tend to be less responsive to spiritual things than women are, (2) to answering why a few New Testament texts seem to demean a woman's role. Above all, (3) it addresses a society that is confused about God's Word and purpose for each gender.

For me, the "unraveling" began by heeding some insights into "the mystery of the male psyche." It started with verse 8:

> *Therefore, I desire that the men pray everywhere, lifting up holy hands, without wrath and doubting.*

The Context: A Quest for Male Leadership

Two new things struck me, both related to the context—the surrounding verses and ideas from verse 8. *First,* these words were directives given to apply what the opening verses 1-7 called for: the Church, at intercessory prayer. *Second,* verses 8-15 led directly to an appeal for men to lead, including a direct elaboration of character requirements for doing so.

I had never noticed those two things before!

Although I *had* often quoted Paul's call to men to open, forthright prayer, (*"lifting holy hands"*), away from angry debate (*"wrath"*—born of male competitiveness or human self-righteousness), and from unbelief (*"doubting"*—produced by the masculine tendency to discredit his spiritual viability, because of failure or condemnation), I had not really noticed the larger context.

Now I saw this appeal as it flowed through the whole passage—all of chapter 2 and into chapter 3—as a complete plea for MEN! Now, reading it in the wisdom of this sound interpretive approach, one thing became exceedingly clear: *The overriding focus of bringing men toward taking their respon-*

sible roles in spiritual leadership and ministry is key to understanding chapter 2:8-15!

In statements before and after these verses, Paul is virtually trumpeting (in verses 1-8): "Men, take your place of leadership in the congregation's prayer-life!"; then (in 3:1-15): "Sir, to be a servant-leader in the Body, these growth-traits need to show!" To see this strategic approach to men in its full breadth is to help us not miss the key to our text (verses 9-15): "Brothers, to rise to your role, learn your responsibilities—as a man!"

These insights help us see how the introduction of "women" issues in these verses has more to do with building *gentlemen* than it does with correcting or criticizing *ladies*. God's Word is seeking to help men see the root of their failure at accepting leadership responsibility, and is calling women to help men answer that call.

A Problem: The Wives' Influence on Their Husbands

First Timothy 2:9-15 is one of three New Testament texts (along with 1 Corinthians 11:2-16 and 14:34,35) that have become notorious through unreformed tradition and heavy-handed interpretation. We can recover a practical, faithful and sensitive application, however, if we unlock it using two keys to understanding.

First, we must remember the context of the passage (especially 3:2,4,5,11,12, which follow) is *very* emphatic in expecting men who are growing in God to also learn the responsibilities essential to a growing relationship with their wives.

Second, we must retranslate the Greek noun *aner* "man/men," as it should be—"husband." This is its foremost use, even though it is also a gender-referencing term for men. But if contextually translated "husband," it sheds light on what is said about "woman/women," indicating "wives" are being addressed specifically, not "women" generically.

Applying these keys, a thoughtful analysis begins to reveal that Paul is not reprimanding women; he is working at releasing men! We need to see that references to "women" are to *wives,* and are purposed at moving their husbands from unresponsiveness and/or neglected responsibility to their roles as "redemptive leaders." These verses were never intended essentially for addressing "women" in a categorical sense, but are to wives in a married sense. (This is not to say the *principles* of the passage are only related to husbands and wives, but the *problems* being addressed are primarily within that relationship.)

Apparently, then as now, the style and speech of believing women—carried over from habits shaped in a pagan society—tended to discourage their husbands' growth toward leadership. As Paul is seeking to embolden men as prayer-leaders and servant-leaders, he is concerned that the men learn to accept their full roles and responsibilities as men. He sees, though, how the worldly patterns of role-reversal and stressed inter-relationship between spouses are working against a God-ordained goal. (As we will shortly see, that goal is *greatly* in the woman's interest, so Paul's motive to have her "help her man grow" is targeted on their joint joy together.)

Paul calls women—especially wives—to contrast their behavior with the world's behavior. He urges them to grow past practices of feminine manipulation through an outward show of style consciousness, and from habits or practices of verbal pushiness, which become completely counter-productive—whether through irritating, discouraging or even intimidating their husbands. To pave a pathway to reestablish men as accountable and responsible for the redemptive role of leadership God desires, the Word of God says:

1. Verses 9,10: *"In like manner also, that the women adorn themselves"* is a parallel exhortation to the one given to the men in verse 8. In short, *both* men and women are told, "Don't take on the characteristics the world has shaped in your gender: *men*, stop your anger and doubt; *women*, stop using your beauty as a tool to allure or a key to your appeal."

2. Verses 11,12 are a plea for the wife to restrain herself in two ways: (a) from being too quick to crowd her husband's own initiative regarding talking about spiritual things (her natural readiness may too easily work against her husband's "coming out" spiritually, and he will likely reflect a man's natural reluctance); and (b) from her inclination to "take over and lead"—a temptation abundantly present seeing as so many men forfeit their roles, leaving responsibilities for their wives to discharge that are their own God-assigned duties.

What About "Woman, Be Silent!"?

Key to our freeing this text to truly "speak" its fullest message, we need to correctly set the word "silence" in the context of its usage here. If anything, this text has too often been used to suggest "real men put women in their place!" This is not the spirit or the truth of this passage, however distorted such emphases may have made it seem to be. In teaching my men, I felt it mandatory that we all see that God's Word here is not reprimanding women for talkativeness as much as reproving men for inattention to their responsibilities. Take, for example, the issue of the apparent statement: "Woman, be silent!"

"Silent/silence" is a twice-used term, in verses 11 and 12, expressed in the Greek *hesuchia,* but the same word is used in verse 2. We have an immediate contextual usage that can clarify *hesuchia*'s contextual usage; still, I have never found a commentator who drew attention to this fact. Rather, a too-quick readiness to subordinate women reveals itself. Most translations/interpretations use a gentler word in describing verse 2's content, and sometimes an almost brutal brusqueness describes *hesuchia* in verses 11 and 12. Although precisely the same word appears, the first *hesuchia* is shown as "peaceful," and the second two times is translated "silence" or "to be silent." The mood communicated too often seems to basically say, "Ladies, shut up!"

However, in context, *hsuchia* clearly means to call women (again, especially wives) to exercise orderly, self-governing spirits. The passage is not

a muzzling "cease and desist" order, but something far more gracious and meaningful. Paul is saying the same thing to wives here that Peter says in his first letter: "Ladies, don't depend upon your talk to train your husband in godli- *HERE IS THE STARTING PLACE ON THE PATHWAY TO RECOVERING GOD'S ORIGINAL ORDER FOR COUPLES, ONE RESTORING EACH TO THE PARTNERSHIP GOD DESIGNED FOR HUSBAND AND WIFE FROM THE BEGINNING!*

ness—gain his release as the man he's meant to be by your walk!" (My abbreviated paraphrase of 1 Peter 3:1-6.)

When we keep focused on the apostle's paramount objective in this passage, it all comes together. His priority is, through the call of the Spirit, to awaken men and women to a dynamic point of spiritual understanding. The power principle at stake is essential to both genders, and the men we teach need to see how crucial their return to responsibility is. Why? *Because here is the starting place on the pathway to recovering God's original order for couples, one restoring each to the partnership God designed for husband and wife from the beginning!*

That statement is the heart of what this text teaches. We need to gain the high ground of God's high purpose, which this passage unfolds: to see how Paul is not diminishing women. Rather, he is trying to say, "Wives, if you'll voluntarily learn to restrain yourself from *pushing* your husband to be spiritual, and if you'll exercise a self-administrated graciousness of loving submission, you'll maximize the likelihood of that man rising to accept his God-ordained role—*and you'll be blessed!*"

That "blessing" is directly linked to a man's rediscovering and reclaiming his role; to restoring male leadership that releases a "redemptive recovery" rather than something that preserves a "masculine preeminence." Herein, the Word of God is pointing us to the "why" of all "men's ministry"—toward Creation's initial program for couples and their communities; toward the possibilities that come within reach when men relearn their redemptive potential. As the apostle Paul continues to press his quest for men to assume their responsible *and releasing* roles of *redemptive leadership* (not "deserved, created preference"), he begins to press the issue of man's responsibility with a penetrating insight.

> *For Adam was formed first, then Eve. And Adam was not deceived, but the woman being deceived, fell into transgression. Nevertheless she will be saved in childbearing if they continue in faith, love, and holiness, with self-control* (1 Tim. 2:13-15).

Become Realistic by Asking Some Obvious Questions

Why has Adam's being "formed first" become an issue? Was it to remind us "Eve belongs in second place"? Why the mention that "Adam was not deceived"? Was it to suggest "He was a lot smarter than 'deceived Eve'"?

A superficial or prejudiced look at this passage has often seen verse 13 as declaring "rank," as though to justify the presumed "muzzling" of the preceding verses. Paul is, however, pointing to the issue of the first man's "responsibility," because Adam's sore neglect, at his pristine moment of opportunity to "protect," became the source of the Fall of the race. Further, the redemptive truth disclosed here is pointing the way "back"—not to a pre-Fall "domination" of woman by the man, but to an understanding meant to motivate men and women to accept the path of redemptive discipleship, to gain that originally intended "dominion" shared by man and wife.

What Was "The Original Order"?

The Bible reveals that at their creation, in the original divine order, an equal rank was given the first couple. From the inception of their being, an equally valuable, noncompetitive role was established by the Creator. The record of the Word clearly shows that the words of our text, "for Adam was created first, then Eve," should not be misconstrued to suggest a descending order of authority, but rather a distinction of roles within their equal assignment as partnering sovereigns over Creation (i.e., under God).

> Some believe that Adam's being created first, and then assigned to naming the animals, was an action designed by the Creator to demonstrate a male role of greater prominence than the female's in reference to Creation. This loaded interpretation insists on securing the man's "head-

ship" on the grounds of the created *sequence* God chose in bringing the original pair into being. To concede this is to irrevocably and permanently reduce the inherent purpose and potential of the woman. It also begets a definition of man's "headship" or "leadership" role that tends to propose a superior status, rather than focusing on the man's servant-responsibility.

In the next chapter, my exposition of the Genesis 1—2 account of God's purpose in the Creation sequence of the original couple focuses on this proposition. For now, however, suffice it to say that the Creator's order—"the man was created first"—reveals something in His "sequencing"; something especially needed in the understanding of men in our generation. Rather than positioning man as preeminent over woman, God created the man first so (1) he would be profoundly impressed with his own distinctiveness, *as separate and apart from the animal kingdom*; (2) he would be profoundly aware of *his own need of a partner*, seeing no creature was comparable to him; and so (3) he would be profoundly prepared *to tenderly welcome and deeply appreciate* the partner he would receive.

Then God said, "Let Us make man (lit. humankind) *in Our image, according to Our likeness; let THEM* (emphasis added, note both genders inferred) *have dominion"* (i.e., sovereign responsibility for all issues on earth, under God's universal sovereignty) (Gen. 1:26).

So God created man; (this time referencing Adam, as witnessed by the following words) *in the image of God He created HIM;* (emphasis added) *male and female He created THEM* (again, both genders are ordained as follows, v. 27).

Then God blessed them and God said to them, "Be fruitful and multiply; fill the earth and subdue it; have dominion (jointly and in equal partnership) *over...every living thing"* (v. 28).

As these words show, the original order was one of complete partnership, neither one being subordinated to the other. Adam's position in the relationship was not elevated by reason of his being first in the sequence of his and his wife's creation. To see this is to establish a critical starting place for a man's understanding, otherwise two things will surface as he begins to seek responsible claim to his role as a man.

First, he will presuppose his assignment is to "rule" his wife and home, (which is a vastly different concept than to "lead" it).

Second, he will fail to see that the "redemptive order" (e.g., the wife's submission to her husband) is intended as a means to restore the original, or "creation order."

It is no secret that God *has* ordered a distinct place for men and women in His creative and redemptive enterprise. The husband-wife and man-woman relationships, however, are largely clouded by sin, pain, confusion and human traditions. So the importance of Paul's words, calling us back to the beginning, becomes all the more important. They are *not* spoken to reinforce a "ranking" of the genders, but to recall a failed responsibility by the "first man" when *his* neglect of *his* assigned partnership plunged the first pair into sin.

THE MOMENT OF THE "BREAK"

And Adam was not deceived (1 Tim. 2:14).

The most devastating moment in the history of our planet and race was that instant when man broke the divinely decreed contract by which his life and ability were maintained to actuate the rule the Almighty had given him over this small part of creation. More "broken" than we know, is that moment described by theologians as The Fall of Man. In the face of that event, one of the most ironic twists in biblical interpretation sustains currency. It revolves around the words "Adam was not deceived."

Here, as a staggering indictment is actually made against the *man,* how often have you heard the reading to somehow appear to rail against the woman? But look: Paul is actually distinguishing between the relative degree of responsibility for "the Fall" where the first man and woman were concerned. The man is focused for his *greater* failure, not lesser. He was *not* "deceived," *he was "disobedient"* (read Rom. 5:12).

Have you, as I have, heard this text elaborated as an argument for "the gullibility of women"? But this idea has *nothing* to do with the text, and when so twisted, the missed idea also appears to suggest that men are seldom deceived, tricked or made the fool! While some see the words "the woman being deceived, fell into transgression" as charging Eve with primary responsibility for human failure (and Paul's "attack" on women to have achieved its final coup de grace) this is not the point. The truth of God's Word (and the focus, I believe, in Paul's argument) is *not* merely to review history, but to see how what occurred has left us with a unique challenge of "getting through" to the male of our species regarding his role.

Two Different Sins

I see verse 14 as drawing a contrast between Adam's outright, conscious and calculated rebellion, and Eve's very differently motivated (but no less guilty) act of sin. They *both* sinned. However, Adam did it with his eyes wide open—he was consciously *disobedient*; while Eve, in contrast, succumbed to carefully crafted stratagem by the serpent—she was deceived.

Romans 5:12 sets the record in categorical terms: *"Through one man sin entered the world, and death through sin, and thus death spread to all men."*

There is more: *"By the one man's offense many died,...by the one man's offense death reigned... through one man's offense judgment came...by one man's disobedience many were made sinners"* (vv. 15,17,18,19).

THE SCRIPTURES PUT THE ENTIRE RESPONSIBILITY FOR THE FALL OF THE RACE AT ADAM'S FEET, NOT BECAUSE HE WAS A GREATER SINNER THAN EVE WAS, BUT BECAUSE HIS *CONSCIOUS* ACTION OF DISOBEDIENCE IS JUDGED A DEEPER FAILURE WHEN CONTRASTED WITH HER *CONFUSED* ACTION BORN OF DECEPTION.

So it is that the Scriptures put the entire responsibility for the Fall of the race at Adam's feet, not because he was a greater sinner than Eve was, but because his *conscious* action of disobedience is judged a deeper failure when contrasted with her *confused* action born of deception.

The Genesis 3 narrative of the Fall of Man sheds light on why "man-the-male" is charged in this way. Let me offer two separate views of Genesis 3:6:

> *So when the woman saw that the tree was good for food, that it was pleasant to the eyes, and a tree desirable to make one wise, she took of its fruit and ate. She also gave to her husband with her, and he ate.*

There are often interpretive differences in opinion here, which center on the words "she also gave to her husband with her." The words raise the question: What is meant by "with her"? *With her when* and *where?*

One view sees Adam "with her" (e.g., *present beside Eve*) *during* the temptation, standing there in full hearing of her conversation with the serpent and in full view of her action-under-delusion.

The second view sees Adam as "with her" (e.g., *in the Garden, but not present beside Eve at the moment of her sinning*) approached by her *afterward*, and though he clearly sees through her deception, he still willfully disobeys.

Either scenario screams with charges of failed responsibility on the man's side of the partnership.

The first evokes the question: Was he simply standing there, curiously watching to see if she *would* die, while he would remain unscathed? Might Adam have intervened, shaken Eve to alertness as her eyes began to glaze under the serpent's spell?

The second makes the inquiry: What might have happened if he had refused to partake? Could his obedience have annulled the woman's unilateral action? Or might the man have acted in some other redemptive way, through obedience to God's will as an unfallen representative of the woman? Let me propose an answer to that reasonable question, offering it on the grounds of biblical revelation; what God's Word shows actually *did* occur at another time and place and with another "pair"—Christ and *His* Bride. Think with me, please.

In Christ, "the last Adam" (1 Cor. 15:45), the Redeemer-Man has been sent to us—the Son of God from heaven. Quite apart from the actual realities of our salvation through His blood, His cross and His resurrection, one wonders if there may not be in *His* accepting responsibility for *our* sin and in giving Himself to redeem us a picture of something that "might have been in the beginning."

The Word of God says, "In Adam, all died," but *what if*? What if Adam, being "with" the woman at the time of her deception and sin, had accepted a redemptive role? Remember, at the time *he* was sinless, and as such might have accepted the responsibility for *his* "bride."

Such questions are moot—the past is done, and we know the reality. We rejoice and praise our Lord Jesus, who *did* refuse the tempter, who *did* die to retrieve His Bride from death and hell, and who *was* "made to be sin for us, who knew no sin, that we might be made the righteousness of God in Him." "In Christ, all are made alive." In His role as the "last Adam," Jesus fulfilled the Father's will where the first Adam failed. Is it possible that His fulfillment of His role as our Savior may also suggest something the "first Adam" might have done, but did not?

A UNIQUELY SCARRED MALE PSYCHE?

In any case, we only know the historic facts the Bible records. Still, one thing is clear: In any alternate speculative scenarios, but both indicative because where the man might have taken spiritually responsible or even redemptive steps, he failed to serve his partnering role—failed to support his wife with spiritual sensitivity and care. So once more, but even more deeply, we repeat the words and feel their consequence: *"By one man's offense!"* (i.e., *by the first male's decisive neglect of responsibility*), the whole race was dashed to destruction!

THIS is the point I believe is underscored in the words of our text (1 Tim. 2:11-14). I propose his experience in seeking to "draw men out to accept leadership responsibility" had caused him to see the crux of *two* issues: first, the obvious *theological* fact of human sin and its consequences for all humanity; second, the crippling *psychological* influence of the first man's conscious spiritual unresponsibility on all men to come.

I propose that in every male of Adam's fallen race lies something of a residue of this conscious failure. My proposition is not that man is more deeply sinful or harder to save than is woman, but that men as *males* are generically more deeply engraved with an undiagnosed-yet-present abiding sense of having been marked by an order of failure that still haunts their identity as men. To my perspective, this is a fact of the male psyche — and it *speaks* in the habits, the responses, the fears and the attitudes uniquely characteristic of the male of our species. It also does the following:

- It explains the reserve men generally show toward things spiritual, because they have an intuitive sense of having once failed the Almighty already, and thereby feel unworthy of credibility now.
- It explains the slowness of men to make commitments they intend to keep, because a residual consciousness of his forebears' failure to keep a commitment argues against his ability to do so.
- It explains the suspicion of men toward other men, because a "doubt toward the likelihood of a man's trustworthiness" is inherent in his own self-doubts.
- It explains the anger of so many when called to spiritual responsibility, because such a call awakens a low-grade, internal sense of certainty that failure is guaranteed, and thereby, any invitation to repeated shame seems motivated by mockery.
- It explains the male "need to win," the competitiveness (or its reverse counterpart—"asserted passivity"), the "I don't really care" attitude that is a symptom of the need to "control," for having so tragically "lost it all" at the beginning.
- It explains the tenacity with which men tend to withhold fervor in worship or spiritual initiative in conversation with their wives or children, feeling to do so may somehow not be taken seriously.

All in all, whether my interpretation is valid or not, the six tendencies of men listed here are verifiable, and I have found men change in those regards. My conviction is that "something is there" in 1 Timothy 2 and that church history's chauvinistic habits have overlooked it. But a reformation in men's ministries is in motion!

CLIMAXING THE CONCEPT

This brings us to the final words of our text:

> *Nevertheless she will be saved in childbearing if they continue in faith, love, and holiness, with self-control* (1 Tim. 2:15).

Critical to understanding the mighty promise and redemptive potential is to note the grammatical difference in the "person" of the verb "*saved*" and "*continue*": the first is singular, the second, plural. This oft-overlooked construction reinforces our point. It disallows confusion about the Holy Spirit's intent in this passage, and it may provide the most supportive verification of the interpretation I have offered. For if this broader text (2:1 – 3:13) is directed toward (1) raising up men, through (2) guiding women to an understanding, which will (3) help men take their place of neglected responsibility, then we should see some "coming together point" as a reward. The text provides that climax.

It is not unusual to hear verse 15 taught in a way that perpetuates the shallow notion that Paul is on a crusade to reprimand and restrict women. I have heard these words twisted to say, in effect, "Now if you girls will all just stay home and have babies, and be spiritual, loving and submitted, *then* you'll have an easier time in the delivery room!"

In sharp contrast to such a condescending approach, the grammar noted in the verb forms introduces a clearer focus: The *woman* is the one referenced in "saved" (singular) and the *married couple* as a "being renewed team" are the ones called to "continue" (plural). No other meaning gives real continuity or sense, and with these words the promise in this passage is unveiled, holding forth the hope in the redemptive potential awaiting the husband and wife whose relationship moves into God's fuller redemptive order.

Let me freely paraphrase and amplify the text to describe this:

> **As the husband and wife together CONTINUE on a path of faith** (believing what God can flourish in their lives), **and love** (patiently learning to live out their roles under the redemptive order), **and holiness with self-control** (submitting to the Lord according to His Word), **then they will both be rewarded; even unto the possibility of a beginning recovery of what was lost when the first pair fell into sin.**

The key is in noting that the *one* (the wife) being "saved in childbearing" is the result of the *two* (the couple) "continuing" to grow together on God's terms.

Genesis 3:16 reveals a twofold consequence for the woman's disobedience: (1) complexity in childbirth, and (2) the loss of her "equal" status with the man. Here, our text offers hope for some amelioration of the first consequence. It seems to hold promise of the woman's indirect recovery from the second: The conditions are clear—a woman and a man, husband and wife, learning to take their place in the redemptive order. The results are seen in a beginning recovery of the original order!

This is redemption's goal under the New Covenant in Christ; not only God "saving souls," but God also restoring the blessings of His original, created design.

We summarize: just as surely as God is returning the hope of endless life (*beyond* this world), so He is offering a pathway to a couple's potential rediscovery of His originally designed full partnership. Why now? Because He wants to demonstrate the beauty of His plan for marriage, and it is intended to be learned and gained in *this* life, because marriage relationships will not exist "*beyond*" it. Thus, once a couple knows Christ, the path and price of personal discipline toward this redemptive possibility is shown:

1 TIMOTHY 2:1-15

1. Husbands (and men in general) need to be open to a role of exercising spiritual initiatives in prayer (v. 8).
2. Wives (and women in general) are called to make their characters, not their appearances, their identities (vv. 9,10).
3. Women (especially wives) are asked to behave in ways conducive to men being open to spiritual things (vv. 11,12).
4. Men (especially husbands) need to confront their habits of fearing spiritual responsibilities or neglecting redemptive possibilities (vv. 13,14).
5. Where these disciplines are accepted and applied, couples may begin to discover new joys as the effect of the Fall is reduced, as mutually accepted **redemptive roles** begin to issue in a recovery of their original designed **created roles** (v. 15).

MOVING TOWARD TRIUMPH

These concepts as I have outlined them are not mandatory to a theology of human salvation, but I do believe they are essential to grasping the fuller degree of God's desire for practical redemption of the roles of men and women.

And I am convinced that before I can lead men to accept their "men first" assignment, I need to help them see it from the standpoint of a fuller body of truth than simply their God-appointed call as men.

Even as believers are "called *saints*," then called to grow in the disciplines of that call's responsibilities, so we pastors of promise must "call" men to manhood, and must back our call with concepts that will enable them to respond with understanding. The issues 1 Timothy 2 unveil are designed to pave the way to that triumph. Its insights are to clarify the intent of a man's assignment to lead:

- It is a charge—a responsibility for ministry, not a privileged status to exercise from a stance of superiority.
- It is redemptive in intent (i.e., man's "leading role" is given to help restore the earlier equality, not to perpetuate a permanent disparity).

As a pastor, however, my ability to help men find the way to these far-reaching possibilities requires that I review and renew my own path. I cannot teach "the recovery possibilities of the redemptive order" without being deepened in them myself, and that will call me back to the altar where my own marriage vows were made.

It is there that the secret unfolds.

REFLECTION QUESTIONS

1. In your congregation of men, do you identify evidence of the "distinct culture" described? Have you noticed any *"machismo"* attitudes of men when they gather? How do you relate to this attitude?
2. Has the feminist movement made guys feel more demeaned, redefined and frustrated? Could this be part of the reason for temptation toward this cocky male attitude?
3. Review this chapter's account of God's original order of male and female creation in relationship to the male psyche. Do you think understanding this order helps explain how men and women should relate to each other? How?
4. Does the explanation of the male psyche related to Adam's failure surprise you? Is this a new concept for you?
5. Do you agree that your own marriage vows hold a secret to helping men and women "recover possibilities of the redemptive order"?

Note
1. Jack Hayford, *Worship His Majesty* (Dallas: WORD Inc., 1987), p. 19.

CHAPTER FIVE HIGHLIGHTS:

- True husbanding is crucial to becoming a pastor of promise.
- According to Ephesians 5, we are called as husbands to give of ourselves to our wives—to set them apart, serve their needs and to nourish and cherish them.
- Whatever the starting place, most stressed interaction between couples is a "revert-to-habit" discussion of "The Problem."
- A return to the "created order," as discussed in Genesis 2:15-25, holds promise for any marriage relationship's enrichment.

For the husband is head of the wife, as also Christ is head of the church; and He is the Savior of the body.

Ephesians 5:23

THE PROMISE OF A LIFELONG LOVE

I was in a restaurant the other day, reviewing a biographical news piece together with a buddy of mine, when I paused midway. The article was about me, but included mention of my wife, describing her as "*a quiet strength and balance* to her husband," when my friend quipped: "*Does that make you 'a loud weakness'?*" Our efforts at controlling our laughter in that public place were almost futile, as peals of laughter followed; a *leaning-on-each-other, unable-to-stop-it, laugh-till-your-stomach-hurts* laughter. Finally, my "buddy" and I fell into each other's arms wet-eyed, hardly caring that those at tables nearby were starting to laugh at us.

My "buddy" is named Anna. She is my wife, and with more than 40 years of marriage behind us, she is not only my best critic and closest friend, but also my companion in scores of such "moments." Her down-to-earth genuineness and fun-to-be-with personality captivated me on our first date, and we have been together ever since. Make no mistake, though: Our marriage has not been without its seasons of high demand, not only by reason of the pressures we have faced together, but also because of the ones that have tried to drive us apart.

Besides the fact that the background influences of family were drastically different for each of us, we are also both quite opinionated, and often at very different points on the spectrum of the subject. We have also weathered storms of difficulty that would effectively dispense at least a lifelong joy in a marriage, if not lifelong commitment to its maintenance.

At one point, Anna's struggle with our ministry situation brought her to the edge of a nervous breakdown; at another, an infatuation duped and nearly brought me into the disaster of an adulterous relationship. In both cases, God's grace spared each of us, and sustained our rich partnership, both in marriage and in ministry. Nevertheless, laughter-filled times such as the one mentioned have multiplied, and though honestly admitting our "less-than-perfectness" as a pair, we both readily consent that we have a "great" marriage.

Whatever success Anna and I have found in our marriage—that we have "lasted," as well as "grown" in our love and life together—probably is the result of one moment more than any other. Amazingly, we had already been married 17 years when it happened!

DISCOVERING "MY WORLD"

Ironically, Anna and I had just come away from trying to help a pastoral couple who were on the brink of divorce. Our conversation with them had begun at the conclusion of a retreat in the Rockies, and had become an almost-all-night travail of struggle, pain and tears. We were heartbroken about this pair, in whose wedding we had participated, and who were so unable, if not unwilling, to reach a hopeful resolution for their marriage's survival. The next morning, Anna and I were alone together, and while we were at prayer for that marriage God spoke to me about mine.

We had exhausted all the words and ideas our own understanding could muster. We had prayed for the couple, the issues and attitudes involved, and everything else we could see about their problem. Then, feeling helpless to adequately unburden our souls, we united in a partnership of prayer "in the Spirit," inviting the Holy Spirit to assist our insight and intercession (see 1 Cor. 14:15; Rom. 8:26,27). After a brief season of this order of praying, I said, "Honey, let's just sing together over their situation."

For us, that terminology is rooted in an intercessory perception that calls for a "spiritual song," employed as an instrument of prayer. So without hesitation, Anna and I reached to join hands together, and continued bearing our concern for that other couple—upward, before God's throne. We had been praying in this manner for only a minute or two, when a "picture" began to unfold before my inner vision. I was not in a trance or in any way other than "right there with Anna" in prayer, but without conjuring anything of my own imaginative powers, a videolike drama took place before my eyes.

The scene was "space," and I was being borne along by the accompanying presence of Jesus Himself. I only sensed His being there, holding my arm as He took me to an appointed location. I did not see His face, but He spoke two sentences that resonated with unforgettable clarity as we arrived, over-looking what appeared to be a "planet" somewhere below our position in this

journey. (Whenever I tell this, I always feel some hearer will be tempted to attribute my "vision" to some "star-trekky" mind-set, but I have never been a sci-fi fan.)

"THAT IS YOUR 'WORLD,' AND HER NAME IS 'ANNA.' YOU HAVE FAILED TO 'SUBDUE' YOUR WORLD."

As the Savior and I had paused now, and He had directed my gaze to the planet below, these words were spoken—with pointed force, but with a patient tone: *"That is your 'world,' and her name is 'Anna.' You have failed to 'subdue' your world."*

The scene immediately closed, but instantly, three things were opened to my understanding. *First,* the poetic reference to my wife as "my world" made sense—transcending the romantic ("You're all the world to me") and under-scoring my husbanding responsibilities. *Second,* I saw a dimension of respon-sibility for my wife I had never perceived before, and how I had "failed" in fulfilling that responsibility. *Third,* I sensed the essential relationship between my learning to serve my "world named 'Anna,'" and effectively influencing a "world" I wanted to touch with effective pastoral ministry.

Central to my understanding was a viewpoint I had about the word "subdue"; not in the sense of conquest, but in the sense of "development." To illustrate: At Creation, the original couple was told to "replenish the earth, and subdue it" (Gen. 1:28, *KJV*) ("subdue"—Heb. *kawbash*). The goal of God's assignment to them was to develop the earth's potential, through responsibly tending to it. Although the verb is a forceful one, including the idea of "treading down," or "mastering"—the objective obvi-ously intended is the begetting of fruitfulness. Now, the words "You have failed to 'subdue' your 'world'" were echoing in my soul, and I understood, oh too clearly. I was being confronted—not with 17 years of fruitless mar-riage, but with years of blind failure in bringing about the *fullest fruitfulness* latent in my dear wife. Let me provide an example by describing what immediately came to my understanding in that moment.

Music Made the Difference

Musical styles and training were among the vast differences in Anna's and my backgrounds. Though we both had a common interest and gifting in music, our exposures were worlds apart. I was from a large church on the West Coast, and had a highly advanced music ministry and a program involving considerable stylized, contemporary music arrangements.

Anna was from a small congregation in Nebraska, and regularly sang in a girl's trio on a radio broadcast that featured more of a Country-Western style of down-homesy music. The chord structures we were accustomed to were, alone, so different in complexity and application that I had often frustrated her with my perfectionist demands when we worked together on music programs. Now, having years behind us, I was suddenly brought by the voice of God to an instant, shocking recognition of a sad fact.

Anna did not sing much anymore!

Oh, she sang in church. It was not that she had "simply stopped" or had retreated to some childish, stubborn refusal to sing, as though consciously rebelling against me. That fact dawned upon me that very moment, and I at once realized I could not remember hearing her sing around the house, or sitting at the piano and playing as she so often had done earlier in our marriage.

This one image and the stark fact it evoked to my awareness caused a turnaround in my whole understanding—both regarding my marriage and my ministry. From that moment of songful prayer with Anna that morning, a flow of *life* began to issue. It began to open new understanding in the Word. It also opened a new season of growth in our marriage relationship, which largely resulted in birthing what has since become a fruitful family-focused ministry in our congregation.

None of it happened quickly—other than that life-influencing flash of humbling self-perspective I received that day. From that day, a quantum leap issued in the promise of my pastoring a church filled with healthy, growing marriages. Our ministry to couples and families began to blossom dramatically, primarily because of what I was beginning to learn about my own responsibility as a husband and as a pastor. My earliest lessons were not simply biblical; they were intensely practical.

"JUST AS CHRIST ALSO LOVED"

No passage in the Bible has ever been used more by the Holy Spirit to process ongoing transformation in my own life than Ephesians 5:21-33. In one mammoth blow to any possibility of any man's misapplication of his role as "head of the wife," God's Word puts it all in perspective: *"As also Christ is head of the church!"*

Although I had never been a "bossy" or overbearing, demanding husband, until the season of understanding that dawned beginning the day of the vision, my sense of "husbandly headship" was based on a false sense of Jesus' style. My focus had been on His authority over the Church, and though I did realize He also died for the Church, my supposition of how that applied to me as a husband was sadly deficient.

If you had asked me then, I would have unhesitantly said, "As Anna's husband, I recognize my role as her defender should anyone or anything threaten her life." In other words, I would be willing to love Anna as Jesus loved the Church—even unto death, if the situation called for it. Although that may be noble, and even appropriate, the fact is that the text said little about my loving as Jesus loved us in dying. The whole passage is, however, filled with things that had never registered with me.

- "Giving myself" (v. 25) was a call to sacrifice my convenience, to lay aside my own self-interest in the same way Jesus laid aside His authoritative role at the Father's right hand in heaven, and came as a servant to redeem us (see Phil. 2:1-7). Headship as "authority" was far less the issue of my husbandly role than "taking the lead" in doing anything that would help fulfill Anna or serve her.
- "Sanctifying and cleansing" (Eph. 5:26a) pointed toward "setting her apart"—that is, doing everything in my power to provide a special place for her. My affection was to be seen in my giving her special time, giving her a listening ear! I could not think of one time when Jesus was too busy with His ministry to hear my cry for His attention; nor any time I have asked Him to hear my heart and found Him impatient with the request. BUT, I *could* remember far too many times when Anna would say, "It doesn't seem like we've had any time together lately," or, "When I try to explain how I feel, you don't hear my heart—you only analyze my words."
- "Washing...by the word" (v. 26b) was translated into a therapeutic ministry more than as a corrective one. I realized God's Word is laden with promises He keeps, not only precepts He declares. I also thought of the number of times I was late for dinner, or altered an occasion with Anna (all for great and grand "ministry" reasons!), then was frustrated when she did not seem all that impressed, or later expressed her hurt or disappointment. My "words" then were usually self-justifying, rather than "washing," just as my "word" had been worthless, and resulted in overlooking her need while I served the needs of others.
- "Nourishing and cherishing" (v. 29) were not even in the picture. Again, my "headship" style was not oppressive, but neither did either of those two words describe it. The idea in the Greek usage of those two words is wrapped in one English word: *tenderness*. My problem was that I usually only reflected that degree or timing of "tenderness" many men do with their

wives: the self-serving care that seeks sexual fulfillment in exchange. Without discounting that facet of a marriage, I came to learn something in my life with Anna. I found that even *those* moments together somehow became more precious when—*day in and day out*—I learned to be *more sensitive* to notice when she needed help with the kids, *more hearing* when she expressed a minor frustration about a situation, or *more understanding* when she was just plain tired, and needed me to "fill in" for something at the house while she took a break.

"THIS IS A GREAT MYSTERY"

Furthermore, although the *definition* of true husbandly headship began to come into perspective for me, the *dimensions* of its meaning and influence on my pastoral role were slow to be fully understood. I was yet to see how crucial true husbanding is to becoming a pastor of promise. It happened nearly 20 years ago now, but I remember the circumstances that occasioned another breakthrough in my understanding as a pastor-husband.

I had been called into a tragic situation; I was asked to help minister to a couple where the husband—a pastor—had fallen morally, and violated sexual fidelity toward his wife. As more and more details were uncovered, through counseling and in the bitter aftermath of his congregation's having to come to terms with his failure, multiplied dimensions of pain and problems surfaced. Without retelling that story, suffice it to say, one devastating fact was distilled from it all: he had been no better a pastor than he had been a husband.

That is not a matter of comment about the man's capacity to teach or preach, or his abilities to lead, direct or manage. He was extremely capable in all those regards. The truth was, he did not *listen* to people, he "told" them; he did not have a *heart* for the flock, he had a "vision" for the church. Notwithstanding a longtime record of honesty in financial dealings, we learned that at the same time his flirtations began with another woman, he began "fudging" in his financial dealings.

In this pained context, in the middle of a conversation with that pastor one day—trying to spiritually wrestle his soul free of the bondage and confusion that had destroyed him—I felt I captured an insight. I saw the horrible parallel between his long-term insensitivity toward his wife, and his "busy" *driven* way of leading as a pastor. I saw how this had preceded his ultimate compromise of trust with his wife, which, of course, disastrously compromised his leadership role with his congregation. Then, for the first time, I felt I truly understood *why* the New Testament requirements for pastoral eldership are so insistent that a man be "the husband of one wife" (1 Tim. 3:2,12; Titus 1:6).

SINGLE PASTORS AND
WOMEN PASTORS

It is not my intent to so focus the importance of the pastor and his marriage that I appear to suggest any other than a married man is disqualified for fruitful pastoral ministry. I do not believe this. I do believe, however, that in the single pastor's absence of experiencing the stress and cost of growing in a marriage, and in the woman pastor's obvious inability to lead men at a man-to-man level, limitations are obvious.

I also believe, however, that the place and value of any dedicated man or woman for ministry should probably never be measured by these facts. First, because the Bible demonstrates the propriety and worth of single leaders, as well as women, who are anointed by God's Spirit for leadership. Second, staff and resources might supplement the primary leader for strategic ministry to men and to marrieds.

Abounding videotaped resources are available in both arenas today. Further, trusted guest speakers or teachers can bring tremendous blessing and vital nourishment in areas of their gifting. The pastor's sensitive scheduling of these ministries can garner the appreciation of those he or she serves for his or her revealing such understanding of need and faithfully seeking to address it.

Besides these suggestions, both men and marrieds would benefit in *every* congregation by making available *and promoting* libraried media resources that may be utilized by the congregation. Books and audio- and video-tapes abound about these themes today. The past 20 years have brought a proliferation of these resources for two reasons:

1. Our society is confused about sexual identity, true masculinity or true femininity, marital commitment and sanctity (as well as domestic health and sanity);
2. The Holy Spirit has answered this confusion with revelation, bringing insight in the Word and practical, workable patterns for applied truth.

Because the need is so manifest and answers are so available, every congregation can be served with effective resources and ministry to men and marriages. These blessings are intended for any assembly, and most of what is recommended here is as practically applicable in the congregation in which a married man is the pastor as one in which a single man or a woman is the pastor.

For most of my life and ministry, I had only heard arguments about the phrase "the husband of one wife." It was used as an argument against a celibate priesthood, as an argument preempting a single man holding a pastorate and as an argument against a divorced man ever pastoring. Whatever

A PASTOR CAN BE NO BETTER A REPRESENTATIVE OF *JESUS'* "HUS-BANDLY" ROLE TO HIS CHURCH THAN HE IS IN FULFILLING HIS ROLE AS A HUSBAND HIMSELF.

use debate made of the text, though, I had now become struck by the far larger issue of a man's *focus*, his *caring* and his *commitment* that is called forth by those words. I now saw this dramatic parallel: A pastor can be no better a representative of *Jesus'* "husbandly" role to His Church than he is in fulfilling his role as a husband himself. That is why my "first promise" to keep as a pastor is my promise "to love, to honor, to cherish" as Christ loves His Church! That is why a pastoral elder is to verify a commitment to "one wife."

- Such a man has no secondary interests, emotionally, mentally or sexually. He is not fantasizing in private or flirting on the side. He is bonded in heart and soul to one woman—and so Jesus says, "I'll trust my Church to a man like that."
- Such a man is growing in showing his patience, his understanding for human frailty, his willingness to give time, heal hearts and show forgiveness. He lives that way with one woman, so Jesus says, "I want him to serve my Church that way, because it's like me."

The focus of all this brings me as a pastor of promise to one grand fact:

Christ calls a man to be a pastor who will first learn to answer His call as a husband, for He knows that a man will only become as loving and caring of *His* Bride—the Church—as he will become of his own bride—his wife.

This is certainly at least one reason Paul, after elaborating the husband's call to Christlike self-sacrifice and servanthood within the marriage, stated, "This is a great mystery, but I speak concerning Christ and the church" (Eph. 5:32). The husband's leading, deterministic role in the marriage either works redemptively, or the options are tragic. Any marriage in which a husband is not committed to grow in learning and living out a Christlike willingness to serve that union is, at best, destined to face the struggles of married living without the redeeming power of love. It is that "leading man," "truly husbanding" kind of love that characterizes true male "headship." And more, it is the foundation upon which true male authority is intended to be built.

BUILDING MEN, MARRIAGES...AND THE KINGDOM

Anna's and my encounter with the distressed couple, following which my eyes were opened as we prayed, came shortly after the call the Holy Spirit issued to me: "Begin to gather men!" The two episodes were so strategic, especially now that I have the advantage of hindsight, that I have come to see them as essential priorities for extending Kingdom life. I am persuaded that both ministries—to men and to marriages—are paired priorities that must command the highest pastoral focus, only preceded in priority by the congregation's worship life. Just as with worship, I can only lead as a pastor where I have first moved forward in my own life—as a man, and as a husband.

Three points of pastoral growth are waiting here: (1) growth as a man as I grow in my own marriage; (2) growth in insight through the Bible's revelation concerning marriage; (3) growth in the marriages of the men I influence, following Christ—the model "bridegroom."

A PASTOR'S GOD-GIVEN "MINISTRY CONTEXT"

The pastoral requirement for roots in marriage and in the family certainly has nothing to do with reducing the value of any pastor without these qualifications. At the same time, no environment like a marriage and family forces the formation of character, presses the demands of patience and grace, or daily calls forth pragmatic faith and love. It does not take a great deal of analysis: simply put, God has forced an issue by the very nature of the list of qualifications He sets up for pastors. It should not surprise us that a leader's wife and children are a key part of Paul's leadership expectations (see 1 Tim. 3:1-13).

According to the Bible, pastors are placed in office by the hand of Christ Himself (see Eph. 4:8-11). As the Lord's designated servants to His Body, leaders are assigned not only to *relay information*, but are expected to *reveal incarnation* as well; to model as well as teach. Because the source of all ministry is the *Father*, and because the saving love to be communicated is found in the *Bridegroom*, these relationships need to be seen in a credible context. So it is that:

- God calls for men whose styles of life in their homes and with their families reveal something of the balance, in patience, order, authority and love, which the heavenly Father wants His earthly children to understand about Him.
- The Word calls for men whose commitments to their marriages reveal something of the character, in constancy, caring and gentleness, which the heavenly Bridegroom wants His earthly Bride to understand about Him. And,

The primary ministry context for preaching and teaching is the home. No setting is more practical, more of a test of the reality of the truth we preach, or potentially more verifying of the glory of the gospel.

This is not merely to wax poetic about marriage and family. It is to cut to the heart of all the Word of God reveals about the eternal order and objective of things. *Creation* is about God establishing a couple intended to beget a global family (see Gen. 1:28; 8:17; 9:1). *Redemption* is about Christ coming to redeem "sons and daughters" unto "Father...from whom the whole family in heaven and earth is named" (Eph. 3:14,15; see also 2 Cor. 6:17,18). Nothing brings greater credibility to the practical, day-to-day reality of the life we have been given in Christ than what a pastoral couple reveals in its relationship, or the pastor's family displays in the long haul!

Probably no single feature has engendered credibility of Anna's and my nearly 30 years at The Church On The Way than the visibility of our relationship as a couple and as parents. Although we have certainly never paraded ourselves as paragons, and have tried to be careful not to violate the individuality or private interests of our kids, we have still been anything but secret about our struggles as well as our joys. Life lessons, as we have learned them in the crucible of the home, have been relayed time and again through testimony and sermon.

Although my seminary training advocated against it, I have often shared stories of my own slowness to learn how to live as a good husband and wise father. One such episode occasioned a breakthrough in my understanding of the power that is released when a husband even slightly begins to learn what it means to "love your wife as Christ loves the Church."

ON PUBLICLY SHARING "PERSONAL LESSONS"

I am not unaware that historically, and in many cases even today, exponents of classical preaching either discourage or altogether speak against any use of personal episodes in a preacher's sermon. Some consider this to be "calling attention to yourself, rather than to the Word of God," and attempt to ennoble this denial of self-disclosure as though it were a form of righteousness. This not only removes the accessibility of our using the most practical illustrations we have—where we have had to come to grips with seeing God's Word incarnated in our own lives as pastors, but it also flies in the face of Scripture.

The entire mood of God's Word is candid, forthright, transparent and self-disclosing. Uncompromising honesty revealing human failure not only abounds in Old Testament narratives, but also considers the frankness with which Jesus' own struggles are recorded in the Gospels ("Father, if possible, take this cup"; "My God...why have you forsaken me?"). Notwithstanding the spiritual dynamic and intellectual brilliance we see in Paul's persona, who can deny that we are most comforted by his honest acknowledgments of weakness; that we are comforted to hear his pained heart cry when feeling rejected or alone?

Although I view and practice biblical transparency as a desirable feature of pastoral preaching, wisdom more than merely recommends certain limits: They should be required!

First, any matters of personal, marital or domestic self-disclosure should never make public what always belongs in private. For example, with sexual instruction—in public teaching or private counsel—never use your own experience as its illustration. Or with financial principles taught from lessons you have learned, the financial facts of your life should never be public information any more than anyone else's.

Second, when lessons learned are shared, they must never be to anyone else's embarrassment more than your own. It is my privilege to choose to disclose my own blindness, ignorance or slowness to see a point, truth or principle. If I describe the failure of another one of my family or anyone else, however, not only will I destroy trust with them, but I will also alienate any audience, however true the story may be.

Third, never share what ought to remain unspoken. For example: (1) angry words exchanged (though the presence of stress might be mentioned); (2) details of interpersonal conflict (other than your own responsibility for its cause); (3) specifics of counsel to your children, or disciplinary action taken with them (either of which exposes them to having the story of their failure repeated to them in jest or judgment).

Fourth, never share in self-disclosure that which has not reached a point of personal, spiritual resolution. Simply describing a struggle, without being able to offer a lesson that helps people to gain hope beyond the struggle, may seem a humble thing to do, but it contributes nothing. My call to refrain in this regard is not to reverse my recommendation of transparency in preaching, but to remove the possibility of trivialization or self-excuse through a recurrent generalization of one's own vulnerability to carnality.

"MY GREATEST DELIVERANCE"

Does anyone else out there have the same revert-to-habit tendency Anna and I have experienced through the years? For us, it has usually happened on the heels of an "argument"—that is, any interaction that follows some kind of misunderstanding or irritation caused by a quick remark, a sharp retort, or even an instance of unintended yet insensitive treatment; or from inflections of impatience in the voice or in gesture. You know, don't you? I mean the kind of things that ruffle the feathers of lovebirds everywhere.

Although the frequency of our arguments has wonderfully decreased through the years, we are still a pair of loving, yet strong-willed people. We still argue; genuine jawbone sessions that sort of start with, "I'm really steamed over what you just said!" Our arguments do not necessarily open with those words, but they do initiate with that emotion. Whatever the starting place (and here is the "revert-to-habit" I mentioned), the "argument" inevitably gets into a heavy discussion of "The Problem." I think every married couple actually and ultimately only has *one*; it is "THE Problem." No matter what *other* difficulty you are discussing, the conversation always arrives back at *this one*!

For us, it has been rooted in the very different ways our respective families communicated. My family was verbal, open and expressive. Everything was analyzed, discussed, explained—and it was possible, indeed, *necessary!*—to TALK. Reasoned, elaborated discourse and interaction were welcomed and encouraged. Whereas in Anna's family, not only did they have less interactive communication (with nine kids, it was probably a survival technique!), but they also had a tendency toward negativity. Consequently, for her (as one of the younger children) it was easy to feel demeaned or diminished if what she said was disagreed with, so silence became preferred rather than to risk disapproval.

Although we dated for nearly two years before we were married, it was not until we were into our marriage that we discovered how much of a problem Anna's learned pattern could present. Disagreements or misunderstandings were harder to resolve than I was used to, because I felt I could not "talk it through" without appearing to be demeaning her. For her part, the problem appeared differently: My habit of "needing to talk" had a destructive emotional effect, more than I could realize, because of my background. The very "talking" itself was exhausting to her; and further, she felt that to respond held a severe threat of proving inadequate. After all, in her childhood, "silence" had always served as a protection against possible pain.

As we came to discover the "what" in our communication problem, efforts at finding a "how" to solve it kept reaching an impasse. To my view, our difficulty was not Anna's fault so much as the fault of how she was raised. Of course, I never said this to any of her family, but I would recurrently find myself being angry. Why could a family not cultivate kids who could interact without fear of criticism? Even though I knew none of them intended or were conscious of doing this to Anna, but it is how I *felt*—and without realizing it, gradual resentment built in me.

Now, as years of marriage have accumulated, Anna and I have learned to handle our "revert-to-habit" thing fairly successfully. But we have no question in either of our minds that the pivot point in resolving a relentless frustration was that autumn day as we drove back from our district pastor's conference in Santa Barbara, California.

Neither of us can remember what brought about the intensity of emotion that day. We were at verbal sword points, and though she was quiet— having retreated to the "safety of silence" habit—I was at a complete point of exasperation. I was controlled, but wanting to give vent to an inner rage born of futility: "Why can't we ever TALK and RESOLVE?" I wanted to scream. I said nothing, however, and was about to settle to a quiet boil, steaming, but without words. Then it happened.

A Divine Grace

Will you die to it? (No words were spoken, but it was what my spirit heard.) *Will you lay it down? Now. Completely.*

At that moment, I did not see this call as related to Ephesians 5, the passage that would become so clear and so important to my understanding later. I did recognize, though, that I was being called to the Cross— *and to take up my own.* It was a revelation to my own heart, for I at once realized I was to *forgive*—but who? Of course, I obviously needed to show a patient regard for Anna, but I knew the issue was much wider. What can I do—how can this syndrome ever be stopped? Then I was confronted by truth: I was made to realize that however efficiently I might have felt I could *"analyze"* the root of my anger, an unforgiving, unwillingness to die-to-myself-and-my-feeling had me *paralyzed*. What happened next is wonder filled.

It is as memorable a pair of events as I have ever experienced.

First, a sweep of divine grace flowed over me. It was divine in its source, and I knew it was mine to receive or reject. The Holy Spirit was not only dealing with me through the inquiry that came to my heart, but now He was also making His presence real—letting me know that if I was willing "to die," He was there to help me.

As we drove down the highway, the silence was deafening: Anna, clammed up from a lifetime, inbred habit; Jack, stifling the scream that wanted to cry out for a shattering of whatever her upbringing had encrusted upon his dear wife. Then, at that moment, the "Who to forgive?" was answered: I knew I needed to release all my feeling of frustration about things I had not seen before as being so binding upon my own soul—*and thereby upon my wife as well!* Because I had never been hateful toward them, I had not discerned the depths of my resentful, unconfessed feelings toward Anna's family. The anger was not personalized toward anyone in particular, but toward what that environment had bred in my wife. Now, suddenly, I knew I had a choice to make—a call to "let go," to surrender my irritation about a history I could not control.

I did. I "let go." It was a conscious decision of saying no to my frustration and yes to the grace I was welcoming.

A peace began to envelop me. It surprised me: I wasn't prepared for the atmosphere change I felt in the car. I didn't know if it was just me, and I didn't feel I ought to do anything more than simply pray—silently—with an overwhelming sense of gratitude for my in-laws, and most of all for Anna.

Then the second thing happened.

Becoming Liberated

It had not been 60 seconds since my "surrender to the Cross," when Anna reached over and took my hand.

"Honey," she said, "we need to pull over by the side of the highway and pray." She paused, trying to find words, then said, "I think I may be about to experience my greatest deliverance."

Naturally, both she and I know and knew that our GREATEST "deliverance" is in our salvation through the Lord Jesus Christ. This was a given, though, and her words at this moment were expressive of that order of expanding freedom 2 Corinthians 1:10 outlines: "[God] *delivered* us from so great a death, and *does deliver* us; in whom we trust that He *will still deliver* us."

I watched for a break in the heavy traffic, and angled toward the side of the road under the shad-ow of an overpass. We prayed, simply, but with a great sense of the pres-ence of the Lord. Every time I think about this event I am renewed in my conviction that Jesus absolutely *rejoices* when a

I AM RENEWED IN MY CONVICTION THAT JESUS ABSOLUTELY *REJOICES* WHEN A HUSBAND LEARNS *HIS* HEART FOR *HIS* BRIDE AND DECIDES TO DISPLAY IT TOWARD *HIS*!

husband learns *His* heart for *His* Bride and decides to display it toward *his*!

Here is Anna's description of what happened: "As we were driving down the highway, I suddenly felt like there was a pressure in my head, which, to me, represented the whole backlog of obstruction to communi-cation in Jack's and my relationship. But then, all at once, I felt *faith*—believing that this moment was filled with hope. I *knew* that I could be free, and that our communication could be more open—powerfully liberated from the oppressive feelings of intimidation!"

It was more than "a moment." That day opened a new era in our life together. Although neither of us think of the years before that as being unpleasant, and our commitment to one another was never in question, still there is no question that something changed that very day. We were not placed on a magic carpet and wafted to a utopian dream world, but the log-jam was broken. We were still the same people, but something new unleashed a "flow" of God's grace, carrying us forward to new possibilities in our marriage. With no judgment toward me, but certainly with great joy and praise to God, Anna agrees with me that our joint experience of "redemptive release" was somehow related to my "dying"—to "loving like Jesus loves the Church."

THE HUSBAND—THE "HEAD"

As it turned out, this deliverance experience became dynamically helpful in my orientation to the whole subject of "male headship." Until that time, although we were not into anything of a cultlike or chauvinistic emphasis on women being "in submission," I operated in a more dominating, tradi-tionalized view of male-female relationships. For example, I had never noticed that the New Testament does *not*—not *anywhere*—place "women" under "men." Biblical "headship," I came to realize, is not a gender issue, but a domestic one. Women are not proscribed a place in submission to men, but wives are called to voluntarily submit to their husbands.

Wives, submit to your own husbands, as to the Lord. For the husband is the head of the wife, as also Christ is the head of the church; and He is the Savior of the body. Therefore, just as the church is subject to Christ, so let the wives be to their own husbands in everything (Eph. 5:22-24).

This is a greater issue than I realized at first. The true implications of Ephesians 5 undercut the crustiness of many "religious" rather than "biblical," attitudes toward the man-woman relationship. *"Husbands, love your wives, just as Christ also loved the church and gave Himself for her,"* establishes a model that is different from the presumptions I held. Those words place the burden on the husband to "win" his wife's trust, rather than putting the burden on her to yield to submission on *any* terms.

The model places the Church—you and me—in submission to a Savior who has died to redeem us, and thereby has won our love and trust. That is a different thing from mandating submission on the grounds that Christ is also Creator. The question is not whether our submission to God is deserved on the grounds of His having created us: it surely is! But the parallel drawn to illustrate and direct the nature of my role in the husband-wife relationship is rooted in Jesus' model as Redeemer, not Creator. Thus, the call to a man is to "win" his wife's love and trust, but not by either romantic exploits or demanding expectations. Rather, we are called to grow in discovering the promise of a lifelong love by serving actual life-circumstance situations with a self-giving willingness to "die" to our own interests.

This is not a surrender of husbandly authority; it is the pathway to it. It establishes the man's "headship" in the sense of the "head" being occupied with the interests of the "body," rather than the body merely existing to serve the interests of the head. The beauty of the model is that it points the way toward genuine mutuality between the husband and wife, while still placing the "leading role" in the hands of the husband. It is a beauty I doubt I would have ever come to understand apart from the sequence of the events I mentioned earlier.

NOTHING OF SECULARIZED "FEMINISM"

Nothing of this line of thought is either motivated by, or a concession to, a secularized feminist agenda. I do believe, however, that if such passages as Ephesians 5:23 were treated fairly, two things would happen: (1) the residue of "sanctified male chauvinism," still a hangover of unfinished business since the Reformation, would soon be removed; and (2) most men and women (especially marrieds) would soon rejoice in the happy realization of God's plan for the progressive restoration of both genders—each to our highest fulfillment and to our fullest personal release!

Our exposition here, as well as in the preceding chapter, is fully warranted by an unprejudiced approach to the texts involved. When we cut to the core of the "redemptive model" issue, this faithful interpretation has a way of "defanging" classic but defeating interpretive approaches:

- *Those which tend to denigrate the image of womanhood in Christ.* They tend toward creating an atmosphere of tension, imposing restrictions and asserting male domination, in contrast to encouraging an atmosphere of trust. When sensitively invited, that atmosphere will prompt women in general, and wives in particular, to wisely and faithfully apply self-imposed disciplines to see God's hand raise men to their place.
- *Those which suggest God's "second-classing" of women.* Some have categorically subordinated women to men, as opposed to calling each *wife* to be in voluntary submission to her *husband*. This more biblical idea is a world removed from the proposition that *all* women are to be subjugated to *all men*!

I believe all men as husbands need to see how the starting place for their "headship" is found in their redemptive "acts," not through being founded on created "rights." Equally essential is that this be seen upon the *biblical* foundation of its truthfulness. We are not accommodating a political "equal status agenda," but are seeking to recover God's original intent for couples—a recovery that is only possible within redemption's program.

The idea to which I had been oriented—of a man's being given a "created right" to male headship—plays to a "prove-yourself-the-man" kind of husbanding. Even if a wife accepts those terms (and, in our life together, Anna was not unwilling to do so), for the man, it is essentially a "cost-free" pathway to domestic leadership. It offers the right to authority without learning the price of service; it exacts the requirement of a wife's submission to her husband's headship without any requirement of his submission to anything. It does not answer at all to the idea of "loving as Christ loved the Church."

A RETURN TO THE "CREATED ORDER"

The biblical order is, of course, always consistent. God has not changed His plan for the marriage relationship, but He has instigated a redemptive pathway for our recovering the "original." As both a husband and a pastor, not only to a wife who needs my ministry to her, but also to men who need my ministry to her to establish a model they can see and follow, we all need God's Word. What qualities in my marriage  **GOD HAS NOT CHANGED HIS PLAN FOR THE MARRIAGE RELATIONSHIP, BUT HE HAS INSTIGATED A REDEMPTIVE PATHWAY FOR OUR RECOVERING THE "ORIGINAL."** will I look for as evidence I am moving back into something more approximate to God's original idea for couples?

Genesis 2:15-25 presents three essential values to be sought and preserved.

1. God starts with the man (vv. 8,15).

The Lord God planted a garden eastward in Eden, and there He put the man whom He had formed. Then the Lord God took the man and put him in the garden of Eden to tend and keep it.

These words were not written to establish a human doctrine of male primacy or dominance, though in the context God does place *initial responsibility* upon the man. From the beginning, irrespective of the personality differences or relative gifting of the husband or wife, God makes the husband responsible to "lead." How should we understand and apply this?

Primarily, we need to see that in starting—or "initiating"—with the man, God only placed the woman as second in one respect—*in sequence, not in significance.* Each one is given a distinctive, uniquely dignifying role. Just as in creating man the responsible "initiator," God makes the woman a nourishing "sustainer." Neither term—"initiator" or "sustainer"—suggests a superior or inferior role for either, nor do the terms negate that in some respects both words could be used for men and women alike. These two words, however, distinguish the beauty and significance of God's primary intent for male and female.

"Initiator" and "Sustainer" seem clearest to the understanding when applied in our most dramatic "in-the-image-of-God" human capability—

our life-begetting capacity for procreation. Look at how each contributes in the original order:

Men are Initiators, a role that is first demonstrated in the *"sowing"* action, which *initiates* life in the womb, unto birth.	Women are Sustainers, a role that is first demonstrated in the *"bearing"* activity, which *sustains* life in the womb, unto birth.

So just as clearly as each gender fills a unique role in the begetting of children, so surely do each fit into a distinctive and dignified place in God's plan for human life and living. To affirm this does not require a positioning of the original couple in a hierarchical order. Thus, my marriage will indicate I am serving my husbandly role, not by my dominance or "control," but by the way I sow "life" into our union, and initiate redemptive renewal (compare again with Eph. 5:25-27).

2. Man and woman were made for partnership (Gen. 2:18).

And the Lord God said, "It is not good that man should be alone; I will make him a helper comparable to him."

The beauty of the words "helper comparable to him" must be linked with the dignity in the words "let THEM have dominion" in Genesis 1:26. If I am to understand my "goal" as a husband with a full recovery of the original order in view, they cannot be separated, even though habits born of history hinder the clarity of this concept.

It is possible that few greater distortions exist in our language than the one begotten by a unique twist of words from the old *King James* translation. To this day, many argue the role of the woman as a "helpmeet" by reason of the words "an help meet for him." What is a "partner" concept in the original plan, came to be defined as a secondary role—a "helper"—which has historically tended to register the woman's place as an apprentice alongside a fully qualified worker. But this does not comply with the full biblical idea of a good wife.

For example, a study of the "Proverbs 31 Woman" indicates a wife whose partnership with her husband is not only praiseworthy in the eyes of God. The text's details show her as a woman who has also been released to a magnificent dimension of responsibility and creativity by her husband. This is completely removed from any paradigm for marriage that produces wives whose gifts are submerged on the grounds that "wifely submission" or to be a "helper" require it.

I believe that the standard of God's intention for husband and wife, according to His Word, evidences my success as a "redemptive" husband to the degree my wife's fullest potential is realized—in all her gifts and giftings. She was not created to be my servant (though we may both choose to serve each other's interests time and again). However, a mind-set focused on a "full partnership" will not be able to measure *my* fruitfulness without a concern for how I am contributing to *hers*, to verify I am an influence toward the maximum development of the creative possibilities in her. After all, isn't that exactly what Jesus' love has targeted for each member of His "Bride" He has redeemed? (Compare again with Eph. 5:27; and remember my concern in noting, "Anna doesn't sing anymore!")

3. Husband and wife are intended to be of unique value to each other (Gen. 2:20-23).

So Adam gave names to all [the beasts]...but for Adam there was not found a helper comparable to him...[and God] made [the rib] into a woman, and He brought her to the man. And Adam said: "This is now bone of my bones and flesh of my flesh; she shall be called Woman, because she was taken out of Man."

Nothing in the Bible stands in more direct opposition to the world's view of life than the Creation record. Contrary to the revelation of the Scriptures, which show specific, determinative and divinely calculated creative action, unbelief asserts a "chance" occurrence of life and its development upon our planet. Contrary to the biblical record of human existence as a "special creation," with a logical accountability to the Creator consequent to the fact, unbelief asserts an "accidental evolution," with a philosophical relativism the logical offspring and its moral guide.

IN THE ORIGINAL ORDER OF GOD'S PLAN FOR HUMAN COUPLES, THE CLIMAX OF THEIR FORMATION FOR ONE ANOTHER ISSUES IN A FULL PARTNERSHIP CHARACTERIZED BY DEEP MUTUAL APPRECIATION, ABSOLUTE COMMITMENT AND TOTAL TRANSPARENCY IN THEIR RELATIONSHIP.

Honesty with the Creation text allows a variety of views on the first "five days," and even reverent, evangelical scholars hold to widely divergent interpretations. Concerning the "sixth day," however, there is little room to escape the blunt demands of the text, especially when the generalized report of chapter 1 is detailed in chapter 2. For the sake of review, let us note two things: (a) The majority of the animal kingdom is created first in the "sixth day's" *initial* action (reported in 1:24,25, then repeated in 2:19 by way of review). (b) Human beings are created as the "sixth day's" *concluding* action (reported in 1:26-31, then this crowning act is elaborated in 2:4-25).

It is in this longer passage that God's work in constructing the male and the female relationship is given important detail. The implications of these two—His "initial" and His "concluding" actions—are enormous, for they establish grand and inescapable principles.

- First, the role of the man's *initiating responsibility* is established, seeing he is responsible to inform and lead the pair in following the moral law (2:16,17) upon which their kingdom will be ruled in partnership (1:26-30).
- Second, the *distinctiveness and value* of the man and woman is accentuated, seeing how God sequences their creation in a manner that will emphasize mutual dependency and appreciation.

Look at God's first action on the sixth day. *In opening,* the Creator elaborates their *distinctiveness*—separate and different from the animal kingdom. God forms the man, then, in marshaling the animals before him for naming, He establishes two things: (a) human distinction from and authority over lower creatures, and (b) the male's aloneness and dependence on God for the provision of a partner of his own created order.

Then, in the sixth day's *concluding* action, the Creator underscores *values* totally unlike any other at Creation. He forms the woman, using a part of the man as a "building block" in beginnings, thereby revealing two basic values intended to undergird their union in exercising the "dominion" they are given in partnership.

1. Worth: verse 23 affirms the first: their absolute equality in worth. *"This is now bone of my bones and flesh of my flesh."*
2. Interdependence: verse 24 asserts the second: the essential need of their mutuality in relationship, separate from others, committed to each other in life and interdependency. *"Therefore a man shall leave his father and mother and be joined to his wife, and they shall become one flesh."*

Their Openness and the Pastor's Call

The finale of this passage describes a marvelous transparency, forthrightness and openness toward each other. "Naked" is far more meaningful a term than merely "nude," the fact that usually preoccupies most artists and writers.

For example, Hebrews 4:13 observes how all things about each of us are "naked and open to the eyes" of God. The point has little to do with being unclothed, and everything to do with full disclosure. So in the original order of God's plan for human couples, the climax of their formation for one another issues in a full partnership characterized by (a) deep mutual appreciation, (b) absolute commitment and (c) capstoned by a total transparency in their relationship.

The elements of this initial order, elaborated with such clarity of intent by the Creator, are by and large overlooked in casual readings of this watershed passage. But God created the man and woman to know a life together that is built on values radically different from the world's. His Word establishes those values at the very beginning, and that text elaborates the value husband and wife are to place on one another.

In the light of their creational significance, I believe extensive pastoral teaching of these principles is required. Three things will result: *individuals* will understand what marriage commitment means; *couples* will understand what marriage growth requires; and *families* will discover the happiness of God's intended plan being filled in their homes.

However, beyond my call to pastoral *teaching*, as a pastor of promise I have a preliminary *personal* call to answer: the call to my marriage. What I am learning and growing in, deciding and demonstrating in humility as a husband seeking to "love as Christ loved," is all that will truly multiply and establish itself in the men I lead and the people I serve.

Pastoral ministry to Christ's Bride ultimately only goes as deep as the pastor's ministry to his own bride. Any spiritual values I teach will finally only be as credible as the value I am perceived to place on my wife—and the mutual value toward me that my leadership begets in her response.

REFLECTION QUESTIONS

1. If you are married, have you experienced a watershed experience such as described in the beginning of this chapter? Do your arguments tend to develop into "THE PROBLEM"? What is it?
2. Are you willing to love your wife as Jesus loved the Church—even "unto death"? How might that most practically be applied, seeing as "physical" death is an unlikely demand?
3. How would a pastor's first promise to his wife "to love, to

honor, to cherish" as Christ loves His Church find practical application with you?

4. Do you share personal stories in your sermons? Do you sometimes use your wife or family in your examples? If so, in what context? Who looks best? What do people learn?

5. Will the discussion of Genesis 2:15-25 help you in resolving any "woman" issue in your congregation?

CHAPTER SIX HIGHLIGHTS:

- The substance of character is fashioned by the accumulated responses of the heart to the Spirit's refining work.
- A pastor-leader needs to find a biblical value system that works—a sense of accountability born of a life commitment to seek and satisfy the Savior.
- There is a threefold "happy fruit" of diligent, steadfast obedience.
- A pastor-leader needs to guard against five vulnerable areas: matters of accuracy, privilege, power, prestige and moral purity.

Keep your heart with all diligence,
for out of it spring the issues of life.
PROVERBS 4:23

THE POWER OF AN UNGRIEVED SPIRIT

It seems like a scenario I have lived out a hundred times.

It is nearing the conclusion of a leader's conference. I have been speaking to gifted church leaders for several sessions—sometimes, two or three days. We have had some interchange before this, but now the floor is open. It is the listeners' turn to talk about anything anyone wants.

What the theme or focus has been usually makes no difference at this point. The subject of my messages or seminar sessions may range from vision casting, worship leadership, staff management, sermon preparation or spiritual gifts to finances in the church, eschatology, men's ministry, family life or whatever else. Still, irrespective of the subject, once I have opened the floor for questions, it has become inevitable that something like what follows will take place.

> **Question:** "Pastor Jack, how many hours do you spend in study each week?" or (and often joined to those words) "How much time do you spend in prayer, say, weekly or on an average each day?"
>
> **My reply:** "Thanks. It's a worthy—indeed—a greatly discerning question. But with respect, let me ask you for two

things—first, your forgiveness, because I would rather not answer that question. Second, I want to ask for your patience, because I'd like to discuss the subject I believe is behind such a perceptive question."

Of course, in responding to those Q and A sessions, I have always made a clear affirmation of the fundamental importance of steadfast prayer as a discipline, and systematic study as an essential for a pastor-teacher. I would not be embarrassed to describe the pattern I employ in each of those two pursuits nor the amount of time involved. My primary reason for not answering the question, however, is because it tends to bypass the "heart" issue of a pastor's inner responses to God. Even the disciplines of devotion and scholarship are capable of being put in place with such systematic style and skillful pursuit that, strangely, it is possible for any of us to still remain unstripped of self-dependency or unwitting carnality.

So after those appropriate explanations, when the question comes, I shortly turn it to a discussion of what, for me, has become the ultimate issue for every leader—*integrity of heart.*

I did not actually "rush" to this life priority, though my earliest influences in life had pointed me in the right direction by reason of my parents and the manner of our home life. I was more "crowded" toward it, however, brought to an early confrontation with my *self*, and with the potential of the heart for secret corruptibility, by reason of the setting of our first pastorate. Please be patient with my explanation, lest it seem either wildly arrogant or disgustingly self-pitying.

ASSIGNED TO OBSCURITY, NOT ABANDONED

Our first pastorate provided the venue for repeated feelings of having been sovereignly assigned to obscurity. Everything was a stark contrast to the recognition we received during my years in training for the ministry. Having been student leader (ASB president), a spiritual leader (college department director in a large congregation), a reasonably accomplished athlete (varsity letters in three sports) and a successful student (*magna cum laude*), general attention was not lacking.

Anna, too, was an honors graduate and a student leader, and when we graduated we had excellent opportunities afforded us by denominational officials inviting us to places of service in their regions.

As we prayed, however, we did not feel the peace of God regarding the most convenient and visibly promising of these offers. Instead, we felt led to pursue the possibilities where no promises were offered at all—except, "Come, and we'll find something."

That is how we came to be in Fort Wayne, Indiana, trying to plant a church in an environment that often seemed unpromising. The limits to our *own* experience almost assured limited success before we even began.

We were young and optimistic, though, and most of all, we believed God wanted us there.

He did. There is not a question in my mind. Irrespective of the statistical unimpressiveness of our first years of ministry, we knew we were in God's hand and that He had something in mind. That "something" He had in mind (and in "hand") was *to shape us*!

WE KNEW WE WERE IN GOD'S HAND AND THAT HE HAD SOMETHING IN MIND. THAT "SOMETHING" HE HAD IN MIND (AND IN "HAND") WAS *TO SHAPE US*!

The setting was remote. Geographically, we were 2,500 miles from our college, friends, family and the concentration of our denomination's numerical strength and name recognition on the West Coast. Culturally, we were in the middle of all the pleasantness that constitutes the heartland of the United States. People, however, though not unkind, were more than merely tentative. We faced a rather "closed" culture—not easy to win neighborly acceptance, especially as soon as we were discovered to be "Pentecostals...from California."

Remember, this is the late 1950s, and our church tradition was regarded with deep reservation—we were tabbed "holy rollers" and every Pentecostal was suspected of snake handling. At the time, our whole nation was far more marked by provincialism and a regional readiness to reject "outsiders" than it is in today's pluralistic, highly mobile society.

The geographical and cultural factors were not the greatest challenge for me, however, but the absence of recognition, of the affirmation we had constantly received by reason of privileged position. We had not been in town for a month when I came face-to-face with the cloying ways of the flesh when it lifts its selfish, moaning cry for it to be fed with other than the simple peace the soul can rest in when the will of God is being served.

As certain as I was that we had processed God's will, and that our relatively fruitless efforts were no excuse for running elsewhere, the flesh was still a formidable opponent. I am thankful I was not surrounded by the general social acceptance of ideas then that are virtually regarded as "gospel" in today's cater-to-the-flesh psychology. The predominance of propositions such as, "I need to feel good about myself," or "If this isn't good for me, it's not good at all," are propagated with self-serving effectiveness. They also often survive in some Christian circles, where they are semi-sanctified with a smattering of Bible quotations conveniently removed from their context, and where the Cross never involved "dying," but is only thought to be a ladder to success.

I was struggling with lost "recognition," and it was not because I had ever sought or relished what small honors I had received. Instead, I was only making the frightening self-discovery of finding how "used to it" I had become, and how important it was once it was not there anymore.

For another pastor it could be something else—a sense of having had "power" in a position he has left for the ministry; or the feeling of carnal depri- vation, where "money" had been more available in a past environment. It is amazing the degree to which the flesh can seem  **I WAS COMING TO THE CONVICTION: WE *HAD* BEEN ASSIGNED TO OBSCURITY—BY GOD, I WAS SURE. BUT WE WERE NEVER ABANDONED.** to justify its argument for its own way, or for having what it wants and does not have. I was discovering how tempting it is to surrender to substitutes for self-affirmation. In the middle of it, I was coming to the conviction: we *had* been assigned to obscurity—by God, I was sure. But we were never abandoned.

We were prayed for by more souls, I am sure, than we ever knew were faithfully bearing us up in prayer. We were also cared for by our regional bishop, Dr. Vincent Bird, and his wife, Connie. Their office was 200 miles away, however, and the nearest church in our region was more than 100 miles distant. So there, in the middle of a city of 135,000 people, but a mil- lion miles from being "recognized," God set about teaching me and develop- ing my convictions about "integrity of heart," and its priority in His eyes.

CONFRONTING "PASTORAL FLESH"

Those early lessons are still clearly remembered, as a young pastor began learning a heart integrity in the face of "pastoral flesh":

- Confronting *jealousy*—upon seeing the success and recognition gained by peers. It was easy to submit to internalized, private irritation with their "getting all the breaks," rather than rejoic- ing in God's grace on their ministries.

> During seasons of God's dealing with me—confronting "flesh" as "the old man" seeks to resurrect itself, I have cried out to God in different ways—among them, in writ- ing my heart cry at the time, such as this poem:

SACRIFICE

Father, show...let me know, let me understand:
Why the bleeding side of Christ, why the nail-
    pierced hands?
Why did thorns rend His brow; Why the stripes
    He bore;
Why the anguished agony? Father tell me more.

Men must know...blood must flow e'er new life
    begins;
So I cast my son apart; spent Him for thy sins.
He expelled from fellowship on the altar died,
Gave Himself a sacrifice, brought men to my
    side.

Child draw near, lend thine ear, and this lesson
    learn
If the lost be ever won, thou thyself must spurn.
Canst thou leave friendship dear, goods and
    gain behind
That through thy own sacrifice men my life
    might find.

Lord in praise, now I raise empty hands to Thee
I have cast far behind all things dear to me,
Thou hast taught how sacrifice fellowship
    restores
Take this worthless life of mine, make it wholly
    yours.

Father mine, let me shine, may I burned-out be;
May the light purely glow drawing men to Thee,
Self-consume, flesh destroy, Father hear my
    plea;
Use this fire of sacrifice for forging men to Thee.

Jack W. Hayford

• Confronting *unholy competition*—upon measuring what small
successes we occasionally realized against others we felt were
not doing as well as we were. (Oh the shame of remembering

my taking inner *comfort* about the failure of a nearby pastor, rather than feeling his pain!)

- Confronting *sexual temptation*—upon innocently coming upon a stash of "high quality" pornography while assisting our youth with a paper drive to raise money for summer camp; (and how I kept the "stash" for my own—for four days—wrestling beyond hiding it for my own self-indulgence, unto my decision to burn it—which I did. Oh the number of dear pastors I have counseled who at some time "didn't," and early on became chained from personal freedom in their ministries).

As a fellow companion in ministry, let me assure you my dear reader, I do not champion the concept of "integrity of heart" with any degree of smugness or self-righteousness. I do know its rewards, however, and for that reason want to invite you to explore the subject further with me.

INTEGRITY OF HEART

Years before I discovered this theme—integrity of heart—in the Bible, I had begun learning this "daily-mid-course-corrections" way of living. Two experiences, 10 years apart, are fixed in my memory.

The first relates to a practice of my mother's in teaching her children to keep an accountable "heart" toward God. As an eight-year-old, I was tempted by a secret event, which, however innocent by comparison then, could well have led to a pattern of soul-numbing behavior.

In that setting, I can remember Mama saying, "Son, I want to ask you a question but, before asking, I want to say, I'm asking you 'in front of Jesus.'"

When I answered her inquiry, her wise and gentle dealing cut through to the core of a child's potential for delusion and eventual confusion.

Mama's "in front of Jesus" summons was not a manipulative ploy, nor were those words frequently spoken, but she used them as an occasional reminder. A wise parent recognizes when a kid can be tempted to dishonesty as a deceitful defense. Her words beautifully framed a picture that accentuated the fact that my Savior was not a distant entity, and that heart honesty was not an optional issue. I never thought this phrase was used to induce guilt or to breed an atmosphere of condemnation. Rather, it was based on a biblically verifiable truth that even redeemed human nature too often forgets to heed: "All things are naked and open to the eyes of Him to whom we must give account" (Heb. 4:13).

The second experience is the memory of the summer I was 17 years old. Each day at lunch, taking a break from my job to earn money for my college education, I memorized Bible verses from the Navigators card-pak

I carried. One verse especially became indelibly etched on my heart as well
as my mind:

> *The heart is deceitful above all things, and desperately wicked; who
> can know it?* (Jer. 17:9).

I can remember asking myself the question: If I can trick myself into
believing something's right and it's not, how can I keep my heart from
being deceived? The following verses became pivotal to my life and began
to govern my habits of thought:

> How can a young man cleanse his way? By taking heed accord-
> ing to Your Word. With my whole heart have I sought You; oh,
> let me not wander from Your commandments! (Ps. 119:9,10).
>
> POINT: It is not enough for me to know God's Word, but
> my WHOLE HEART must be kept consciously available to
> His Spirit's correction so I will not inadvertently wander in my
> own way or supposed wisdom of my own flesh.
>
> Search me, O God, and know my heart; try me, and know my
> anxieties; and see if there is any wicked way in me, and lead me
> in the way everlasting (Ps. 139:23,24).
>
> POINT: Only by daily welcoming the Lord to walk the cor-
> ridors of my heart can I know the blessing of HIS PROTEC-
> TION against the subtlety of my own rationalizing of my sin,
> my own toleration of my selfishness or my own defending of my
> arguments that seek to justify my preferences without humble
> correctability before the Lord.

In brief, I began to come to terms with what I am convinced is the
shaping power, the forming hand and the essential terrain of true character. The shaping power is the truth of God's Word, the forming hand is His
Spirit's "dealings" and the essential terrain is the human heart kept fully
open to instruction, correction and refinement. I began to learn that God
is not so interested in what I am as He is in what I am becoming. I was
launched upon a journey of daily opening my heart to Him for scrutiny;
not as an exercise in self-flagellating or berating introspection, but as a
practice of maintaining sensitivity to His Spirit's "voice," keeping integrity
with His dealings in my heart.

The Bible candidly states, "As he thinks in his heart, so is he" (Prov. 23:7).
Jesus pressed this same issue with His disciples, calling them past the superficial to the essential to teach them that what makes a man is not the appear-

ances of his words or deeds, but the true and inner thoughts of his heart (see Matt. 15:10-20). This is the reason the writer of Proverbs says:

Keep your heart with all diligence, for out of it spring the issues of life (4:23).

A leader's character will never rise beyond the flow level of his or her obedience to the Holy Spirit's dealings with the heart. Although our standard of character is outlined in God's Word and person of Christ, the substance of character is fashioned by the accumulated responses of the heart to the Spirit's refining work.

AFFAIRS OF THE HEART

At the core of everything a Christ-honoring pastor seeks to do is a biblical value system—a sense of accountability, and presumably a life commitment to seek to satisfy the Savior. Our pursuits and their objectives are laid over a grid of convictions rooted in revealed truth, and our personal priorities are dictated from heaven. At least that is where we start.

These values that guide decisions and motivate action are ultimately "heart" issues because they transcend the intellect. The mind is often too quick to rationalize, but the heart, at least at *first*, realizes—that is, it "knows" and "feels" the deep-down yearnings of the heart of God. Our responses at this dimension are rightly spoken of as "affairs of the heart." They determine the actual "balance of our life's personal and moral accounts," in the same way our financial "affairs" determine how much currency we have to expend. A shortness of accounts reduces our present-moment capacity to do the business we have been called to do as pastors because the fountain of the outflow of our life as a leader has been clogged. Its heaven-born stream of true "becoming" has not been cared for.

As a shepherd of souls, my own heart's "fountain" must be fed by more than a self-developed set of philosophical principles. Although my grid of convictions is rooted in biblical principles and the absolute authority of the Word of God, my applications may too easily be administered in my self-interest or flavored by my opinion. Thus, joined to God's objective Word must be a more subjective integrity. It will determine how I "live out" the objective statements of His Word. The following is a combination of promise and problem:

- The "promise" is in God's divinely trustworthy, objective revelation in His Word, given once-for-all by His Holy Spirit;
- The "problem" is in my humanly fallible, subjective perception of God's will, and my need for daily correction by His Holy Spirit.

Without my acknowledgment of the "problem"—and thereby, my constant availability to the Holy Spirit's adjusting corrections to my attitude, understanding or perspective—I will inevitably have occasions when I "fool myself," no matter how much objective truth I may know.

For example, that is the reason "good pastors" tolerate bitterness and unforgiveness toward others, and justify their attitude on the basis of their being the "violated party." It is why some leaders allow themselves the privilege of speaking critically or condescendingly about leaders who hold different doctrinal emphases than they do, then self-justify their judgmentalism on the false supposition that God sees them as "more right" than others are. It is why otherwise moral, godly shepherds have been known to become deluded about the nature of an inappropriate relationship; to tragically fall into the confusion of moral compromise, to tolerate an infatuation—supposing it "under control" and so not violating his marriage's trust. That the heart is capable of becoming "desperately wicked" is the greatest reason for its being given primary attention in our honest quest to walk with God.

GOD'S PRESENCE IS GIVEN TO EVERY REBORN SON OR DAUGHTER OF THE MOST HIGH, TO TEACH US HOW THE FATHER'S WILL FLOWS INTO THE MOST PRACTICAL DETAILS OF OUR LIVES.

Honesty calls me to see that my character as a leader will be determined by how well I know God's Word. It will also depend on how willingly I permit His Spirit to continually refine my imperfect capacities for receiving and responding to His will in the moment-to-moment details of my life. My character is not shaped by the sum of my *information*, but by the process of a *transformation* that is as unceasingly needed in *me* as God's Word is unchanging with *Him*.

There is more to my character formation than having learned a set of ideas—even if they are God's. I not only need to *turn to the Bible*, but I must also keep *tuned to the Holy Spirit*, for with the "grid" of values His Word gives me, He provides His Spirit as the ultimate umpire who comes to apply that Word to my living. His presence is given to every reborn son or daughter of the Most High, to teach us how the Father's will flows into the most practical details of our lives.

The purpose of His monitoring is not to produce a mysticized brand of supposed "holiness," but a dynamic quality of wholehearted, clear-eyed people; people of a character described in one word—Christ's! My character as a pastor is not that I prize the highest values in God's Word, but that they are being woven into the fabric of my life—growing me slowly but certainly into the image of Christ. This happens *only as I "walk in the Spirit."*

The phrase—"walk in the Spirit"—becomes a pivotal issue in the determination of my character. It is the secret to finding the promised possibilities of a heart committed to integrity. It means I need to learn to recognize when I "grieve" the Spirit (Eph. 4:30), and to readily respond with repentance and confession in each situation I find He corrects me.

REFUSING EVEN "MINOR DEVIATIONS"

As a pastor, my commitment to walk with integrity of heart calls me to refuse to allow the most minor deviations from honesty with my *self*, with the *facts*, and most of all, with *the Holy Spirit's corrections*. They are either prompting your soul, stinging in your conscience, bringing restlessness to your mind or an inner pain to your "heart."

Contrary to the scorn of those choosing a less-demanding standard for their lives, to make such a commitment to integrity is not to become the victim of a wearying legalism or the exploited subject of a dignified guilt complex. Instead, this is to commit to a healthy mind-set; to an "inner-heart lifestyle" lived in the joy of God's grace and in the fullness of peace we are given in Christ. It does call, however, for an abiding willingness to constantly invite and allow the Spirit of God to make me sensitive to matters that make a difference to God—*however small, or however unperceived they may at first be to me.*

The Happy Fruit of Obedience

Having decades now behind me of seeking to keep this openness to the Spirit's correction, I can only rejoice about both His patience and His ways. I have found that the happy fruit of a diligent effort at steadfast obedience to such dealings is at least threefold:

- Because the heart of God is sought and His purity of character made a leader's priority, a holy intimacy of fellowship with the Father continually increases. *"The secret of the Lord is with those who fear [reverence] Him, and He will show them His covenant"* (Ps. 25:14).
- Because the practice of confessing one's failures to those on the human plane is biblical (see Jas. 5:16), as well as the obvious need to confess and repent before God (see 1 John 1:6-10), an amazing freedom from our human preoccupation to constantly defend oneself is found.
- Because a commitment to walk in submission to the Holy Spirit's prompting and correction is pursued (see Eph. 4:30; see also vv. 25-32), a clearer mindedness comes to the voice of God

and a sharper sensitivity to the will of God, as well as a more ready discernment of the works of darkness (see 5:17,18).

The Scriptures clearly instruct and warn regarding this importance of integrity of heart. In my book for men—*A Man's Integrity* (one of the "six-pack" set published by Thomas Nelson Publishers, Nashville)—I have developed the following outline in greater detail. Notable for any leader's study is an examination of "integrity of heart" as revealed in the lives of men who learned God's ways through integrity, or its violation.

- Abimelech (see Gen. 20:1-6): As we witness his confusion as the result of a lie being told him, we then see the PRESERVING POWER of *integrity of heart* as God introduces us to the truth that He will keep us in spite of our honest mistakes if integrity is present.
- David (see Ps. 25:19-21): As we discover his integrity in depending on God's sustaining grace as his defense—God's PROTECTING POWER— rather than political diplomacy. (See also David's *first* source of leadership ability and resource— *"integrity of heart"*; Ps. 78:70-72).
- Solomon (see 1 Kings 9:1-5): As we hear the Lord's covenant relayed to this new king, declaring that *"integrity of heart"* has a PERPETUATING POWER that will sustain us unto the realization God has promised if His ways are faithfully maintained—from the heart.

FIVE VULNERABLE AREAS

In the light of both—the manifest rewards and the biblical blessings attending a heart of integrity—let me point to five areas of vulnerability calling for the pastor's guardedness. I have found these to be danger points I need to keep sensitive to maintaining a correctable, teachable heart that sustains fullest integrity.

1. Matters of Accuracy

A leader should require of himself absolute honesty of heart in communication to those he leads. Nothing is more tempting than to exaggerate numbers; for example, church attendance figures. (This is sometimes done in the self-deceiving guise that "people need the encouragement," when in fact the inflated figure is used as ego support for the leader himself.) "Blurring" the information, so as to make something sound better than it is, is another common ruse of the flesh. To surrender to either of these or similar habits is to dull the ear of my soul to its call to maximum integrity.

Of course, an honest mistake in disseminating information might be made, and such a *faux pas* ought not be called a "lie" or a violation of integrity. A mistake is not a lie; it is an accident in understanding. A violation of integrity is something else, however, and the honest heart will acknowledge that inner "twinge" to the soul and stand corrected, and also acknowledge as much to anyone to whom he has knowingly misrepresented the truth. On the other hand, mistaken facts have not compromised the heart, and though correction may be made, no embarrassment is necessarily to be borne.

2. Matters of Privilege

Along with the responsibilities of leadership, occasional privileges may also be enjoyed. These should be known to at least those to whom the leader is first accountable, and they ought not to be hidden from those the leader leads. It is also critical to my maintaining an integral heart that any privileges I might enjoy ever be sought and never be exploited. What naturally is given may be received, and seen as a grace or gift, but even the privileges of God's grace are not to be insinuated upon, and so it should be with whatever privilege a leader may have.

One of my first lessons at this point of inner accountability took place when I was in my first pastorate. An order for church supplies from one catalog afforded the premium of a small transistor radio—free with the order.

"Ah-hah!" I at first intoned, seeing this small "gold mine" as a treasure to be snatched for myself as the official making the order. Self-justifying reason would have it that "certain benefits" are deserved on one's own advisement.

The argument—I'm paid so little I ought to be able to enjoy some privilege of office—has captured a million minds, dulled as many souls and stumbled thousands of leaders. So I did place the order, but I did not keep the radio for myself. Privileges *are* acceptable to be enjoyed—but not secret ones. If there is a privilege to my office, it ought to be sanctioned by those under whom I serve and understood in that way by those I lead.

3. Matters of Power

The pastor's role obviously incorporates significant authority, or "power" in the personal sense (as opposed to spiritual sense). The meaning of "authority" (i.e., the right to a realm of dominion for the service of a task), is biblically intended to focus on "power for the purpose of serving people." This is Jesus' insistent emphasis (see Luke 22:24-27), and its violation will inevitably destroy the very realm of rule intended to the one assigned the authority. (Study Rehoboam's "show of power" and the folly it created, resulting in splitting the kingdom—1 Kings 12.)

One of the wisest observations I have ever noted about the exercise of power I heard from the late Dr. David Hubbard, who was the president of Fuller Theological Seminary in Pasadena, California. David and I were members of a panel interacting with a group of pastors on the subject of "the submission of a leader." In that context, this dear brother spoke words that welded a concept into my own soul: *"I never exercise the full extent of the power inherent in my position."* I registered that wisdom, understanding very well that to ever feel the *need* to exercise the full range of my powers makes it likely I am in a situation best resolved by a team rather than by myself, unilaterally. It is also far less likely that power *shared* will ever crush a person being chastised. At the same time, sharing my power moves me to a greater distance from the possibility of my ever becoming enamored with what power I may have.

4. Matters of Perceived Prestige

As a pastor, just plain "human vanity" is also a highly vulnerable point to which I must pay heed. Often even kindly intended remarks, offered to affirm or recognize me, involve either positive or negative comparisons with others. This "mirror" tactic of the adversary of our souls is untiring, seeking to draw me to compare myself with people rather than the standard of God's Word. I dare not let my heart be stolen by even the most sincere praise or most gracious approval. It *is* right to accept kindnesses and affirmation, and it *is* inconsiderate to fend off such remarks with pretended piety. At the same time, I am wise to recognize that nothing I may have I have not received (see 1 Cor. 4:7).

This principle works both ways, too. It is far too common for a pastor to pander to the pride of an individual or the congregation—playing to an individual's or corporate body's human sense of quest for superiority. For example:

> "Helen, you're the finest leader our women's group has ever had." "You're the greatest choir this town has ever seen!" "Church, you're the greatest congregation in our denomination!"

What may innocently be intended as encouragement can very quickly develop a spirit of smugness in any group, and any loyalty gained at the expense of compromising this principle is built on sand. It is not necessary to compare in order to commend. Note Jesus' words, "Well done, good [not better or best] and faithful servant" (Matt. 25:21).

Early in my present pastoral tenure, I wrestled with a case of my own fear of losing "prestige" when responding to a request for a magazine article. As I came to a point in writing where I wanted to use an illustration I received from a fellow-pastor friend, I did not want to credit him as the source for fear my mentioning another leader would distract from my own prominence in the mind of the reader.

"WE WOULD WORRY A LOT LESS ABOUT WHAT PEOPLE THOUGHT OF US IF WE REALIZED HOW SELDOM THEY DO." —ETHEL BARRETT

It is too long a story to tell, but I confronted the fear of lost prestige and as a result of mentioning the other pastor, a woman who read the article visited his church and received Christ! One wonders how many self-protectionist ruses I may have used through the years of my leadership might have been at the expense of similar results.

I am right to presume that, in the case of the magazine article, the likelihood of *any* reader having any notions of my "prominence" were nil anyway! I love to quote my dear friend—the author, Ethel Barrett—who said, *"We would worry a lot less about what people thought of us if we realized how seldom they do."*

5. Matters of Moral Purity

Aside from the obvious mandate the Bible gives to moral purity in sexual, financial and relationship dealings, the spiritual leader wanting to cultivate a heart of integrity must come to terms with his mind as well as his body. Especially today, considering the proliferation of pornographic resources and the capacity for absolute secrecy while deeply involved—or the abounding mental and media resources for feeding fantasies, then justifying them as "personal relaxation without moral compromise"—integrity of heart is all the more to be sought and maintained.

Some years ago, I was speaking at a retreat where the joyousness of the collegians found warm expression in everyone's hugging one another at the conclusion of each service. Nothing was inappropriate: The Bible fully endorses the practice, and the expressions were void of either giddiness or mushiness. The memory I relate is embarrassing—not because I continued in any violation of my integrity—but shameful to remember that my mind, for even one moment, was compromised by incipient carnality.

I had "holy-hugged" a half-dozen youth, both guys and girls, when a rather short girl reached out in simple purity to embrace me—the respected Bible teacher. Without intent, as I reached to hug her, by reason of her small size my arms circled her to the point that my reach extended slightly under her upreaching arms, lightly touching the fullness of the side of one breast. Because the contact not only was innocent and brief, and without any intent of a potential impropriety, it went entirely unnoticed—except to my mind.

As I said, it is embarrassing to confess (which I did, to my male associate and roommate, who was traveling with me on the trip). At the moment, however, I suddenly was faced with a horrible realization of my mind's conniving potential. For a few shameful seconds, I thought to myself of how such an apparently innocent action could become a means for periodic self-gratification. At the same moment, the inner pinching of the heart—prompted by the immediate grief of the Holy Spirit about my mind's indulgence—called me to take a stance of integrity: "Never again!"

Our congregation is a loving one and has a constant habit of embracing one another, and to this day I participate as freely as anyone. That one day, however, the discovery of a fleshly ruse was encountered and refused. I, of course, have stood firm in that grace—vowing within my own soul never to violate integrity with either my own heart before God or my own sisters in Christ.

I have risked relating the story on the possibility of being judged unkindly by some critic. Because I have had to counsel too many leaders who have violated points of integrity, only to fall deeper into failure and loss for having taken the first step, I have decided to confess that moment's test while testifying to the victories heart integrity can win. May God's tender Spirit cause my sharing to possibly warn some dear but weakened pastor away from any compromise of His call to us all to integrity of heart.

AN OVERLOOKED ISSUE

While noting primary issues in "keeping the heart," I would like to ask you, my fellow-servant, to consider joining me in introducing to the list of "integrity issues" one very overlooked matter of the leader's "heart-set" (as compared with a "mind-set"). Would you agree with this?

Every Christian leader is constantly confronted with pressures to take sides against other believers, to criticize styles and doctrines that are different and to pass judgment on leaders or ministries that don't suit their tastes. "Spiritual suspicion" has almost become an article of faith in North America—a deceptive notion fostered by "experts" who pursue their critiques of some other Christians in the spirit of the jaundiced investigative reporting of secular news writers.

Whatever may be the actual number of cases of actual error or violation of trust in ministry, it is certain that far more mud slinging and attack verbiage is employed than ever could be justified. In this atmosphere of what often deteriorates into a junkyard dog-eat-dog style of attack against brethren, however failing, I am deeply of the opinion that it is time for the rise of a new breed of Christian leader who sees such lovelessness as a violation of integrity. Could you agree that we would all do well to take note that the biblical warning against *last days error* provides no warrant for *end times judgmentalism* or snobbish posturings against one another in Christ's Body?

Is it possible that the highest call to integrity spiritual leaders may need to hear today is the call to love one another as we have been loved—to be forgiving of one another as we have been forgiven? It is often hard to hear the Holy Spirit whispering this call to my heart if I have been schooled in systems that argue for their own righteousness over others without ever suspecting the righteousness of such an attitude.

I have neither preachment nor illustration to make at this point, but my appeal is that we learn to defend one another rather than to attack. Illustrations are prevalent, from assault registered about the Christian media to privately barbed commentary made in personal conversation. Certainly, differences of viewpoint, practice and preference will exist

WE WIN WITH OUR HEARTS, NOT OUR HEADS, AND A HEAD SET ON INTEGRITY IS THAT PRIMARY ESSENTIAL THAT WILL SHAPE THE WINNING HEART.

among the members of Jesus' Body—His Church—until He comes again. Yet knowing this, our Savior Himself prayed: "That they may be one just as We are one: I in them, and You in Me; that they may be made perfect in one, and that the world may know that You have sent Me" (John 17:22,23).

Because that prayer, as much as any that has been prayed, was surely offered in the power of the Holy Spirit, we can all apply a point of wisdom with confidence. We can be certain that if we all "tune in," the same Holy Spirit, in the gentle grace of our Lord Jesus who interceded for unity, will increase our sensitivity to avoid anything we do or say becoming a contradiction to our Savior's heart cry. Will you join me in "tuning" to that station?

BEYOND THE "MARKETING"

The common denominator of these issues is that they call us all beyond technique—beyond, to use a contemporary term, merely learning to "market" the Church. Although I have no condemnation to register upon any whose skills and analyses are offered to help us "speak" to our generation with sensitivity and clarity, let us remember that our *gains* will never be made without *pains*. The true "cutting edge" that penetrates my culture will most likely be that edge of the Spirit's sword that circumcises my carnality and releases the dynamic that flows from a blend of purity and love—a holy heartbeat for the hurting in my world.

Decades of serving the Church and watching the world—and of seeing the world ever and always trying to shape the Church—have produced a settled conviction: We win with our hearts, not our heads, and a head set on integrity is that primary essential that will shape the winning heart.

FRUITFUL LEADERSHIP IS NOT THE ABILITY TO "PRODUCE RESULTS," BUT THE CAPACITY TO BRING THOSE I LEAD UNTO THEIR DEEPEST ENRICHMENT AND HIGHEST FULFILLMENT.

Nothing is more *chic* in today's management technique than answering the present mandate that every corporation project a concise mission and vision statement with a companion set of "core values." It is a good idea, focusing the central reason for being, and the controlling principles for being that. Whatever the Church's mission, in the final analysis, the character of the leadership will determine its fruit. The "heart" will be the final measure of success, whatever else may have been achieved.

The deepest and highest point in the personal life of a pastor centers in a private venue—the heart. It pointedly runs in diametric opposition to his or her being controlled by visible evidences of success, acceptance or recognition. Furthermore, the criterion of a spiritual leader's ultimate measurement comes from a plane higher than human origin. The character of a true shepherd requires an answer to a call that sounds from the *highest* source and shapes him in the *deepest* personal corners of his soul. "Success" at these levels—at the highest and deepest—can be found, but will only be realized when I choose a leadership style committed first to an inner accountability question: *Am I keeping my heart "with integrity"?*

Such a heart, tooled by the hand of God and dedicated to serve with practical wisdom and earnest zeal, will reveal an order of truly effective pastoral leadership (irrespective of how "efficient" he may or may not be). He will be the kind of leader who builds *trust* (and thereby never needs to "demand loyalty"); and the kind who realizes long-term *durability* (born of abiding substance that outlasts transient "style").

Best of all, that pastor will realize true *fruitfulness* in leadership, as that term is properly defined. *Fruitful leadership is not the ability to "produce results," but the capacity to bring those I lead unto their deepest enrichment and highest fulfillment.* It is not in getting my people to fulfill my goals (or even my God-given vision for our collective enterprise and good), but in helping each person to realize God's creative intent for his or her life—personally, domestically, vocationally and eternally. Integrity to that vision, driven by a heart showing integrity toward God and man, invites God onto the scene—to prove good His promise.

FINALLY—INTEGRITY'S PROMISE

Finally, then, nothing is more demanding of my character as a leader than to yield humbly to the corrective or adjustive promptings of the Holy Spirit. He is the One who has drawn me to the Savior! He is the One whose power has brought regeneration—new birth to my spirit! He is the One who has come to grow in me the traits of Jesus' character as surely as He wants to fill me with the words and works of Jesus' power!

That promise is ours to possess as pastors; the "promise" given in God's Word, ultimately assuring a flow of Holy Spirit grace and power wherever a heart of integrity can be found.

> *For the eyes of the Lord run to and fro throughout the whole earth, to show Himself strong on behalf of those whose heart is loyal to Him* (2 Chron. 16:9).

What a promise! God "showing Himself strong" in our midst!

Let's lay hold of it—bearing one another up; refusing any path or pursuit that offers a *perception* of achievement without the *penetration* of true holiness. It is too shortchanged an offer for us who are called to heaven's long-range vision—to see the eternal, and to maintain a heart that values its rewards above all.

REFLECTION QUESTIONS

1. In this chapter, "the ultimate issue for every leader is *integrity of heart*" is discussed. How has a quest for "integrity of heart" developed in your own life and ministry?
2. Can you identify with being assigned to obscurity? But not being abandoned?
3. In honesty to yourself, has "pastoral flesh," as mentioned in this chapter, presented problems for you at some time in your ministry?

4. Do you think a pastor's responsibility to principles is called to a higher standard than those he leads?
5. Review the five vulnerable areas a pastor needs to guard. Have any of these issues been problems for you during your ministry?

CHAPTER SEVEN HIGHLIGHTS:

- A directive suddenly ignited my whole field of understanding.
  My two "houses" (family and church) were in need of an order
  of priestly "prayer covering."
- The tentlike "tabernacle" concept conveys the idea of "covering" in prayer.
- By applying a true principle of "submission," no one will ever
  be exploited, manipulated or dominated by another.
- God speaks to every human being by both general and specific revelation.
- An outline on the theme of submission focuses the semantics,
  significance, specifics and the spirit of submission.

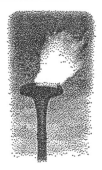

*Assuredly, I say to you,
I have not found such great faith,
not even in Israel!*
MATTHEW 8:10

CHAPTER SEVEN

THE WAY TO KEEP "COVERED" WITH PROMISE

It was 4:00 A.M.

The lighted digital dial on the bedside clock was more than a time indicator: It seemed to beckon me personally. I knew I had been awakened to get up and pray.

Perhaps you have had similar experiences, for it never ceases to amaze me the way the Lord can communicate with us as His own kids. Knowing I was called to an "appointment," I slipped silently out of bed so I would not bother Anna and, picking up my robe from the chair at our bedside, I walked softly down the hallway, sliding my arms into the sleeves and cinching the belt around my waist. As I padded toward the living room, a phrase was whispered to my soul:

The tabernacle is falling.

It came as a directive, answering my prayerful inquiry why I was being called to prayer. You understand the feeling—our common experience of how the communication of just one sentence or phrase can mean volumes. Within a longtime, personal relationship, a gesture—not to mention one or two words—can indicate a bevy of things. A single sentence spoken by someone who knows you well can mean paragraphs, and such was my experience that morning. The Lord impressed on my mind a phrase that suddenly ignited a whole field of understanding to me.

PRAYER FOR "STICKY SITUATIONS"

I immediately understood that I was being directed to pray for a cluster of sticky situations. Key to my understanding was my familiarity with the quotation involved: My mind flashed to the words of Amos, the prophet:

"On that day I will raise up the tabernacle of David, which has fallen down, and repair its damages; I will raise up its ruins, and rebuild it as in the days of old" (Amos 9:11).

Until now, however, I had only thought of this text as a reference to promised restoration, and not as a picture of impending desolation. In that short instant, I recognized the Lord was pressing my attention toward some personal issues—things that, if left unattended by prayer and careful seeking of His counsel, could become serious problems.

A plethora of the nitty-gritty—all kinds of "stuff"—seemed to congeal into the "not-so-nice." Little things had seemed to be accumulating during recent days—continuous "happenings"—resulting in minor points of confusion, unusual amounts of wasted time and frustration escalating into flights of temper. Furthermore, various family members were having recurrent bouts with minor ailments and sicknesses—all of us at home, on through the whole family right down to some of our grandkids.

Besides these happenings, I was also experiencing sporadic moments of depression. If they had lasted longer, or if it was an ongoing problem, I would have done something about it. I would have invited elders to anoint and pray for me. I might have reviewed my diet or made sure I was sleeping enough, because physical explanations for such things are a possibility. In my case, though, these moments would come like clouds blown by a high wind, blocking the sun for only a few minutes. No apparent natural reason explained it. A wave of depression would strike, along with an acute feeling of loneliness or helplessness; then it would pass. Although they were temporary, it was still clear that such "moments" could become a sustained bout with despair if they stuck around.

Then too, although no strife was present in Anna's and my relationship, I was forced to admit a need. The honesty of this encounter with God alerted me to "a something else" that seemed to be occurring in the house—something I could not pin down but that was there nonetheless. In retrospect, I called it an "absence of one accord." We certainly were not at each other's throats, but we seemed "out of sync" with each other. Hectic and sometimes conflicting schedules stampeded us in different directions of daily duty. A season of high intensity and compounded responsibilities for us both were not so much driving us apart as they were preventing our togetherness. Valued times of intimate conversation beside the fireplace during late evening hours had not happened for weeks.

THE SIGNAL FLAG WAS RAISED

Now the signal flag had been raised in heaven: *The tabernacle is falling.* I recognized that God was shaking me awake in more ways than getting me out of bed. My "house" was tossed and blown by winds of circumstance, as a tent is blown around in high winds, and something drastic was needed to secure it.

Perhaps these kinds of things happen to you, too. I am amazed at my remarkable capacity to tolerate an accumulation of a kind of "situational garbage" without recognizing something larger behind it all. I miss seeing the pattern and become consumed with an effort at juggling the increasing number of minor problems and, if unwarned, as I was, continue the juggling effort until—*crash!* So although I had not seen the pattern in those things until that morning, the words *"The tabernacle is falling"* brought a sudden new perspective. A mental picture appeared that helped me respond with prayerful sensitivity and practical wisdom.

I saw a giant tent, not unlike the old-fashioned big-tops used for the circus. The only difference was that this tent was not flamboyantly colored, but was a plain, neutral shade. Supporting it were two towering poles, constituting its primary upward thrust (I sensed that these represented Anna and me). Within the broad area covered by the giant spread of canvas were unidentifiable people and objects, and these, I knew, represented the "circumstances" I by now perceived as badly needing pointed prayer.

The most notable feature of the vision was that the ropes tying the tent down—strung from the bottom sides of the canvas to stakes surrounding the mobile structure—were either loosened or slack. Worse yet, the four primary ropes—larger ones placed at each corner of the tent—were completely loose and flapping violently in the wind.

As I studied the scene, it was clear that the sweep of the gale sought to come under and into the tent, rising upward as would a geyser of air, bent on tearing the tent from its supports and exposing everything within it to the ripping blast of the storm. Seeing this picture, I was dynamically motivated to take action—first, in prayer, and then in further other actions I will describe in a moment. First, here is what I understood from the "prayer-picture" just described.

Anna's and my "house"—our family circumstances, our home-life's atmosphere, our joint enterprise in ministry—was under pressure. Just as tornadoes are the product of two radically different weather systems at drastically different temperatures, so the peace of our house was threatened by a hostile force we were encountering. As I said, we were not actually at odds with one another, but neither were we unified in identifying and resisting the forces that were marshaled against us.

The tent (tabernacle) was en route to a collapse; that is, the people and things constituting our arena of responsibility— which we "covered" through our prayers and agreement—were vulnerable to *exposure*. Should the wind whip away the tent, the two poles would still be standing in close proximity—that is, our marriage was not in danger. But we had children, grandchildren, other family, a congregation, a ministry— all involving people and circumstances that our prayers were responsible to "cover." We needed to be certain this covering was secured by our prayers about these matters.

THE PROMISE OF A LEADER'S LIFE WILL ONLY BE FULFILLED TO THE SAME MEASURE HE OR SHE IS WILLING TO LEARN AND LIVE IN THE SPIRIT OF SUBMISSION.

The four larger ropes snapping in the wind, pulled by the wind's pressure on the tent and now tossed like threads, represented four distinct areas of duty we needed to address prayerfully—*now*. It was clear in the vision and clear in my soul—*The tabernacle is falling, unless you pray right now!*

CALLED "TO COVER"

In a few minutes, I want to finish that story—actually, a testimony of an important prayer encounter. Before I do, however, I think it is important first to express how much the significance of that moment was rooted, *not* in a prayer vision, but in strong convictions about that central priority for spiritual leadership I want to focus on here. The whole point of this and another testimony I am about to relate is to sharpen one point: *The promise of a leader's life will only be fulfilled to the same measure he or she is willing to learn and live in the spirit of submission.*

The "tabernacle" concept was a natural image for the Holy Spirit to use in prompting me to concern and prayer because the tentlike sanctuary so perfectly conveys the idea of "covering." My perception of the principle and pursuit of a life of "submission" is that we are all called "to be covered, and to cover." That is, every leader needs to live a life aligned with God's divine order for authority for him or her personally. It relates both in reference to whom we are submitted, and to whom we are given authority to love and serve.

My grip on the priority of this truth (or, rather, my being gripped by it) came about by three means. The first two were (1) my upbringing, and (2) my belief that this was a biblical truth to which every believer is called. I would never have caught the depth and the practical application of the concept of submission for a pastor-leader's life except for a third factor, (3) a merciful visitation that took place one night. Before I relate this pivotal awakening to the pastoral implications of "biblical submission," however, let's look at the subject in God's Word.

THE ROOTS OF REAL SUBMITTEDNESS

Although "submission" has often been a twisted truth and a distorted emphasis, the roots of biblical submittedness are not burdened with the heavy-handedness the flesh often brings to the theme. If we see and apply the principle of "submission," first to ourselves, and always according to God's Word, no one will ever be exploited, manipulated or dominated by another. Rather, the Scriptures show submission as a concept and submittedness as a practice being rooted in a highly practical life of love, care and responsibility. A passage in Matthew's Gospel gets to the nub of it.

> *Now when Jesus had entered Capernaum, a centurion came to Him, pleading with Him, saying, "Lord, my servant is lying at home paralyzed, dreadfully tormented." And Jesus said to him, "I will come and heal him." The centurion answered and said, "Lord, I am not worthy that You should come under my roof. But only speak a word, and my servant will be healed. For I also am a man under authority, having soldiers under me. And I say to this one, 'Go,' and he goes; and to another, 'Come,' and he comes; and to my servant, 'Do this,' and he does it." When Jesus heard it, He marveled, and said to those who followed, "Assuredly, I say to you, I have not found such great faith, not even in Israel!" Then Jesus said to the centurion, "Go your way; and as you have believed, so let it be done for you." And his servant was healed that same hour* (Matt. 8:5-10,13).

First, although the *word* "submission" does not appear here, still, (1) the actual derivation of the *term* is present in the setting, and (2) the *heart* of the *concept* is demonstrated by the centurion's response to Jesus.

The text introduces us to a military setting. The centurion is a captain of men, saying, "Jesus, I tell my soldiers, 'Do this and they do it.'" *Hupotasso* (Greek, to submit) was literally and culturally used to refer to an arrangement of troops *under* proper order; each private, corporal, sergeant, lieutenant and captain relating correctly right up the line through majors, colonels and generals—to a commander-in-chief. So in this Scripture text, the centurion is well versed in the relationship of power and authority when he says, "I am a man *under* authority and I *administer* that authority according to a specific order of *alignment*."

This soldier understood that *his* submission, or alignment with authority placed above him, was the source of that power available to manifest itself through him as he submitted to it himself. His power or authority was not self-derived. It was delegated through an appointed order (military or governmental in this case), and his acceptance of his role as a "submitted" man was what gave rise to the power or authority he exercised.

Second, the centurion proceeds to use his position of authority, not only to make an analogy in his comment to Jesus, but also in the way he shows care for a person of lesser position than himself. He reveals his recognition that Jesus is one who can be trusted to use His "authority given" to apply the "power available" in the interest of human need. In effect, he says, "Jesus, just as I have military *authority*, which can apply military *power* at will, I know You have authority in another realm, and an ability to bring power to bear on a matter of concern to me. All You need to do is to speak a word."

Don't miss seeing the centurion's own heart to serve or care for others, when, as an officer, he could show an almost brutal indifference with a degree of impunity. Studied closely, the whole scene unfolds multiples of insight in providing the finest understanding of how true authority is to be exercised. The blend of attitudes, words and actions all breathes of the spirit of the New Testament idea of submission.

This is verified in Jesus' response: *"I have not found such great faith, not even in Israel!"* Jesus' explanation at once confirms the man's faith and commends his perspective, understanding and spirit. What follows is a beautiful story in which the Lord exercises power over affliction and brings healing to the centurion's servant. Seeing this, every thoughtful pastor must inquire about the possibilities waiting our release as we willingly learn God's order of alignment for our lives. To function in submission to that order, what are those points of divinely appointed order I need to accept? Just as the centurion's servant was healed through faith born of a leader's perspective on true humility, and Christ's power born of true authority, so who or what under my leadership awaits healing, wholeness or recovery if I learn submission's power?

These principles, though revealed in the Scriptures, were *not* clear to me in my early ministry. But *another* "night-time experience"—this one *before* I went to bed—brought that third and pivotal point of understanding I mentioned.

SURPRISED BY GOD'S OPINION

It was past one o'clock in the morning. I sat in our living room rocking chair, my robe wrapped around myself against the late-night chill. I was waiting on the Lord in prayer, when at one point, as I paused in my intercession, a question asked with crystal clarity surprised me.

You don't believe you're in My will, do you?

I could not have agreed less or been puzzled more. Why? Because I *did* believe I was in God's will. Yet His question directly asserted that I didn't, not really. I kept my mouth shut and my mind open, and He whispered again to my waiting heart.

Do you believe you are to be pastoring?

I nodded affirmatively, as though He were seated across from my chair.

Do you believe you are to pastor in Van Nuys?

Again I affirmed as much.

Do you believe you are to pastor the Van Nuys Foursquare Church?

Of course, I did! What kind of quiz was this? God had suggested I did not believe I was in His will, yet everything He asked I was affirming.

Then came the punch line—a knockout blow leaving me flattened—in complete, but enlightened disarray:

You believe that being in the Foursquare denomination is your own idea.

⋯⋯ ABOUT MY PERSONAL DESCRIPTIONS

In some of the life stories I relate, I will often say, "The Lord spoke to me." This terminology can be sorely misunderstood, so when I say "God speaks," I am making a specific statement predicated upon certain scriptural truths.

First, I certainly do not see myself as preferred above anyone, more as a candidate for new revelations. I believe, however, that God speaks to everyone—to every human being, by both general and specific revelation.

- The starry *heavens* bear testimony to His eternal power and Godhead (see Ps. 19; Rom. 1:20).

Creation itself testifies to its Creator, which is the reason an internalized awe and "sense of God" moves us when we gaze at the night sky, ponder the relentless tides of the sea or look into a baby's eyes.

- The *conscience* is an inner voice of God (see Rom. 2:14,15). This secret point of inescapable awareness and accountability is present in one way or another in virtually every person. Conscience may be smothered and silenced—even seared or burned over—but it cannot be escaped.

- God speaks in the *Bible*, the conclusive written Word of God (see Rom. 10:17). Here is the source of His clear and analyzable revelation, where propositional truth is synthesized and practical understanding made fully and accessibly available.

- God has spoken in His only begotten Son, *Jesus* of Nazareth. The character, actions, miracles, teaching, life and death of Jesus are all expressions of God's living Word. He has spoken in Christ—and continues to speak through the testimony of Jesus, which you and I bear to others.

- God speaks to people in the *church assembly*, as the Holy Spirit prompts someone with a word from the Lord (see 1 Kings 19:12,13; 1 Cor. 14:1-5). Such subjective words must always remain in alignment with established principles of His timeless Word. The Spirit of prophecy never speaks to add anything to the Scriptures, but to apply the eternal Word of the Scriptures—practically, powerfully and vitally to us—at given points of needed understanding.

- He also speaks by the example of godly *relatives* whose influence marks so many, through their characters and by prayer (see 2 Tim. 1:5).

By these means, then, humans experience direct messages from the almighty God, to whom we will all have to give account. So you can understand why I am not hesitant to say, "God spoke to me." Since He communicates so fully and freely with us, even *prior* to our new birth, it should not be surprising He *continues* to do so in even more personal ways once we become His children.

For my part, the "voice" of the Lord comes in different ways. When describing it, at times, I feel virtually able to say, "And I quote." Yet at other times I am only referencing impressions, a sense of prompting, or a quickening of memory. As tens of thousands believers do, I believe it is important for us to learn to hear and respond to such dealings of the Holy Spirit. I also yearn for the day and am hopeful we may find a time when arguments, reticence or critical rejection of such intimacy with God will be past.

"HOW STUPID OF ME!"

My mind reeled. A dozen streams of thought converged at once. For the next several moments I attempted to sort them out. What the Lord had just said to me was true, but it was not anything I had consciously "thought out" before. I *was* in the Foursquare denomination. I was not unhappy about it, nor was I thinking of leaving for another group or planning to take an independent posture.

Upon analysis, though, I realized I *did* believe "being Foursquare" was my own decision. I had come to a Foursquare Bible college for training years before, and the natural flow of events seemed to draw me into that fellowship. But I accepted the point.

Sure! I guess I *did* think "denomination" was a matter of natural choice. I mean, after all, isn't being in a particular group anyone's own decision? Surely God doesn't care which we choose. I mean, wouldn't you suppose He is basically indifferent to the whole ecclesiastical hodgepodge? He only "really cares about people," not church groups, I would have argued. Wouldn't you?

But now my thoughts were interrupted by a direct impression from God's heart to mine: It was His will for me to be in the Foursquare Church! I suddenly saw the picture—*How stupid of me!* How ludicrous to suppose that I could claim to be in God's will while *pastoring* the Van Nuys *Foursquare* Church if the "Foursquare" part of the equation was immaterial to Him! They were two parts of an inseparable proposition—the church, the denomination and God's will for me were one and the same. *Amazing,* I thought, *that this obvious fact has been wholly imperceptible to me until this moment.*

Further, the Holy Spirit used that same instant to bring immediate recognition of another fact: Because *God's* providence had placed me in this denomination, I was startled by the conviction I suddenly felt about the implications He was bringing to my mind. The Spirit was profoundly pressing a point. Now, my participation in the policies of my denomination's ways of operation were not merely a matter of my opinion, of human politics or of mere cooperation. My submission was a matter of obligation to God, not man! Ouch! Now, please understand me. I am not saying that God sees any denomination's polity or policies as perfect, since Scriptures do not reveal any conclusively correct format for church ecclesiastical structures. But my clarified view about the issue of God's will and my church relationship nailed down one issue, which I think applies to all pastors: We are *called by God to function with a spirit of submission in whatever circle He places us in His Church!*

My exclamation, "Ouch!" is rooted in the memory of that night. God hit me right between the eyes. I was not functioning with an understanding of submission—not because I was a troublemaker, arguing or sowing discord. But my submittedness was reflected in my limited participation in a significant program of the Foursquare Church. Let me explain.

A "TOKEN"? RIDICULOUS!

Our denomination funds its offices, programs and church expansion by a monthly "extension tithe" from the member churches. This policy is not policed with any harshness, so the guideline calling each congregation to send 10 percent of its general tithes and offerings each month to the regional office becomes virtually voluntary. Accordingly, although the corporate bylaws of the denomination expect this point of participation, many local pastors had, through the years, participated at widely varied degrees of consistency, and the spirit of voluntary cooperation was commonly violated. Now, though I was not alone in this limited pattern of cooperation, God was calling me to account. The bitter pill He was having me swallow was this:

We were sending a "token tithe"—only $100 per month, though at that time our small church's monthly income was about $2,500, and warranted more. The fact that others did this caused me to rationalize this practice. However, I had just been stripped of my case!

Further, what a ridiculous term! *Token tithe*! Rewrite Genesis 14, imagining Abraham saying to Melchizedek, "You know, sir, the plunder from this victory is so great that it seems unreasonable to give you a full tenth. If you please, I think I'll simply give you this token—I'm sure you'll agree that's quite enough, won't you?"

It is sadly laughable, for the Bible says that Abraham, in whose footsteps of faith the New Testament tells us all to walk (see Rom. 4:12-16), "gave him a tithe of all" (Gen. 14:20).

An Inevitable Trickle-Down Effect

Now, I not only stood corrected regarding my leadership, but the encounter also brought me to a crashing confrontation with what I now know is an inescapable issue for the pastor-leader. I saw that whatever "spirit" governs me—at any point or practice—will determine the mood, life and practice of the whole congregation! If the spirit of poverty could lure me to rationalize a withheld tithe, motivated by the fear *We won't have enough*, it could and would trickle down over the Body and limit financial obedience and support.

I SAW THAT WHATEVER "SPIRIT" GOVERNS ME—AT ANY POINT OR PRACTICE—WILL DETERMINE THE MOOD, LIFE AND PRACTICE OF THE WHOLE CONGREGATION!

Then too, there was that loveless, vision-warping attitude toward the denomination: *They don't need all that money anyway.* But here, in the light of God's presence and the middle of a nighttime confrontation, I saw how my own submission in His eyes was at stake. I also saw how the effect of *any* unsubmissiveness on my part could infect our congregation. The stark fact was this: My people will be either released and enlarged, or hindered and shrunken by my response!

As a result of that pivotal encounter, I learned a crucial lesson, and during my years of ministry I have noted a general principle. It may not explain *all* church problems, but I am convinced that many conflicts within congregations are but the sad projection of a pastor's own lack of submission to some aspect of God's will in his own life.

Enormous *blessings are* available through any disciple's willingness to learn the spirit of submission, but especially a pastor's! A glorious release of *power* awaits the individual, the congregation—indeed, the whole Body of Christ—if we learn to submit ourselves to one another in the fear of God" (i.e., "in reverence for His divine order"). It is overwhelming to conceive the possibilities, if our fears and fierce independence, which so readily crowd out mutual love for and submission to each other, were to be cast aside!

FREEDOM'S UNBIBLICAL COROLLARY

The Bible is very clear: there *is* a God-ordained order for every facet of our lives. None of us are simply to "stand alone." Of course, we *do* stand individually responsible before God in terms of our relationship and accountability to Him—*first*. Life, however, consists of many other dimensions, relationships and factors. Especially for us who lead, it is tempting to arrogate to oneself a broad individualism on the supposition that *I'm called, and I'm a free creature under God.* Inevitably, though, some add an unbiblical corollary to that proposition: *Because I'm free, I can do just what I want—or think best.* Or, worse, *I'll do What God tells me no matter what anyone else says* (irrespective of the person's maturity in Christ or spiritual role of biblical authority in reference to insisting on his own way).

You and I are called to something wiser and better—to a fullness of possibilities and promise that flow when the wisdom of full-hearted submittedness guides our hearts, our living and our ministries.

- I cannot expect any more unity, giving, love, submission, service—anything—in my congregation, than I exhibit in the way I myself obey God.
- How I lead my household in love and peace will reveal itself in the church.
- My attitudes toward those whom God has placed over me in government, be it civil or ecclesiastical, will duplicate themselves in the way the people I lead generally respond to me.

It is the inevitable law of sowing and reaping: We get what we plant! Submission to God's arrangement and order is not to rank people above others, but to serve the interests of all, so "the whole army" comes to victory. The submitted disciple learns that a "tactical advantage," a mutual protection takes place through (1) *committed involvement* with a church family, (2) *submitted service* as a member of the Body and (3) *acceptance* of a personal *accountability* to others in Christ.

MY ATTITUDES TOWARD THOSE WHOM GOD HAS PLACED OVER ME IN GOVERNMENT, BE IT CIVIL OR ECCLESIASTICAL, WILL DUPLICATE THEMSELVES IN THE WAY THE PEOPLE I LEAD GENERALLY RESPOND TO ME. IT IS THE INEVITABLE LAW OF SOWING AND REAPING: WE GET WHAT WE PLANT!

So it is, within the several dimensions of a spiritual leader's "call," that nothing is more essential than to learn the interdependence of the central issues of authority and submission. Though I had learned principles of submission as a child, and the Bible on the subject as a student, the late-night encounter shook me awake to the practicality of "the spirit of submission" for me as a pastor. From the context of having begun to learn to live that Holy Spirit-taught principle, I have found a certain confidence and boldness in life and leadership. When tough times or trials come, when challenges or confusion surrounds, a certainty rises—because I know I am aligned with the throne of "all power."

BACK TO THE OPENING STORY

Thus it was, when the 4:00 A.M. wake-up call took place, and the picture of the "tabernacle falling" came dramatically to my view, that I felt a boldness in prayer. I also found the Lord reminding me of my need to "submit" to two things: (1) immediate action in intercessory prayer and (2) an almost embarrassing (even though I was alone) literal "exercise" of applied faith.

At least two "houses" were at stake: my *paternal* (family) and my *pastoral* (church) realms were in need of an order of priestly "prayer covering." The graphic scene of the flapping ropes and the sagging tent brought to mind the ancient charge the Levites received, to both raise and maintain the tentlike structure of the tabernacle (see Num. 10). I also remembered how Isaiah prophesied concerning stakes and ropes (see Isa. 54:1-3), and knew I was being called to see that mine were "strengthened."

Division clearly raised the question: To what degree is my life and ministry either "tied down" or "blowin' in the wind"? The answer is the same for each of us. Ultimately, it will be to the exact degree I (1) abide humbly under the "cover" of that authority God puts over my life and (2) apply faithfully the prayer and ministry "cover" my pastoral duty requires.

To note our pastoral responsibility is not to deny that God alone is the strength and the foundation of our "house" (i.e., [1] my home and family, as well as [2] my congregation and its families). It is to assert the inescapable fact that a pastor's "headship under Christ" is only as effective in its function to the degree that I "submit" to my role. I am called to:

- *Submit to my role as chief intercessor for the local assembly.* This does not mean I am necessarily the most effective or discerning prayer warrior in the congregation; it simply means that the prayer life of the Body will never exceed mine.
- *Submit to my place as the initiator of worship in my congregation.* This does not mean I am necessarily an integral part of the music ministry; but it does mean that no more worship will flow to God from the people I lead than is expressed by my own will to walk and worship with humility before Him—and them.
- *Submit to my place as the releaser of funds through my congregation.* This certainly does not mean I present the largest offering from week to week; but it does mean that the spirit of giving in the Body will never exceed that which flows from my own obedience and generosity in the light of God's Word.
- *Submit to the Holy Spirit's showing me this principle at any point in my life or leadership,* when I may either question, "Why aren't things happening here?" or where HE says, "Why aren't you overseeing things here?"

In the final analysis, *life* in a local congregation flows (1) from the throne of God the Father, (2) as Christ the Son is honored, (3) by the power of the Holy Spirit. God's ordained order is that this "life" flow over the Body from the "head" down, irrespective of the local church's polity or the spiritual ministry of the pastor. Submitting to his or her requirement to pray, worship and give sets the pace—and the limits. A happy, unified Body flows from "headship under Christ" that realizes its authority is only as dynamic as its submission.

Behold, how good and how pleasant it is for brethren to dwell together in unity! It is like the precious oil upon the head, running down on the beard, the beard of Aaron, running down on the edge of his garments. It is like the dew of Hermon, descending upon the mountains of Zion; for there the Lord commanded the blessing— life forevermore (Ps. 133).

I want to live like a leader whose "headship under Christ" makes possible His "commanding the blessing" where I serve.
LIFE FOREVERMORE!

REFLECTION QUESTIONS

1. Recall times you have been awakened to pray for something specific. Do you feel comfortable to assert that God was "speaking" to you at those times?
2. Why is it important for a pastor to live a life of submission?
3. Review the Matthew 8 account of the centurion, and ask, Can I relate to such a view of submission?
4. Does the terminology "The Lord spoke to me" bother you? If so, why? How would you express this concept?
5. How have financial stress, obedience or problems been a sore spot in your ministry? How did you handle these?
6. What points of personal response do you recognize may be being summoned in your own heart's submission as you have read these pages?

CHAPTER EIGHT HIGHLIGHTS:

- Nothing is more basic to a pastor than regular, direct, personal and intimate contact with God.
- "Devotions" call for discernment in mood and focus; simply being "with" the Lord may be more life engendering than efforts at heavy "pastoral intercession."
- A private walk that builds spiritual strength is assisted by thanksgiving, praise, confession, cleansing, order and obedience.
- "Singing to the Lord" and "praying in the Spirit" are proven "life sustainers" for a vibrant devotional time.
- A periodic getaway with God, a "vacation" for the human spirit, can contribute to a healthy "spiritual maintenance" program for spiritual leaders.

For I received from the
Lord that which
I also delivered to you.
1 CORINTHIANS 11:23

CHAPTER EIGHT

RENEWING THE PROMISE—IN HIS PRESENCE

Few things are as necessary to a pastor as regular, direct, personal and intimate contact with God. Note each of these four adjectives, please:

> regular,
> > direct,
> > > personal,
> > > > intimate.

- *Regular,* because as surely as I need to be fed with "daily bread" for my own soul's need, I also need to be "daily led" by the great Shepherd. As one charged with the direction and tending of that part of His flock placed under my care, I dare not plot paths without His wisdom, any more than I dare pursue them without His power.
- *Direct,* because no place in God's Word suggests we are to live on secondhand experiences. I may be taught, cared for and nourished by the help and counsel of others—my mentors as well as my peers—but the one who saved me *for* Himself, and

has called me *unto* Himself, also desires to draw me closer *to* Himself.

- *Personal*, because He is the One who "knows my downsitting and my uprising," who knows "the thoughts and intents" of my heart, who "knows each word before it is spoken from my lips" and who "numbers the hairs of my head." Such biblical evidence of His personal attention indicates more than merely God taking *statistical* notice of the facts of my existence. It demonstrates His desire to be *personally* involved with the details of my life—continually.

- *Intimate*, because as the Almighty, God is not only grand and glorious, and as the Holy One He is not only splendid in the beauty, perfection and completeness of His being, but also as Love-Above-All, He is the lover of my soul and yours. He wants to be close, to disclose Himself to us, and to hold secret interaction with us (see John 10:15,16; 14:25,26; 16:13,14).

Who would argue with that agenda? The pastoral call is a call to promise—one renewed daily as it is reviewed that way—requiring *regular, direct, personal, intimate* contact with the Lord.

SUBTLE, EROSIVE THREATS

Each one of those four criteria is crucial. Each one is basic and biblical. Yet each one is subtly threatened or eroded today by pastoral pressures: the demands of administrative duty, the tincturing effect of a professionalism and its consequent loss of simplicity, added to suspicions of theologized doubt or the acquired passivity of carnal neglect.

This observation is surely as troubling to you as it is to me. It is not made as a self-righteous judgment from one man's high mountain of presumed, superior attainment. Virtually every pastor begins answering his "call to promise" with a simple brokenness before God. Nearly every one of us knows how time seems to harden the edges of that earlier softness of heart in the presence of the One who has commissioned us.

To maintain a pliable "Thou-art-the-Potter-I-am-the-clay" stance of the soul is to engage in a lifelong struggle with everything from my own natural resistance to godliness to an oft-professionally accepted brand of rationalized righteousness. "Intimacy with God" seems to be classified as the province of mystics—as a gift for a few, but probably not to be expected by the clearheaded. To expect and pursue "a childlike walk, close to Jesus" is, in the circle of some church leaders, viewed as little more than a smarmy, emotionalistic quest for privatized piety devoid of practical value.

However, "*spiritual* leadership" is, by definition, supposed to have some kind of genuine touch with the unseen. So it is peculiar that the norms in much conventional church life often indicate fearfulness of the possibility that a pastor-leader might become "too spiritual." Even a degree of the peer pressure among fellow pastors discourages open conversation regarding one's personal, spiritual intimacy with the Lord. Such talk is not prohibited, but it is simply either not expected at all or it has become socially unacceptable—seen as "parading piety," or pretending an unrealistic brand of righteousness.

A Lone Voice?

I feel a real hesitation in pressing this point, for fear of sounding as though I think myself a "lone voice" in the wilderness. So let me hasten to assert that

I am *not* declaiming against a lesser breed of leader than I see myself as being. I have no illusions about my own righteousness. I am as anxious as the next guy who hopes to retain pastoral credibility, not wanting to be designated as a "mystic" or "hyperspiritual." Still, it also

TO EXPECT AND PURSUE "A CHILDLIKE WALK, CLOSE TO JESUS" IS, IN THE CIRCLE OF SOME CHURCH LEADERS, VIEWED AS LITTLE MORE THAN A SMARMY, EMOTIONALISTIC QUEST FOR PRIVATIZED PIETY DEVOID OF PRACTICAL VALUE.

concerns me that as we stand on the edge of the third millennium, a host of church leaders may be intimidated against intimacy. I see a combination of factors causing this struggle.

First, though they are only a handful, a ready reserve is prompted in most pastors by an ever-present, small band of self-proclaimed "prophets." The lamentable verbal struttings of the pretentious, if not arrogant and pompous, preacher who claims a private hotline to heaven—and who dominates the gullible with his manipulative claims—is enough to discourage us. Who would dare discuss my own intimate times with the Father when I run the risk of appearing on the verge of seeming like that?

Second, a spiritually desensitizing and neutralizing force has been generated by "cool-minded" intellectualized systems in some of our academic sectors of contemporary evangelicalism. For example, an instantly available, tight-fisted, almost-angry doctrinaire resistance has evolved against anything that suggests the possibility of a pastor-leader (much less anyone else) "hearing the voice of God."

This denial of the visionary or prophetic is usually well-intentioned, where an effort is being made at cautioning the unwise against personalized "revelations." But today this disposition rises with a virtual "papal" order of assault on *all* such experiences in relationship with God. Opposition takes the worst stereotype of the confused, suggesting it reflects the normal behavior of those who expect and receive vision, insight and illumination in prayer. This resistance has, to my view, contributed to a collective fear among many spiritual leaders, which has all but castrated their passion for intimate intercourse with the almighty God.

Generally speaking, while sometimes allowed, today's spiritual leader seeking an intimate walk with God had best keep it private and quiet, or risk drawing fire for "heresy." It is frightening to me to witness the ease with which accusations are made: "So-and-so has tripped upon 'New-Age-ish error,'" simply because the person is open enough to describe an encounter with the Holy Spirit, a vision while at prayer, or having received "a word" from God. Thus, in only one generation, we have passed from a time when the hymn "In the Garden" was sung with joyous expectancy to a day when the heart's tender quest of close, daily communion with the Lord has become suspect. If a pastor today claims, "And He walks with me, and He talks with me, and He tells me I am His own," he is more likely to be questioned than commended.

This is no small issue.

A Twist on Truth

Notwithstanding that the Bible overflows with case studies of God's speaking to people personally, by name, giving insight, instruction and direction at specific points in their lives and leadership duties, a devastating twist on "truth" has taken place. In far too many quarters, accepted orthodoxy only believes those recorded  THE DOGMA THAT "GOD DOES NOT SPEAK TO ANYONE TODAY" IS GAINING STATUS ALL THE TIME. encounters "happened," but it is considered unorthodox (indeed, *presumptuous*!) to think they do "happen."

The dogma that "God does not speak to anyone today" is gaining status all the time. A pastor-leader "should not expect God to personally relate to him: nobody should!" Of course, this proposition is always veiled and paraded on the basis of a presupposition; that to claim to experience God's "voice" today is essentially to lay claim to the right to add to the Bible. The truth is, cases of such nonsense, arrogance, deception and error are rare on any terms, and virtually unknown among pastors. Far and away, the majority of pastor-leaders are wise enough and well enough trained to be invulnerable to any notion of playing with the Bible.

It's Okay to Know God

This has become of increasing concern to me as I have navigated the past four decades in pastoral leadership, because I have watched a process of erosion occur. I can readily remember the liberty with which Christians spoke of God's dealings with them, and especially the ease I knew among fellow pastors in discussing the Holy Spirit's promptings. Testimonies describing how "the Lord impressed me," or "the Holy Spirit seemed to be saying" or "God showed me that," are fewer and fewer in occurrence. Someone might argue that this is only because many have acquired a "learned reticence" to openly or personally relate their private interactions with God. I believe it reflects a great deal more than that; it reveals a distressing surrender to intellectualism, to a cold objectivity with spiritual things.

HAVING SERVED AS AN UNDERLING OF THE GREAT SHEPHERD FOR NEARLY A LIFETIME, I CANNOT IMAGINE "LEADING AND FEEDING" HIS FLOCK WITHOUT HEARING HIS VOICE AND KNOWING HIS TOUCH.

Everything within me wants to rise and shout to pastors, "Hey, it's okay to KNOW GOD!" It is okay not only in the sense of exulting in the glorious truth His Word reveals, and to revel in the wonder of His presence as we worship, but it is okay to "converse" with Him too; to express your heart at a personal level, and to have occasions when He speaks to you too.

It is unfortunate to feel, even as I write, that some self-appointed "policemen" out there will doubtless take my words in the preceding paragraph and divorce them from both (1) my lifetime commitment to the centrality of the Word in my life and ministry and (2) my ceaseless conviction that the Bible is a closed canon and that, truly, no additions are possible, needed, desired or to ever be considered. Still, I must run that risk to pursue this chapter with you, my fellow shepherd. Having served as an underling of the great Shepherd for nearly a lifetime, I cannot imagine "leading and feeding" His flock without hearing His voice and knowing His touch.

Let's Be Done with a Carping Spirit

I realize a dozen pastors may describe their relationships with the Father, Son and Holy Spirit in a dozen different ways. I feel no compulsion to require anyone to describe the intimacy of their walks with God the same way I do. I desperately wish we could be done with the carping spirit of criticism that picks at the words of proven servants of the Lord, and has such a manifest way to intimidate the host of rising, younger leaders. This breeds a fear of openness toward God, and feeds a skepticism toward "the knowledge of the Holy."

TO DENY THE READINESS OF GOD TO PERSONALLY AND INTIMATELY SPEAK, PROMPT, ENCOURAGE, LEAD OR "GIVE A WORD" OF KNOWLEDGE OR WISDOM TO A LEADER TODAY IS TO DENY THE BIBLICAL EVIDENCE OF GOD'S OWN REVEALED "STYLE" OF WORKING WITH LEADERS.

To deny the readiness of God to personally and intimately speak, prompt, encourage, lead or "give a word" of knowledge or wisdom to a leader today is to deny the biblical evidence of God's own revealed "style" of working with leaders. It is absolute dishonesty with the Scriptures to contend for their *inspiration* as they disclose God's ways with His own, then deny their *incarnation* in our lives today. That is why I plead this case, and why I want to issue a pastoral call to fellow shepherds. Wherever resonance to my words is found—wherever shepherd hearts, hungry for intimacy with the One who called them exist—I want to urge your expectancy of a *regular, direct, personal and intimate contact with God.*

I am not holding forth with any belief that I am likely to change the mind of anyone set against the possibilities of such an intimate walk with God. The seepage of doubt, fear and criticism (in the name of "contending for the faith") has cut a swath across some precious souls that may not be healed this side of heaven. But for those who recognize that the call of God is not merely an objective idea, and that a walk with God is more than simply a matter of schoolish, legalistic obedience, I want to discuss the pastor's private relationship with the Lord. Let me begin with a testimony of a "recall" He gave me.

A WAKE-UP CALL

I sat on the edge of the bed rubbing my eyes.

The bedside alarm had just announced the time: 6:00 A.M.—my regular time to get up to pray. Yet, I was about to receive a startling word from God about my own neglect of a specific aspect of prayer.

Without any forewarning, and without any reason on my part to expect He would speak to me, the Lord breathed these words from His heart into my mind: *You have forgotten the discipline of daily devotional habit.* The words came with a sense of urgency, but without condemnation. I thoughtfully weighed them, thinking, *That's really true!*, both surprised and stunned by the understanding and revelation spreading over my soul.

My surprise was related to my awakened perception: "devotional habit." You see, this "wake-up call" was not at a time I had been unfaithful in my general habits of prayer; but the words spoken to me heart specifically addressed my

WITHOUT ANY FOREWARNING, AND WITHOUT ANY REASON ON MY PART TO EXPECT HE WOULD SPEAK TO ME, THE LORD BREATHED THESE WORDS FROM HIS HEART INTO MY MIND: *YOU HAVE FORGOTTEN THE DISCIPLINE OF DAILY DEVOTIONAL HABIT.*

devotional habit. Instantly, I perceived the Holy Spirit's intent, distinctly drawing my attention to gradual but crucial change in my patterns of personal prayer. Let me explain.

I came to Christ when I was a ten-year-old boy, and early in my teenage years I was positively influenced to shape habits that gain the wisdom and blessing of *daily devotions*; that daily practice of a time set aside for regular, personal Bible reading and prayer. As well as that solid tradition had been laid in my own habit, however, an unusual thing had taken place during the season just preceding my early morning wake-up just described.

Obviously, what *was not* unusual was that I was up to pray. As I told you, I had just awakened for that purpose when the prompting *"you've forgotten"* came. Now I was suddenly seeing how God was gently correcting me with explicit counsel that I had "forgotten" something *about* prayer— not prayer itself. I think it's something the general course of pastoral duty and responsibility has a way of crowding out of all our lives. It's easy to lose discernment on the difference between the heavy *demands* of pastoral intercession my leadership requires, and the tender *devotion* of simply being with the Lord—alone—with no heavy prayer agenda. Just *Him*.

How significant a distinction that is!

That is the distinction I want to focus on with you, fellow-servant. For I am not writing to you as though you are a prayerless pastor, but as one like me, who might not be allowing the Pastor of pastors time enough to adequately shepherd *you*. Doubtless you *do* pray: I did, but He was still calling me to something I had *forgotten*.

By the time that morning encounter occurred, I had authored a widely distributed book about prayer, led my congregation up pathways of prayerful pursuit, hosted a three-year-long television network series of teachings about prayer, and committed myself to being a person of faith and bold praying. Yet, here the Lord Himself was calling me to something I had unintentionally begun to overlook. He did not discount what I had learned, but He was insistently requiring that I not forget, that I retrieve the systematic exercise of the original *basic* in prayer—*being with Him.*

Now, having received that morning's call to renew the earlier acquired simplicity I had learned as a teen, I bowed and prayed: "Jesus, I am ready to learn again. Please renew whatever you want in me, and teach or review me in the ways that 'first love' requires."

It is a little awkward for me—frankly, "humbling" I guess—to remember and write about the simple details of that morning to seasoned pastors. I can remember how, as I moved from the edge of the hotel-room bed to sit at the table, and opened my notebook, I felt self-conscious then, too. I felt as though I were a teenage boy again. The notes I jotted down were accompanied by the simplest references—verses I was almost embarrassed to write because my professional maturity tempted me to bypass recording them. Just as I am confessing it to you, I confessed this subtle, just-perceived intrusion into my soul then—and as I did, the following hour opened the way to a wonderful refreshing—right then, and in the days that followed.

I am always blessed by the way Jesus promises anyone who will "become as a little child"—even godly, gifted, faithful and well-trained pastors—may enter "the Kingdom." While the promise of "the Kingdom" into our earthly setting is ultimately futuristic (see Matt. 18:3), I gained a reward then and there. I found it in the way the Holy Spirit opened fresh dimensions of "kingdom joy"; that unadulterated simplicity available to all of us who will come to Him with a childlikeness in spirit. That expression of "Kingdom" rule and reign reveals itself mightily, not so much in power as in *presence*—in a broadened and deepened flow of Christ's *life*. And that day, I found that parts of my soul were thirstier than I realized, as my call back to "devotions" brought me to a fountain I had unwittingly neglected.

In just a few minutes I had jotted down the following outline. I offer it here because I've found whenever I have—irrespective of the relative spiritual youth or maturity of the group—pens and pencils *fly*. Why not? All of us welcome resources that build spiritual strength and deepen our relationships with our Lord. Here is what I wrote that day:

I. Thanksgiving and Praise:
I begin by presenting my *self*—my whole being—to Him (see Mark 12:30).

    A. I daily think of a fresh reason to do so (see Ps. 100:4; 118:24).
    B. I present my body in worship (see Rom. 12:1; Ps. 63:3,4).
    C. I sing a new song to Him (see Ps. 96:1,2; Col. 3:16).
    D. I invite Holy Spirit-assisted praise (see Jude 20; 1 Cor. 14:15).

II. Confession and Cleansing:

Next, I present my *heart*—diligently seeking purity (see Prov. 4:23).

   A. I ask the Lord to search my heart (see Ps. 139:23,24).
   B. I remember the danger of self-deception (see Jer. 17:9; 1 John 1:6-10).
   C. I set a monitor on my mouth and heart (see Ps. 19:14; 49:3).
   D. I ask help for keeping His purposes and goal in view (see Ps. 90:12; Phil. 3:13,14)

III. Order and Obedience:

Then, I present my *day*—submitting to His ways and rule (see 1 Pet. 5:6-11).

   A. Presenting the day's details (see Ps. 37:4,5; 31:14,15; Deut. 33:25).
   B. Indicating my dependence upon Him (see Prov. 3:5-7; Ps. 131:1-3).
   C. Requesting specific direction (see Ps. 25:4, 5; Isa. 30:21).
   D. Obeying Jesus' explicit instructions (see Matt. 6:11; 7:7,8).

PRESENT YOUR BODY IN WORSHIP TO HIM

When we approach the Lord in worship, it is both scriptural and practical to involve our bodies. The Bible shows worship to be a physical act as well as a spiritual and intelligent one: "Present your *bodies* a living sacrifice" (Rom. 12:1, emphasis mine). David's exclamation, "I will lift up my hands in Your name," is but one of many such statements in the Word (Ps. 63:4). The body is a living temple of God's Holy Spirit (see 1 Cor. 6:19) and was never intended to be passive in worship.

I have found responsiveness to these biblical injunctions to hold purpose and to prove helpful. Various postures and physical expressions if for no other reason help me keep alert. Oswald J. Smith, the great missionary-statesman of the past generation, admitted that he walked back and forth during most of his daily quiet time with the Lord, and that the conquest of lost concentration or dozing was a hidden benefit of doing so. However, I suspect God has a greater reason than merely keeping us awake when He calls us to "present your bodies." There is an intrinsic call to a *total man* "humbling" of myself in such private prayer responses. Look! All of the following are physical, worship expressions found in the Bible:

- Kneel before Him, as your Lord;
- Lift your hands unto your Source;
- Stand in praise before your King;
- Clap your hands with rejoicing;
- Kneel before Him reverently;
- Dance with joy as a child;
- Bow your head in humility;
- Lift your head in expectancy;
- Prostrate yourself in dependency.

These are not mere calisthenics, for each of them expresses a stance of the soul. Take time not only to *do* each of these (not all on the same day, of course!), but in the *doing* also thoughtfully consider what each physical position reflects in a spiritual sense.

Example: Upraised hands may express adoration, thankfulness, surrender, hunger, receptiveness; *kneeling* may express submission, obedience, devotion; your *uplifted head* may reveal a confidence of your acceptance by Him, your joy in coming to Him. Each day you will find its distinct physical stance reflecting a different feeling of your heart and your hunger for God on that particular day.

IN ACTUAL PRACTICE

In my actual application and practice of the simple "pathway" I jotted down that "wake-up call" morning, I allow enough flexibility to avoid a "sure-death" regimentation. I don't mean I avoid the *discipline* of devotions, but I refuse to be caught in the death trap of rigid, self-imposed *demands*. So please, as you see what I have offered, see it as a resource to assist focus rather than a requirement to achievement or performance.

Legalism can haunt the soul more viciously than an agenda that grinds out the simplicity of being refreshed in the presence of the Savior. It can be imposed internally or externally—by your own self and set of values or by another agency. Requirements, or even outlines like the one I show here, that may be refreshing when first applied, can before long become a burden rather than a blessing. I have found two original practices to be especially helpful in maintaining freshness and avoiding mechanical habit—which inevitably becomes deadening: "singing to the Lord" and "praying in the Spirit." Let me suggest these wonderful and scriptural practices as "life sustainers" for a vibrant devotional time.

"SINGING TO THE LORD" AND "PRAYING IN THE SPIRIT" ARE WONDERFUL "LIFE SUSTAINERS" FOR A VIBRANT DEVOTIONAL TIME.

Sing Unto the Lord

If I am tempted to issue a mandate for your devotions, I'll repeat God's: *"Sing unto the Lord a new song!"* Of course, the original command is His, appearing in about a half-dozen places in the Bible. He apparently likes new music, and the best things about it are: (1) He never compares our vocal qualities as singers and (2) He will never complain about the relative virtues of our songs! I do, however, think He may very well be checking out the degree of our responses to His Word's command to *"Sing!"*

I think a pastor's devotional life cannot be complete without singing in the presence of the Lord.

- Singing brings an uplift that resists discouragement and releases joy. We are called to sing "with grace in your heart to the Lord," thereby opening that His Word may "dwell in you richly" (Col. 3:16).
- Singing invites being continually "filled" with the Holy Spirit, and drives out the flesh's quest for carnal substitutes to fulfillment: singing "psalms and hymns and spiritual songs" (Eph. 5:18,19).

In reading the writings of almost all great leaders, especially when discovering their own devotional practices, singing is recommended in one's private walk just as readily as it is an essential part of corporate worship. I always keep at least one hymnal at my place of devotion, and enjoy gaining inspiration from reading the lyrics whether I sing them all or not. This wisdom is recommended by Christian custom of long history. As recently as early in this century, hosts of believers carried their own hymnals to and from church gatherings, just as they did their Bibles.

Alongside your hymnal, consider using your Bible as a source for singing in your private time with Jesus. In William Law's "Serious Call To A Devout And Holy Life," that eighteenth-century leader instructed every believer to open each day with a spontaneous, freely sung or chanted psalm. You can sing your own tunes or ones you already know. Be assured, though, Father God will receive any "new song" as a "sweet, sweet sound in His ear." Rise with David to declare, *"I will sing and give praise. Awake, my glory! Awake, lute and harp! I will awaken the dawn"* (Ps. 57:7,8).

Pray and Sing "In the Spirit"

Worshipful song often naturally leads to the beautiful exercise of Holy Spirit-assisted praise that, whether sung or spoken, is surely appropriate for my agenda as a shepherd in the Lord's presence as the day begins. Paul's frequent references to singing are probably telling us something about the apostle's secret to spiritual joy, notwithstanding the incredible burdens, trials and pressures he faced. Paul said, *"I will pray with the spirit, and I will also pray with the understanding. I will sing with the spirit, and I will also sing with the understanding"* (1 Cor. 14:15). His stated *action of the will* deserves to be noted: "I *will* sing with the spirit,...I *will* sing with the understanding!"

Of course, in this verse Paul is making clear that worship, praise and thanksgiving are appropriate *both* in languages that are known or understood by the worshiper, as well as those he does not understand, but that the Holy Spirit helps him speak. As I have been privileged to travel and minister throughout the whole Body of Christ, I have been impressed by the large number of pastors—in every denomination—who have made a personal admission to me.

"Jack, I'm not a charismatic, but I speak and sing in a Holy Spirit-assisted language regularly in my private worship."

Why is this worth mentioning? Because contrary to the abusive and destructive things that have been said and done with "speaking with tongues" (both within and without Pentecostal and charismatic circles), God's Word assigns an edifying value to their employment in prayer and praise. That is probably why Paul was moved to acknowledge with gratitude the fact that he exercised this form of prayer more than anyone else did (see 1 Cor. 14:18).

In discussing this aspect of our private walk with Christ, I have no cause to serve other than your edification as a fellow servant. I have found that when I give myself anew to the Spirit of God, and invite Him to *enlarge* my worship as well as *enable* it, He delights to do so. He is the best assistant any of us will find when it comes to knowing and glorifying Christ.

RECEIVING FROM THE LORD

Besides family prayer in the parsonage;
Besides pastoral prayer for the congregation;
Besides worship preparation and leadership;
Besides directed intercession at prayer meeting;

Jesus wants the pastor-shepherd to be alone with Him, to be in His presence—to be taught as a child, nurtured as a son of the Father, schooled as a teacher of the Body, and, to hear His voice!

I have sometimes wondered how the Early Church leaders conducted their own devotional lives. What does John mean when he says, "I was in the Spirit on the Lord's Day" (Rev. 1:10)? Is this an announcement to self-verify the authority of the word he is relating, or is he saying, "I was at prayer one Lord's day—praying in the Spirit—and suddenly He visited me!"?

When Peter was visiting at Simon the Tanner's house, he was apparently having his regular time of devotion, and I am amused at this, because I have often felt the same way when kneeling down to pray: *"He became very hungry and wanted to eat"* (Acts 10:10). Check the text: Dinner is being prepared, and the aroma is wafting up to the rooftop—and the Holy Spirit uses this moment of *physical* hunger to lead to sensitizing Peter with a *spiritual* reality—through a vision. The point is, unveiling leaders' understanding of God's purposes in their lives is modeled for us in the Scriptures as happening in the course of a normal, daily devotional relationship with Him.

Have you ever wondered how Jesus "served communion" to Paul? Look at the apostle's highly significant introduction to his elaboration of the Lord's Table in 1 Corinthians 11. His words, *"For I received from the Lord that which I also delivered to you"* (v. 23) employ an expression that raises an interesting question. Is Paul describing his "receiving" through the oral tradition of the earlier disciples? Or is he using speech that is intended to say, "The way I teach about the Lord's Table came from an encounter"?

SPIRIT-FILLED, YET VERY HUMAN

As we read the "eternal words" that flowed from the pens of the apostles, let's not forget we are reading the testimony of leaders who walked with God in Spirit-filled-yet-very-human ways. When Paul says "I received from the Lord," I doubt that the resurrected Savior actually reappeared and arranged a table for communion. I do think, however, Paul was probably alone with the Lord in prayer one day, in a rather ordinary setting customary to the habit of his own devotions. I would suggest that his words are intended to convey that then and there—at a point in private with the

Savior—came a vivid sense of the presence of Jesus. Now, in this letter, he is describing how something he already knew at an academic level was transmitted to a deeper dimension of grasp through his personally "receiving from the Lord." In short, being with Jesus (was he partaking of the Table at that moment, perhaps alone in prayer?), a deeply stirring, insight-filled unfolding of truth took place, rooted in what had already been relayed to Paul by faithful witnesses. In short, consider that each of the apostles may have been more shaped by intimate dealings of God with their heart; that their intellect was ignited on their knees with Christ than by their powers of analysis. Their encounters hold promise for us.

- John was lifted above the struggle of Roman-imposed exile on Patmos (and the question marks that could bring to anyone who was wondering, *Is Jesus* ever *going to come?*).
- Peter was delivered of sectarian, racial bigotry and qualified to pursue his next step of mission (and prepared to face the initial opposition of peers who would doubt his good sense and propriety).
- Paul was "served" by the Savior with a perception of the *immediacy and relevancy* of the Lord's Table (and equipped to describe and minister it with timeless authority beyond tradition).

What could be more practical? Can you see why we just might be missing the key to effective ministry by the present trend toward codifying proposals against the intimate "walking and talking with God"?

I am convinced that a fallacious approach to the matter of "how God speaks" is motivating a number of leaders to inflict many pastors and laymen with a cold, even error-prone attitude toward the possibility of an intimate, communicative walk with God. A salvation that only receives the "witness" of the Spirit at conversion, and thereafter is incommunicado with the Almighty save through the Bible until death, is dangerously close to depersonalizing the deity who "became flesh" to walk and talk with us.

THE RELENTLESS ARGUMENT AGAINST PERSONALLY "HEARING FROM GOD" IS ALWAYS LODGED IN AN INSISTENCE THAT TO DO SO IS TO RISK CONFUSING PERSONAL REVELATION WITH THE CLOSED REVELATION OF THE SCRIPTURES.

The relentless argument against personally "hearing from God" is always lodged in an insistence that to do so is to risk confusing personal revelation with the closed revelation of the Scriptures. But that can only take place when the Bible is left out of the equation, and our proposed personal, devotional walk with God—including "hearing" from Him—is rooted IN the Word, not separate from it.

To face the facts with honesty, much of contemporary Protestantism is guilty of the same thing we have criticized in historic Catholicism. In the same way Catholic traditions "closed up the Book," through limited access or disallowing the right of the *laity* to interpret the Scriptures, Protestant practice is today "closing the door" on the right of *anyone* to expect God to speak directly to his or her heart.

Because I am writing to pastors, I am presuming that there is no need to elaborate the obvious: guidelines should be secured so the God-intended blessing of "hearing" from Him is not distorted. When wisdom is regarded, the authority of "prophetic words" to a person or congregation will never be confused with the authority of Scripture. The personal, subjective nature of any private stirrings, promptings, insights, illumination and edification—*all from God*—ought always to be understood as subject to "judging" by elders when necessary. Above all, the objective of *all* "revelation"—whether found in God's written and closed revelation of the Holy Scriptures, or realized by the Holy Spirit's personal dealings in a believer's heart or understanding—is *always* edifying and *always* consistent with the *whole* Word of God.

A "GETAWAY WITH GOD"

Sustaining the vibrancy of our pastoral call;
Maintaining the confidence of God's promised purpose for us;
Keeping the warmth of God's heart for people, through
staying close to the Savior's side.

All these and more are by-products of a pastor's pursuit of a steadfast, private walk with the Lord of our lives. But I have also found the need for a periodic and distinct break from the usual.

A "vacation" for the human spirit is necessary; not necessarily requiring as long as our bodies and minds need and receive, but every bit as important.

For example, I recently felt a kind of "hollowness" in my soul. If I had been consciously compromising anything of a biblical life standard, I would surely have known it, as well as known that I needed to *repent*. But there was something else nagging at me, and I didn't have any definition for my feelings—only a sense of "empty."

One morning, not long after I had been alone at prayer—without much energy, and with some degree of latent frustration—I was passing through the kitchen on the way to my study at home. Anna looked at me, and her words confirmed my feeling: "Honey, do you think you need to go up to the conference a day early?"

She was referring to my scheduled speaking engagement at a mountain retreat that weekend, and suggesting I make arrangements to arrive there early Thursday afternoon. I can hardly describe the "leap" within my spirit: She had not only sensed my need, but had also recommended action. Though I had taken "days with the Lord" before, I was too tied up in my own frustration to think of the possibility of leaving early.

It would take paragraphs to describe what those few hours meant. As I drove toward the mountains, I wept before the Lord with gratitude for His goodness and promises to me. I poured out my feelings of emptiness—my sense of "hunger"—and, in a way that made the verse seem as though it was the first time I had ever heard it, Matthew 5:6 was breathed into my heart like liquid hope. I felt I was being filled with faith. I had confidence I was headed to a rendezvous with my Redeemer!

Blessed are those who hunger and thirst for righteousness, for they shall be filled (Matt. 5:6).

Suffice it to say, as I did little more than walk mountain paths, alone and in spoken communion with Jesus, *He visited me*! Words can hardly attempt to describe the exhilaration of being refreshed by "an overnight with Christ," but I still like to look back in my journal and be reminded of His faithfulness to refill—fully and readily.

Of course, I am not proposing that a 24-hour breakaway is a cure-all for every time a pastor feels a need for renewal. I do believe, however, that a *pattern* of acknowledging that need—and prioritizing it when the first signs of "empty" are sensed—can contribute to a healthy "spiritual maintenance" program for spiritual leaders.

ONE ELDER'S EXAMPLE

In my teaching time with the men of my congregation, I have often strongly encouraged taking periodic, short-term "Getaways with God." One of our men, a brilliant scientist and a capable writer, recorded his practice of this wisdom—getting away for a day to gain personal focus on your life, your family, your work and your future, *in the presence of God alone.*

I became Dr. Vern Grose's pastor more than 20 years ago, and have been honored that this man, who was already a committed, mature Christian when we met, acknowledges my part in his further growth in leadership and success in his life and vocation. Vern, who along with his wife, Phyllis, became elders in our congregation, calls his periodic "getaways," FIELD Days—for *Fasting, Intercession, Empowerment, Listening, Direction*. Today he lives in Washington, D.C., where he moved when he received a presidential appointment to the National Transportation Safety Board. Today, he is a consultant to several corporations, a college and seminar lecturer and author; perhaps the foremost analyst on the risk factor in industrial accidents and disasters. You have probably already met him; he frequently appears on CNN and other networks as a technical resource of information when disastrous accidents occur.

Having received Dr. Grose's permission, I am including this example of the practical power of applied devotions, along with a special application to the possibility that you, as I have so many times, might find help toward the potential of a "Getaway with God."

FIELD DAYS
BY DR. VERNON GROSE

Concept Background: In the early 1970s, I began to feel the need for a better means of communicating with God than I had previously experienced. I had experimented over the years with a variety of formats and approaches for *personal spiritual development*—quiet times, daily study guides, Bible reading schedules and devotional outlines. However, I never felt that these programs really provided the type of intensive, in-depth results that I needed.

Fasting, as a regular weekly regimen, had been adopted by 1975. But this only accentuated the need for some technique for coupling it with a dedicated time of hearing from God. Because of my "Type A" personality, it was difficult to totally devote myself to spiritual matters for any length of time while in my office or at home.

So I decided that I would try to schedule an entire day to be alone with God. A code word to easier explain my absence from the office was coined—the acronym *FIELD Day*. Over an extended period of time, a general structure for my FIELD Days has developed: First, I load three to four versions of the Scriptures, a tablet and *Strong's Exhaustive Concordance* into the car. Then, I drive to some location as close to undisturbed nature as possible. The objective is to get free, if possible, from people and things built by them; while at the same time, being able to see and appreciate the physical world God has created. In California, I would drive to the crest of the Santa Monica Mountains or to a beach area. In Washington, I tend to find a secluded spot along the Potomac River.

Based on Pastor Jack Hayford's teaching regarding prayer in the Spirit (see Rom. 8:26,27; 1 Cor. 14:15; Eph. 6:18; Jude 20) as a means for "restoring my soul," I have adopted the practice of praying, praising and singing in the Spirit for at least 60 minutes at the start of each FIELD Day—avoiding any English and attempting to commune with God in His idiom. It seems to purge my too-active mind of issues unrelated to God's agenda.

Invariably, toward the conclusion of that first hour, a theme or topic begins to be impressed on my mind. I accept that as His direction for our time together. Sometimes that initial theme becomes the focus for the entire day, while on other occasions, it will lead to several subsequent topics.

Documenting what transpires during this day has gradually developed as a discipline. In that sense, it resembles what others might call a *journal.* Remarkable results have come from these notes. For example, the 16 May 1984 notes became the foundation for my teaching and application of the subject of *Christian calling.*

FIELD Days do not occur unless they are deliberately scheduled. At times, I have observed them monthly. However, no particular frequency has been established, but I now often teach the value of this discipline when I am invited to do so, speaking at men's retreats.

At Pastor Hayford's request, I am also sharing the following example of the notes I take; reflecting the kind of things that occur in my mind and soul when I set aside FIELD Days with my Lord Jesus Christ.

Notes from FIELD DAY, 10 September 1992:

- I enjoyed an unbroken hour of praying, praising and singing in the Spirit from 0840 until 0940 while walking in a luxuriant—almost Garden of Eden—setting on Dangerfield Island adjoining the George Washington Parkway in Alexandria just south of Washington National Airport. This communion in spiritual language was deliberate and I intended to purge or cleanse my thoughts as I prepared to hear the voice of the Lord.
- It seemed as though it was possible for me to almost reenact Adam's walk with the Lord God "in the cool of the day" (Gen. 3:8). At one point, a brilliant cardinal flew and sat on a branch right in front of me.
- At the very end of the hour-long communion I received a strong impression that the Lord wanted us to discuss "the rest of your life." This thought was not the least bit morbid or fatalistic. It was as though we were simply to talk about the "wrap-up phase" of my time here on earth. (Today is my parents' sixty-fifth wedding anniversary. Because I was conceived within two weeks of that date, my existence in history was initiated nearly 65 years ago.)
- That realization—together with the Garden of Eden analogy—

caused me to ponder first the *beginning* of life in the first three chapters of Genesis. (Of course, those chapters also explain why my earthly life must also *end*—2:17 and 3:6,19.) As I waited for direction about how our discussion would begin, I was impressed that I should study the "wrap-up phase" of 10 men in the Scriptures—*Abraham, Jacob, Moses, Samuel, Saul, David, Simeon, John the Baptist, Jesus,* and *Stephen.* This study was to be focused on hopefully answering three "wrap-up phase" questions for these men's lives that would, in turn, provide guidance for me in that phase of my life:

1. What kind of *awareness* did each man have regarding the time of his departure?
2. What *obligations*, if any, did each man have to complete prior to leaving?
3. What specific *tasks* or *actions* were required to complete those obligations?

Abraham: Genesis 23:1—25:10 tells us that he lived for 175 years. One obligation was incurred when Sarah died at 127 years of age, causing him to seek a family burial plot in the cave of Machpelah. It would turn out to be the burial place for Abraham, Isaac and Jacob.

Although he remarried and had six more children after Isaac, he also felt strong urging to secure, in obedience to God's command, a godly lineage for Isaac prior to leaving. He even prophesied that an angel would lead them to find Isaac's wife, Rebekah.

Another act he carried out was to deed everything he owned to Isaac. While he gave gifts to sons of his concubines, Isaac alone inherited the family estate.

Jacob: Genesis 45:25—49:33 recounts his "wrap-up phase." In a vision, he received from God (1) *direction* to go to Egypt with the Lord at his side, (2) *promise* that his descendants would return out of Egypt and (3) *notification* that he would die in Egypt.

Although he was ready to die just as soon as he saw Joseph, he lived another 17 years in Egypt to the age of 147 years. During that time, he felt obliged to bless Pharaoh on two occasions.

As he became aware that he was dying, he made Joseph promise him that he would be buried in the cave of Machpelah. When Joseph later heard that Jacob was sick, he brought his own two sons to Jacob for his blessing. Jacob deliberately blessed them in reversed birth order and then gave a special blessing to Joseph.

His final blessing of his 12 sons immediately preceded his drawing up his feet into the bed and dying.

Moses: Numbers 27:12-23 and Deuteronomy 31—34:7 define his "wrap-up phase." Moses lived 120 years—three 40-year periods initiated by an impulsive, illegal act. The third act—*striking* the rock at Meribah instead of *speaking to it* as the Lord had instructed—meant that Moses knew he would die in the wilderness for his rebellion.

With that awareness, he asked God to identify his successor for Israel and allow him to commission him. God selected Joshua, and Moses commissioned him. Telling Moses that he would soon die, the Lord ordered Joshua and him to jointly receive instruction for taking the Promised Land.

Moses then recited a song to all Israel, with Joshua at his side (see Deut. 32). That very same day, the Lord told Moses where he would die.

Giving Israel his final blessing (see Deut. 33), he climbed the mountain where he was to die and viewed the entire Promised Land from a distance. Though he had the strength and vigor of youth and possessed perfect eyesight, he died and was buried by the Lord.

Samuel: His latter days are recorded in 1 Samuel 8; 15; 16; 19:18-24; and 25:1. He ended Israel's era of judges—partly because his sons failed to have integrity and follow the Lord and partly because Israel demanded a king instead of judges.

After anointing Saul as king, he still functioned as the voice of the Lord to Saul. When Saul disobeyed the Lord's command to kill King Agag, Samuel did it for him. That was the last time Samuel ever saw Saul, yet he long mourned for him afterward.

Though fearing Saul, Samuel obeyed the Lord and anointed David to succeed Saul as king. It was his last act as judge, although he was later used by the Lord to cause Saul to prophesy. (An ironic note is that Samuel was sought after he died by the witch of En Dor at Saul's command. He spoke to Saul and prophesied his death the next day.)

Saul: His "wrap-up phase" probably started with his disobedience (see 1 Sam. 15:10-31). It was downhill from there. Though he did repent and worship the Lord subsequently, the Spirit of the Lord departed from him. His life thereafter was filled with bitterness and resentment toward David, his successor. He seemed to have a distressing, on-again, off-again relationship with God that tormented him all the rest of his life.

One of the apparent "obligations to accomplish prior to departure" was to persecute David—and even kill 85 priests of the Lord (see 1 Sam. 22:6-19). Samuel, though dead, prophesied Saul's day of death. He died just after his three sons were killed in battle with the Philistines, when he fell on his own sword. Ironically, the Philistines did to Saul precisely what David had done earlier to their hero Goliath—cut his head off and put it on display!

Although Saul committed suicide, it is also recorded in 1 Chronicles 10:14 that the *Lord* killed him because he did not inquire of Him.

David: His "wrap-up phase" is recorded in 1 Kings 1:1—2:12. He paid a high price throughout his life—and to the very end—for failing to discipline his sons. His son Adonijah attempted to take the throne away from David, even as his older brother Absalom had done earlier.

Only through a conspiracy by Nathan and Bathsheba was he enabled to carry out his promise that Solomon succeed him as king. However, it was a joyous time for him to see Solomon be anointed king while he was still living.

He evidently was aware that his departure was near when, as his last act, he charged Solomon to "prove yourself a man" who keeps the Law of Moses. It was a unique charge that is both general and specific.

Simeon: Luke 2:25-35 contains all we know about Simeon. But the account starts during his "wrap-up phase"—he is *waiting* to die. The Lord had revealed to him that he would not die before he saw the Messiah.

Three admirable aspects of his life are described. He was (1) righteous and devout, (2) looking for Israel's consolation and (3) walking in the Holy Spirit. Of the three, the *anticipatory* aspect of the second seemed of particular significance to me.

He more than fulfilled his expectation of *seeing* the Christ. But as he held Him in his arms, He became the channel of a mighty and sweeping *prophecy* by the Holy Spirit, which opened the possibility for me, a Gentile, to partake in God's kingdom.

Incredibly, he offered to the Lord a terminal benediction on his own life and evidently departed shortly thereafter into the presence of Him with whom he had just been speaking.

John the Baptist: All four Gospels record his "wrap-up phase"— Matthew 4:12; 14:1-12; Mark 1:14; 6:14-29; Luke 3:2-20; 9:7-9; and John 3:23-36. So clearly, the Lord intends that we remember what was accomplished at that time.

Because he was just months older than Jesus and died before Him, he probably lived only about 30 years. He was fearless in telling the truth, and that characteristic set up the termination of his earthly sojourn. He rebuked Herod for his illegal marriage to his sister-in-law Herodias, and thereby provoked Herod to put him in prison.

Yet Herod respected him and even gladly listened often to him. His truth-telling about Herodias, however, embittered her. When her daughter extracted a promise for *anything* from Herod, Herodias got her to ask for John's head on a platter.

I have often wondered what John's last thoughts or words were, how much background they gave him prior to his execution, and whether he showed any resistance to his beheading.

Jesus: In a sense, His "wrap-up phase" began with His birth—He was born to *die for a purpose.* Yet the details of His death are gripping in

Matthew 26:2-12,31-56; 27:1-50; Mark 10:45; 14:8; 32-42; and Luke 12:49-50; 22:1-6,41-54; 23:1-46.

He was totally aware of when, why, how as well as by and for whom He was going to die.

His obligations included: (1) having to be tempted with every sin of mankind without yielding to it, (2) faithfully carrying out every command of His Father and (3) sacrificing His life voluntarily.

Among the specific acts He performed as He wrapped up His life were (1) healing the ear cut off in His defense, (2) making provision for His mother and (3) asking forgiveness for His crucifiers.

Stephen: His selection—by the Spirit and the Church—as a deacon established almost immediately his "wrap-up phase" as described in Acts 6—7.

I have always imagined him to be quite a young man—partly because everyone who heard him speak on the last day of his life "saw his face as a face of an angel." On the other hand, he was well-known before then as being full of grace and power, someone through whom God performed great wonders and signs. He also possessed wisdom and indwelling of the Spirit in measure that overwhelmed everyone.

One can only wonder whether he was aware that his invited defense against trumped-up charges would lead to his murder later that day. However, he obviously felt a strong obligation to set the record straight concerning Jesus Christ.

He completed that obligation by boldly and clearly demonstrating a remarkable, integrated knowledge of history and spiritual insight, which resulted in massive conviction of his entire audience—and led to his murder by a mad mob. His last words are still ringing in the ears of the world: "Lord, do not charge them with this sin."

"WRAP-UP PHASE" ANSWERS

These 10 men all completed their lives in different ways and under different conditions. What can I learn from them about how to live "the rest of my life"?

Question 1 (awareness) produced varied answers because all 10 men departed of different causes:

Abraham, Jacob, Samuel and David to aging;
Moses to rebellion;
Saul to suicide in battle;
Simeon to prophecy fulfillment;
Jesus to obedience;
John the Baptist and Stephen to hate-provoked murderers.

To summarize, most had no advance notice or awareness as to *precisely* when they would depart. On the other hand, most seemed to be aware that their lives could terminate at *any* time. So we could say they were really quite average regarding such awareness.

Question 2 (obligations) also revealed a variety of answers. Where obvious predeparture *obligations* existed, they involved addressing—on several subjects—those who would remain behind or succeed these men:

1. Importance of following God's laws;
2. Urging marriage to godly spouses;
3. Final declaration of their own faith; and
4. Being forgiven.

Question 3 focuses on the *actions* or *tasks* these 10 men completed to carry out their perceived obligations. They took different forms, such as:

1. Declaration or charge;
2. Blessing;
3. Warning;
4. Absolving;
5. Eliciting promise; and
6. Directing for the future.

PERSONAL APPLICATION

As I pondered the effect on my life of the composite answers to the three questions, it seemed reasonable for me to ask the Lord: *What counsel or direction are You giving me regarding the rest of my days?*

In fairly rapid fashion, seven specific charges came to me. I accept them as His response to my question and believe they will govern my remaining days:

GOD'S COMMANDS FOR THE REST OF MY LIFE— VERNON L. GROSE / 9-10-92

1. *Remain aware* and *sensitive* regarding unfulfilled assignments given to me by the Spirit in accord with Ephesians 2:10. These may involve people, principles and projects.
2. Increase my *boldness* to speak and live out truth as moral degradation increases all around me. This boldness applies equally to believers and unbelievers.
3. Understand, expect and welcome the return of Jesus Christ by developing a *triumphant*—not an escapist—mind-set that anticipates the ultimate and total destruction of evil.

4. *Anticipate*—rather than dread—the release from my temporal body to join the Church triumphant.

5. Influence my grandchildren in *Kingdom principles* in every way available to me—example, word, actions, encouragement and exhortation.

6. Purge world-mindedness and carnal values from my personal life—as an ongoing exercise of my *will*.

7. Recognize and acknowledge God's *sovereignty* increasingly in new dimensions—in world events, natural phenomena and individual lives.

MOVING ON AS A MAN: A MAN OF GOD

Whatever the component parts—personally applied schedule, means for keeping the soul refreshed—a Pastor of Promise will only *keep the promise* alive in his soul as he walks with the Giver of Promise.

The disciple's cry is, "Lord, teach me to pray."

The disciple's Lord says, "I will instruct you and teach you."

The Teacher never ends this lesson—"school" opens each morning for a lifetime. The student may be faithful or irregular in attendance, but the Teacher is always there—and always ready to spend all the time we need to "walk with Him and talk with Him." In those moments, His "promise of a lifetime"—of purpose, fruitfulness, fulfillment and victory—is renewed in our souls that it might keep unfolding in our lives.

At the same time, an enemy—though he knows he is bound to lose—is unceasing in his quest to quench the promise. Just as he once sought to blind us to the Ultimate Promise Keeper.

REFLECTION QUESTIONS

1. How would you evaluate your regular, direct, personal and intimate contact with God? What regular schedule do you attempt?

2. Does "seeking a closer walk with God" seem unrealistic? Do you fear being perceived as "too spiritual"?

3. Have you ever "forgotten the discipline of daily devotional habit"?

4. Do you or have you kept a prayer journal? How has this contributed to your prayer life, or brought you new insight?

5. Have you ever had a getaway with God, such as described in this chapter? Did it affect you personally? Your ministry?

CHAPTER NINE HIGHLIGHTS:

- The four influences that shape my points of conscious "accountability" are relationship with my wife, friendship with other brothers, stewardship of my money and my interaction with the Lord.
- Self-scrutiny and openness to God establish real and lasting grounds for a functional accountability.
- Highlights the theme, "Staying True to Your Call," using Paul's *"This one thing I do"* commitment to priorities in Philippians 3:12-21 as a text.
- Personal entries and prayers from the author's private journal offer possible patterns of responding to God.
- Focus on "Nine Things That Can 'Remove My Edge.'"
- Focus on "Three Things That Will Help Me 'Keep My Edge.'"

*Since we have received this
ministry,...we have renounced
the hidden things of shame,...
commending ourselves to every
man's conscience in the sight of God.*

2 CORINTHIANS 4:1,2

ACCOUNTABILITY AND THE PASTOR'S PROMISE

In the wake of the media ministry crashes of the 1980s, a great hue and cry arose, which precipitated a reawakened sense of a spiritual leader's absolute need for accountability. "Accountability" has continued to be a buzzword in ministry circles, matched only by "integrity" in verbally facing us as pastors with the most obvious of facts:

1. People ought to be able to count on the trustworthiness of leaders.
2. Leaders are human, too, and need to apply means to assure they do not fail that trust.

Appropriately, then, a rash of articles, sermons, books and other preachments have understandably and justifiably called spiritual leaders to accountable behavior. Although there is no questioning the need all of us have for the *morale* boosting assistance of others, and the occasional *moral* reinforcement of peers, I feel a certain concern about the recent roar demanding "accountability." I have listened and read (and spoken and written about this myself), urging pastors and others to "cultivate a circle of accountability." Among these, no one *says* anyone is to depend on man more than on God. But in a peculiar and ironic way, "the arm of flesh" has become increasingly the focus. I see undiscerning responses beginning to supplant personal moral accountability ("because I ought to"), and reliance on a group-enforced "doing what we require of you."

Without seeming to be an opponent of this biblical discipline, I want to signal the need for balance. The subject has gradually come to a point of grinding—not so much to a stop, but to a point of bogging down with excess baggage.

ACCOUNTABILITY OVERKILL

First, the problem of overkill is growing in the projection of law-enforcing systems of "accountability." Pointing to the need to project plans for personal accountability, the formulation of projected guidelines has begun to push beyond the edge of true principles of Christian discipleship. Faced with the challenge of "out-accountable-ing" the last accountability program designer, some systems now approach the suspicion-born, member-grilling styles of a communist cell group. Sentrylike systems prescribing the "how" a leader should "live accountably" now approach a watch-dogging legalism between believers, rather than the "have care for one another" spirit intended to prompt mutual encouragement and support (see 1 Cor. 12:25; 1 Pet. 3:8).

Second, I see a problem in a tendency to nurture an inappropriate dependency on others. The human encouragement we all need, and well may receive through an "accountability" group, can subtly become a humanistic device rather than a biblical discipline. Today's humanistic, relativistic society has a way of eroding discernment between the way of the

MY LEADERSHIP IS *CALLED BY GOD*, AND MY PRIMARY POINT OF DEPENDENCY IS TO BE UPON *HIM*—THE ONE BEFORE WHOM MY ACCOUNTABILITY *BEGINS*.

flesh and the will of the Spirit. Group dynamics can easily devolve to intergroup responses that become more preoccupied with "feeling good" than with "doing right." Just as a mechanical dynamic may cause a small group to become coldly legalistic, so a humanistic dynamic can reduce it to a warm, fuzzy "support group" that distracts from learning to find one's support in *God*.

Central to my concern is how this concept is vulnerable to being carried to a point of dependency. However valid our intent at retaining purity within the ranks of Christian leadership, we are wise to be cautioned against becoming infected with a virus of falsely prioritized human dependency that fails to teach disciples how to "lean on the everlasting arms." A host of witnesses have proven the sufficiency of this prior point of strength in maintaining their integrity.

OUR PRIMARY DEPENDENCY

Without the benefit of an accountability group, David Livingstone lived a life of moral purity in the midst of a pagan culture, and for years without the presence of his wife or other peers. Similarly, David Brainerd pressed his evangelistic efforts into demon-infested regions, laboring with unflagging fidelity, though he had little partnership or human comfort. He writes of his dark feelings of discouragement, yet he finished his mission without complaint—and with fruitfulness. These are reminders that my leadership is *called by God*, and that my primary point of dependency is to be upon *Him*—the one before whom my accountability *begins*.

"Walking with brothers" (which *is* of great value in God's eyes, and certainly valid in mine, too), dare not be allowed to evolve to a place of substituting for "walking with God." You and I—and those we teach—are wise to remember God's Word and the Holy Spirit's call to obedience as our *fundamental point of* reference in "being accountable." This observation is all the more important in a day so dominated by psychiatric and sociological systems that do not know the difference between *being accountable* and *becoming dependent*.

None of this is to suggest I don't need fellowship, and it certainly doesn't mean I'm not to be subject to the assistance, protection, correction or adjustment by others. I *do* need those who will help support me, or who will help me note and guard against lack, neglect or failure. I also need to be warned against what might generate an undue dependency upon man, however, when my foremost accountable relationship is with God.

LEARNING "THE ROPES"

Because I am often asked about how I form and keep my own "circle of accountability," I recently took time to reflect upon this issue at a new dimension. Earlier thinking was clarified further, as new feelings I had been accumulating became focused ideas. In that process, I realized how much larger my "accountability circle" was than usually described. My usual answer described the men I relate to, but upon more complete consideration of how I actually process my life, I realized there was much more. I saw how my "accountability plan" actually involves the force of *four influences* I welcome, allowing each to be systematically brought to bear upon my life. I now see the picture of these *four* as being somewhat like the ropes that shape the perimeter of a boxing ring. These four influences that shape my points of conscious "accountability" are:

1. My relationship with my wife;
2. My friendship with brothers;
3. My stewardship with money;
4. My interaction with the Lord.

The boxing-ring figure is appropriate for many reasons. First, it reminds me of my own responsibility to "fight the good fight," to abide by the rules, and although I am driven to the ropes at times, to *stay in the ring!* The ropes establish a perimeter, guarding me from accidentally transgressing appropriate boundaries, but they do not substitute for my own *external* per-

A SPIRIT-FILLED WOMAN IS A NAT-URAL CONDUIT FOR THE OPERA-TION OF THE GIFT OF DISCERN-MENT—*IF HER HUSBAND WILL LEARN TO LISTEN!*

formance, *internal* responsibility to fight by the Rulebook or my *personal* actions in the eyes of the Referee.

Second, to be engaged in spiritual leadership is to be encircled by spiritual warfare. The "ropes" are restricting, both confining me to the arena of my service, but also reminding me that there is no way to run from my own responsibility in the battle.

I not only have discovered the rewards of my own obedient response to God's sovereign and providential dealings through this analogy, but I have also witnessed the personal disasters of leaders who have neglected *any* of this quadrangular "circle" of accountability. Let me briefly explain how I see each of them.

THREE-IN-ONE

1. My Wife

How Anna thinks and feels is a deterministic issue in the matters of my life. This is not because she is a demanding woman, and she certainly is not a difficult one either. But contrary to my earlier years of marriage to her, when I failed to see how "superior" I felt my judgment to be about matters, I have learned to draw on the amazing resources of what we usually call, "a woman's intuition." In the case of a redeemed woman, who loves and worships Jesus Christ, this "intuition" becomes much more than the oft-seen suspicious or critical spirit demonstrated by the worldly. A Spirit-filled woman is a natural conduit for the operation of the gift of discernment—*if her husband will learn to listen!*

That is immeasurably important because often—certainly in Anna's and my case—a husband and wife's *styles* of communication can differ drastically. For example, I have found that if I do not take the time and patience to hear what Anna is *feeling* (which is sometimes described in nontechnical, unacademic terms), I can lose a fortune of wealth in practical insight or wisdom she has. That is the reason I spend at least an hour or two each week just sitting together with her, usually quietly sipping tea as we talk over the current matters I am dealing with. As much as I enjoy these times, they don't come easily. I find I have to require myself to reserve them. Both of us have complex schedules, so I make a point of arranging time, not only to pray together, but also to discuss issues—to "talk through," not just skim things. I won't let my soul be comfortable about the direction I am moving in *anything* if she is not confident about it too.

2. My Brothers

Through the years, I have sought to build and maintain relationships with peers or partners in ministry. Early on, I discovered how easily a small inner circle can either become a team of brothers or a locker-room gang. There's a difference between "brotherhood" and "jock-talk." In my first years of ministry, times together with guys my age and in my calling involved my learning the ease with which the privacy of such partnership can become an attempted "escape" from accountable behavior rather than a pursued "entrance."

I have witnessed pastors engaging in private conversation together that they would never risk or indulge among their members. That is not "fellowship"; it is self-deception, pretending a demeanor that pedals as candor what is actually carnal.

My earliest challenges at "building" a group of mutually accountable men (fellow pastors) was in partnering with other guys to find the way to be *real*. Seeking the help of a lot of ordinary men/pastors like myself, I came to learn and to define the *real* spirit of fellowship, brotherhood and—eventually—truly accountable relationships. In the spirit of true Christian discipleship, I believe this order of "real" means to have personal or small group relationships in which you are able to:

   a. Joke and have fun together;
   b. Relax, to "let down" from mutual professional pressures;
   c. Become transparent regarding personal need or concern;
   d. Enjoy and be unaffected in discussing spiritual matters;
   e. Be forthright in communication—encouraging, critiquing,

supporting and making observations about each other;

f. Submit to gracious "iron sharpening iron" confrontation;

g. Pray together without pomposity, judgmentalism or mere formality—but with tears for each other's needs, with faith for each other's blessings and with joy in each other's hopes.

The reward of pursuing this kind of relationship has brought me great protection among both peers and subordinates. With my own pastoral staff, though technically "subordinate" to me, I have worked together to build bonds of kinship and trust. I am open with them, and insist on cultivating a relationship that makes me as subject to them *as a brother* as we together are to Christ *as coshepherds*.

The New Testament contains a stream of reminders that our lives as believers are inextricably linked as members of one Body, and that this is to be acknowledged by the way we relate to one another. Perhaps you will find this list of "one anothers" a useful study (or call!):

Romans 12:5; 1 Corinthians 12:12,26; Ephesians 4: "You are *members* of one another."

Romans 12:10; Ephesians 4:32: "*Be kindly affectioned* to one another" (*philostorgos*-family).

Romans 12:16: "Be of the *same mind* toward one another" (see Phil. 2:1-5).

Romans 14:13: "*Judge not* one another." (The New Testament notes difference in condemnation/evaluation.)

Romans 14:19; 1 Thessalonians 5:11: "*Edify* one another."

Romans 15:7: "*Receive* one another" (refers to acceptance and recognition).

Romans 15:14: "*Admonish* one another"; Hebrews 13:13: "*Exhort* one another" (correct/comfort).

1 Corinthians 11:33: "*Tarry for* one another" (considerately take time in prayer together).

1 Corinthians 12:25: "*Have care* for one another"; 1 Peter 3:8: "*Having compassion* for one another."

Galatians 5:13: "*By love, serve* one another."

Galatians 6:2: "*Bear one anther's burdens.*"

> Ephesians 4:2: "*Forbearing* one another in love" (hold them up; bear them up; assist).
>
> Colossians 3:13; Ephesians 4:32: "*Forgive* one another."
>
> Ephesians 5:21; 1 Peter 5:5: "*Submit to* one another."
>
> 1 Thessalonians 4:18: "*Comfort* one another" (especially those in bereavement).
>
> Hebrews 10:25: "*Provoke* one another to good works." (Meaning: to elicit best responses.)
>
> 1 Peter 4:9: "*Use hospitality* toward one another."
>
> 1 Peter 4:10: "*Minister* gifts to one another." (Meaning: those abilities you have are the common share of the Body.)
>
> James 5:16: "*Confess* your faults to one another."
> "*Pray for* one another."

Of recent years, strong, transparent, trust-filled, faith-inspiring and life-shaping peer relationships have been my privileged experience with: (a) a long-time friend, who is engaged in a Christian counseling ministry; (b) a local pastor, who is one of America's best-known leaders; (c) a pastor I discipled, who has become a brother as well as a son; and (d) a geographically distant leader with whom I share confidences and concerns by telephone and on sporadic occasions of personal contact. I also submit general matters of my personal finances to the elders of my congregation. Details of the same I submit to two of them, whose professional as well as spiritual counsel not only confirms my accountability to integrous ways, but whose practical wisdom also assists me in planning.

3. My Money

When accountability is discussed, I've noticed that this arena of personal integrity is too seldom included. Yet, from the standpoint of one's subjective thought life and evolving attitudes, I don't know any more fundamental point of essential evaluator.

As a general rule, "financial accountability and integrity" seems only to be judged on the basis of what may be seen externally; what may be measured quantifiably, then either exposed for correction or commended as acceptable. The requirements of circumstances, however, have occasioned unsought discoveries in the course of conversations with good men who, as pastors, entertained attitudes and practices that surprised me. Without prying on my part, but usually in the context of answering inquiry or providing requested counsel, I have been amazed at the presence of twisted thinking. For example, I have encountered with alarming frequency:

- Stinginess with their wives, in the name of frugality; with their giving, in the name of limited funds; with their providing guest honoraria, in the name of wisdom;
- Selfish preoccupation with securing oneself, spending undue time in investment pursuits, manipulating known sources of benefits;
- Keeping for themselves what properly belongs to God, interpreting undesignated offerings as "personal," not submitting their own tithes to the church.

It is interesting to me that I have had more positive comments from pastors about my writing in reference to one of my books more than any other: *The Key to Everything.* It is a book about the liberating spirit of giving and forgiving that flows from a right view of the Cross and our finances.

I don't think this is a happenstance.

I think we, as pastors, are uniquely targeted by our common adversary—not to mention our usually limited financial situation—to be kept "small" where money is concerned. To whatever degree the flesh or the devil succeed in shrinking our souls in this regard, a spirit of poverty gains rule over our hearts as well as our circumstances.

For example, in the just-mentioned book, I honestly relate a pivotal moment in my own leadership. As a husband-father, I was frustrated to the point of anger with God when, following the birth of Anna's and my third child, the financial crunch of a young-pastor level of income evoked an outburst.

"It's not right!" I shouted at Him (alone, at home, when no one was around to hear). *"I've tithed—and You've promised!"* (What I *did not* include in my complaint was that I had unilaterally ceased a giving pattern begun years before—giving added missionary offerings beyond our tithe.)

"And neither is it right that you've stopped trusting me as your Provider." The Voice was both stern and pained; clearly postured to disallow my backtracking to less of a stature in giving than I had learned.

The story is longer when told in its entirety, including the miraculous unfolding of divine provision at great and gracious dimensions following my repentance for retreating from patterns of faith through vain supposition. I had submitted to the oh-too-human notion that by ceasing to give I could manage my own financial sufficiency more effectively. But this *NEVER* works, and if anyone must remain privately accountable before God in allowing His Word and His Spirit to control his attitudes toward money, a pastor must. It is my passionate conviction about this point of vulnerability to self-protection, self-deception and smallness that prompted a recent remark I made to a group of spiritual leaders.

The subject of the pastor's accountability was the agenda, and in a passing remark of mine, not intended to shock, but certainly illustrating the depth of my conviction, I seemed to stun the group.

"There are three things I never do: I never fornicate, I never fail to give tithes and offerings, and I never lie."

When I looked at the surprised faces, which were not shocked by the mention of fornication, but by the union of those three concepts, I elaborated.

"Make no mistake, brethren," I said. "There are three fountains of life which flow from each of us: (1) biologically, our seed; (2) financially, our money; and (3) verbally, our words. All of them have life-giving or death-dealing capacity, depending upon how they are administrated. Only when I reserve each for the arena of God's intended purpose for my life can I see the life intended not only preserved, but see it multiplied.

ALL HUMAN HELP AND ACCOUNTABILITY IS ONLY AS EFFECTIVE AS A PERSON'S INITIAL COMMITMENT T("WALK WITH GOD IN INTEGRITY."

"If I deposit my biological seed anywhere else than where the covenant of my marriage requires, some order of *death* will ensue. If I refuse to honor God's Word that 'the tithe belongs to the Lord,' and withhold offerings born of faith, the *life-giving, multiplying* spirit of grace cannot be released because my money isn't being put in the circle of obedience. If I speak words which dishonor the truth, which is my God-ordained arena of covenanted living, another dimension is deprived of life, and a withering, *dying* effect follows."

This illustration and explanation are offered to emphasize what I have seldom heard mentioned: A pastor's personal accountability *in all his living* will inevitably be very closely related to the way he handles his money, *and his heart attitude*, concerning finance. *We cannot serve God and mammon*—we pastors, above all.

4. My Lord

In actual practice, the fourth "rope," *my interaction with my Lord,* is the starting and ending place of the other three *forces* that shape my personal accountability. I realize that saying so can sound either trite, arrogant or pretentiously hyperspiritual.

I contend, however, that all *human help and accountability* is only as effective as a person's initial commitment to "walk with God in integrity." We discussed this in chapter 6, but here I want to refer to a distinct method of responding to God's private dealings with our souls. By *"interaction,"* I am not now referring to my devotional worship, but to *my interactive efforts at processing and registering what I feel God is showing me about myself.*

I do this by means of a nonregimented program of journaling. I don't "journal" every day, but my foremost use of the practice is a means of *interactive response* to moments that the Lord corrects, instructs or encourages me, or recalls my attention to a matter.

Journaling is an aspect of being *"quiet and before God,"* and it contains a dynamic that has helped multitudes in *every* era. Although it is seen and studied in the lives of many spiritual leaders of the past, and sometimes viewed as too introspective or passé by our streamlined society, I am convinced—today more than ever—it is needed in the pressure cooker of a pastor's world.

In my book about the 10 disciplines of Spirit-filled living (*The Power and Blessing*, Victor Books, 1994), I detail an approach to the practice of journalizing. Writing as I am here, though, to experienced pastors, the basics of approaching this private practice are probably unnecessary. However, it's still worth noting how the Bible shows the importance of coming before the Lord to let our hearts be examined in His presence. Paul's words in Philippians 4:8,9 are helpful to see the pathway of the balancing habit of thoughtful, meditative thought and written expression—as the Lord teaches, corrects and adjusts us.

> *Finally, brethren, whatever things are true, whatever things are noble, whatever things are just, whatever things are pure, whatever things are lovely, whatever things are of good report, if there is any virtue and if there is anything praiseworthy—meditate on these things. The things which you have learned and received and heard and saw in me, these do, and the God of peace will be with you.*

The verb expressing *"think* on these things" is a mathematical or bookkeeping term (*logidzo*). It points toward reflection as a means to take time and "tally the goodnesses of God," literally *keeping score of the good things!* Otherwise, the most godly among us can easily become preoccupied with things that *are not* so good. I think these words point to *reflection* in times of quiet *with* God, just as the two previous verses (vv. 6,7) pointed to supplication in times of prayer *before* God. They model how the anxiety release of passionate prayer—"supplication" here, the "binding/loosing" form of dynamic prayer—is to be wisely joined to times of quiet, pensive *thinking* about God's goodness.

I have, however, found it practical to journal "bad things"—but in Jesus' presence! It is amazing that in just writing them down on paper, two things about "bad things" almost always are found to be true. (1) There are not as many bad things as I thought. The dust cloud of confusion begins to be dispelled, simply in pausing to clearly define what is really happening. (2) When I write the bad things down *before the Lord*, it seems as though the mere "writing before Him" *shrinks* their threat and *starts* their solution.

Immediately, I find I will begin to sense direction for handling the situation, and I experience peace as I put the matter *on paper*. Even more importantly, as I write, I put them *under the blood* of Christ's redemptive power and works. Something about defining those problems that appear to be monsters helps when reducing them to words on paper. Amazingly, when they are moved out of the fog of struggle and turmoil—and exposed in the presence of Jesus—they are reduced to their *true* size (primarily, because before Him, they seem a lot smaller!).

> This is illustrated in the book of Psalms, the "all-time great Journal" of history. Many of the psalms help us understand why David gained the reputation any of us would wisely covet—to be described by God as a man after His heart. David is candid, self-disclosing, self-examining and unpretentious, and the record in the Word points to a path of such humility for any spiritual leader. Just two examples are enough to lead us into the Scriptures to see how complete is David's heart cry to God: (1) He calls as a child to his father in Psalm 38, responding to the chastening and correcting of God, *writing down his thoughts*. (2) He cries as a sinner, a broken soul imploring his Redeemer in Psalm 51, as *he writes his confession for sin* before the Lord.

These two practices, accepting correction and making confession, are in constant need for my life as a leader. As I journal these matters, they round out the "ropes" that keep me "in the ring."

THE HOLY SPIRIT'S DEALINGS

Something about being in an atmosphere of honest self-scrutiny and openness to God establishes the real grounds for an accountability that will "stick." Only if I will listen to God will I listen to my wife. Only if I am honest with Him will I be honest with my brothers. Only if I "let go" in His presence will I "give" with faithfulness and trust. If we allow time for His dealings, the Holy Spirit *will* often correct us, and when He does that, journal it.

That is what David is doing in Psalm 27:8. He says to the Lord: "When You said, 'Seek My face,' my heart said to You, 'Your face, Lord, I will seek.'" Can you see it? The Holy Spirit spoke to a person's heart, the person recognized it and wrote his response: "Lord, what You're saying to me by Your Spirit, I'm saying back right now. I'm going to do it."

True spiritual growth—the ultimate accountability point in our lives—is essentially the sum of our responses to the voice of God. As He speaks to me through His Word and by His Spirit, I am not only called to *listen*—but also to *interact*. The first step to His directing, refreshing, correcting or renewing is to *obey*, and I write what I understand Him to say so I will be more likely to remember it.

- Writing out my prayer of repentance;
- Expressing my insight or clarified perspective;
- Confessing my sin, smallness or shortsightedness;
- Detailing a point of guidance for review;
- Standing corrected for neglected disciplines;
- Recording points of action He is calling me to take.

Essential to my own "accountability" is remaining honest to God as He "puts my feet to the fire" regarding what I call "creeping carnality"—the slow-grow, usually-rejected-but-suddenly-found-tolerated violations of disciplines. It is embarrassing to discover how subtly they rise—perhaps self-righteousness is the worst!

That is the one that tempts me to avoid acknowledging what follows, because these are items about which at one time or another the Lord has had to confront me. HE *made me accountable* in private moments—and I journal them to register my shame, my confession and my commitment to His way. The following are some of those things. Do you recognize any?

- Impurity of speech: profane (angry speech); tolerated-though-discretionate "street-talk"; negativism or contradiction of His Word as it addresses my situation (i.e., "doubt talk"; see Eph. 4:29).
- Indulgences of the mind: allowing irritation toward others, justified because it was unspoken; unworthy TV viewing (even though not pornographic) excused as a "controlled reprieve" (see Song of Sol. 2:15).
- Faithlessness and fear: cowered or crippled by "what people think" through reverencing and fearing men (see Prov. 29:25).
- Judgmentalism: discovering an attitude toward another leader and finding myself guilty of failing to "take the beam out" (see Matt. 7:3,4).

- Forgotten/neglected disciplines: fasting, warfare, memorizing Scripture (e.g., "Could you not...one hour"; see Mark 9:29).
- Pride or self-importance: Reminded of a "Yeah?! Well, we'll see," swaggering moment, I could feel the pride in the strut—the way I was walking, the tone of my voice, the "fix" of my countenance. Reminded of the biblical warning against "impudence" (see Ezek. 3:4).

> Such basic points of personal confrontation with a thorough ongoing response to the Holy Spirit on my part are also critical to maintaining a circle of complete accountability. Perhaps it may help to illustrate how I seek to do this with some references to my own journal.

YIELDING TO GOD'S HEALING

What follows is a selection of responses that, hopefully, evidence one soul's effort at maintaining a spirit that *lives* accountably in all arenas and relationships because of a prior choice to *yield* accountably to God in life's ultimate relationship. I have provided a brief context for each entry.

"It's Pentecost Weekend"
(*The following is a word of stirring!* As I was moved in prayer, I knew I was being charged to reach out and lay hold of *promise* for the weekend that was forthcoming.)

Friday, May 24
Dear Lord—and my God:
   "IT'S PENTECOST WEEKEND!"
   Those words were spoken into my spirit this morning. I receive them from You, Lord. I know they are (1) a call to prayer, and (2) a sensitizing to expect—to awaken expectancy!!
   Something is unfolding in the heavenlies.
   I believe this is Your prompting, and You give notice to prepare my heart to pray in faith. ("I will do nothing except first I show my servants the prophets.")
   Holy Lord, I call faith a release of Your divine SPIRIT of GRACE and GLORY this weekend at our church. I ask for a visitation of Your presence—Your *VOICE*—speaking to hearts and calling them to seek Your face.
   Like a rushing wind, whirl in from the north and let a vacuum be created in hearts around which You move—that they will *FEEL* and CALL upon You for an inrushing of Your POWER.
   Explode—Shatter—Splinter! Break through in a host of hearts!

Come, O Lord, and verify Your *pleasure* with the *direction* I feel You leading.

Come, O Lord, and manifest Your *presence*—revealing, "As I *was* with...so *am I with*!

(After this prompting came in prayer, I shared this with two of the principal pastoral team who joined me in prayer to receive this word. No public mention of it was made. That Sunday there was a great moving of the Lord throughout the whole congregation and, among the various results, more than 60 respondents to the call to receive Christ.)

❊ ❊ ❊ ❊

(Often, heading into a weekend, I feel especially accountable to be certain there is "nothing between my soul and the Savior." On this particular weekend, a rash of demanding situations were before me. As I awakened and spent time with God, the following heart searching and confession took place.)

May 4, 4:55 A.M.
Precious Lord Jesus,

I am touched today with a sense of Your great goodness toward me. I am stirred in my soul; called to prayer. For the past hour I've laid in bed, thinking not only of my message to be brought tonight at the Azusa Pacific University commencement, but thinking on the combination of honors and trials to and through which You bring me.

Proverbs 29:25 came to mind: *The fear ("reverencing") of man brings a snare, but whoever trusts in the Lord shall be safe (i.e., "set on high/secured").*

I pray today, Lord, that You will forgive me and keep me from *ever*—to any unperceived degree—"fearing" man. I think of the trembling I felt yesterday when dictating my response to the two calls that came, harshly attacking me because of one Christian radio broadcaster's comment against me. It wasn't "fear," but an upset of my soul over the unrighteousness of such accusatory, pecunious trafficking in gossip. (*Gossip*: a person who habitually reveals personal or sensational talk, rumors or reports.) That's the only true description of such dishonesty.

My heart is pained—I think it's not as much for my own sake as for the wretched smallness this exposes in us who constitute Your Church.

Forgive us, O Jesus!

I think of my own behavior on the same day, and my need to make two calls of repentance: one to Jane for my cowardly, poverty-minded need to remark regarding BT's tunnel-visioned view of things (notwithstanding his beautiful spirit of evangelism and devotion to You, and *more*, that he is my friend! And my suddenly-realized-I-had-done-it moment, when I stooped to a shameful repetition of what I thought was a humorous remark about another person; one which, rather, was a mocking remark, demeaning and grotesque—at least as I expressed it in private to AC.

I did confess and speak my repentance, acknowledging its unworthiness to the person I spoke it to. Now, I write it here before Your Throne: *Please forgive my sin! Wash me and I shall be clean; purge me and I shall be whiter than snow.*

So, dear Savior—thank You for pointing out *my* sin; for reminding me that *I* am a sad source of entry for the same smallness that wounds me. Let me be reminded again and again, O Lord. And thereby, let me be an agent of health and healing, of understanding and graciousness being increased in Your Church—Your Body.

Now, please help me greatly these next 32 hours—with my preparation for APU (and ministry), our Deacon-Elder Council meeting, our weekend services, and the projection of the building repair fund tomorrow. Dear Lord God—grant a great grace of release in confidence and faith by our people, with a full sufficiency of funding.

❀   ❀   ❀   ❀

(The following is a heart cry I raised as I stood on the threshold of a New Year, feeling hungry for God [though bloated with holiday overeating] *and desiring to purge all surplus of anything that could obstruct the promise of a new calendar's possibilities* [though unsuperstitious that a New Year makes anything new unless the One who "makes all things new" puts His touch upon it]).

Dear Lord,
I pray the following, *feeling* the worst is true, but *hoping* somehow these statements are only moderately so—and *trusting* in Your mercy to forgive, compensate for and correct my failures. I confess my sins:
    As a *shepherd*,
        who doesn't know his own sheep;
    As a *leader*,
        who is weary and complains or winces over duties;
    As a *soldier*,
        who has been AWOL at certain times of warfare;
    As a *father*,
        who prays too little for his children, and who doesn't do
        well at knowing how to talk with them;
    As a *husband*,
        who needs to "nourish" his wife more effectively;
    As a *Christian*,
        whose devotional habit is in shambles; though not void,
        still *so* erratic;

As a *son of Yours*,
> who seems too "taken" with all You've given me, and too self-centered to even know with clarity Your *perfect* will;

As a *believer*,
> who is vulnerable to not *"fight"* in prayerful faith at times because of "too settled" a theologized comfort, presuming at times that Your overarching sovereign purpose removes the need for my passionate concern.

As a *peacemaker*,
> who is caught in uncertainty as to *how* to relate to some I love, because they seem to reject my efforts on showing mercy or conciliation.

O Lord, at these points—and all else you see that I do not—help me...that I may move unshackled into the tomorrows of Your purpose.

❊ ❊ ❊ ❊

(The following was born of a picture of myself I saw in prayer—a picture of physical insensitivities illustrating spiritual deficiencies, as our staff and congregation were anticipating a new season.)

September 17

Dear Lord God,

At this portal of possibility and promise...

I feel like my eyes are scaled and need a surgery of fire to burn out the overlay of film that accumulates either from looking on things Your holy eyes would never tolerate or expend time in gazing at;

or, from habitually "scanning" rather than *searching* (1) the scenes of situations or (2) the souls of people—which *frames out* what You see and only sees what man sees.

I want to ask You to give me *eyes to see*—so that I not succumb to the portion of those who "have eyes but they see not." I want to SEE THE RADIANCE, WHITE-LIGHT GLORY OF YOUR FACE, JESUS! As John saw Your eyes of fire, let me—that *my* eyes may be burnt out of the lesser and that they be freshly purged to see with the pure, penetrating and life-infusing vision of Your eyes.

I want my ears to hear the slightest whisper of the Spirit's moving—the sounds of Your wisdom only learned in silence. Oh Lord, please dissolve and flush all wax from my ears—resensitize hearing lost by reason of the rush and din of a hurried, harried, verbose, pomp and palaver-filled world.

Soften the hardened, scarred tissue of my soul's hearing; flush all accumulated debris away—and let me hear heaven's songs and let me sound the depths of Your heart and Your Word as it SPEAKS to me again.

I feel like my hands are gloved; like they are disabled to render the tender, life-and-love transmitting touch You are desiring and capable of extending through them. I bring my hands—lifting them up into Your presence—extending them beyond the layers of earth's pollutants. I want to hold them before You until You have washed every crease of the oils and dust of human production; until You have reprinted my fingertips with Your identity, and reprogrammed my touch to feel with Your feelings.

Great Physician, give me Your surgical sensitivity that I may be an instrument of healing the sick; perceiving their pain and being enabled to remove it. And, let these hands cast out demons by the sweep of Your arm overthrowing the adversary at the same moment You reach through me to grasp the hand of the fallen and bring the aching into the grip of Your mighty power. Removing the callused thickness of hands which cannot feel human need, let my palms become open windows for the healing rays of heaven to course through.

❈ ❈ ❈ ❈

(Having grown weary one day, as the result of a series of factors—encounters by mail, meetings and otherwise, where the busyness of good men [pastors] evidenced in a virtual passivity/disinterest in "even bothering" to partner with some who were seeking to bond and band pastors in our city for prayer—I prayed...)

Dear Lord,

Today I come to You with a sense of burden for the fact that so few of us, Your shepherds, are able to capture a *vision* or *heart* for unity. We are the products of systems, first being separated by denominational, theological, cultural, societal and economic frameworks. Then, we are separated by our circumstances—our geography (in too large a city), our schedules (in so busy a world), our ethnicities (with the cultural tendency to misunderstand the other) and by our languages (in which I characterize the typical American who only knows *one!*).

We have had our *eyes plucked out*, so we cannot *SEE* the vision of the Body's leaders together. We have had our *hearts emptied of hope*, so we cannot *FEEL* the heartbeat of Jesus for the unity of His own.

As I pray this day, I am weighed down with this burden of a call and responsibility to Your *vision* and Your *heart* in these regards.

❈ ❈ ❈ ❈

(I do not remember the context of the following, but I include it because it features a confrontation with those things that sacrifice "confident faith in God alone," while bowing at the altar of human systems to manipulating achievement. This is a ploy to which all of us who lead are frighteningly vulnerable.)

May 25, 4:30 A.M.
Dear Lord,

Today I declare: *I CHOOSE THE SPIRIT OF FAITH*—

I reject dependence upon human wisdom, and call upon You for divine wisdom.

I reject the confusion that attends condemnation, and receive the joy and clarity of soul that is mine in Your righteousness.

I come to *SEEK YOU*...to be unburdened of *flesh*: of self-imposed demands of duty, of any self-constructed structures of ego support. I submit to You *all or any preoccupation with human acceptance, recognition, fleshly comforts* or *material abundance*.

August 19, 20   Psalm 36:5-9
O Lord, I come to present myself to You for a *new season*—
• *Of devotion to You, through fellowship.*
Renew me in *warmth of heart, joy of Presence.*
Remove dullness of soul; Neglect of time with You.
• *Of worship to You through new song.*
Renew me in freshness and spontaneity, praise-filled true thankfulness.
Remove familiarity which brings lost sensitivity; Novelty which misses intimacy.
• *Of sanctification by Your Holy Spirit.*
Renew me in purity and tender sensitivity.
Remove encrusted evil resulting from exposures to a corrupt world; (Bathtub ring—mineral deposit=world spirit); tarnish, corrosion.
• *Of transformation through Your Word.*
Renew my mind to bring availability to repentance at points where I presently do not perceive need; Psalm 19:7-14.
Remove all presumption; All self-righteousness.
• *Of revelation in the Scriptures.*
Reveal things both new and old that I may steward Your Word—serving fresh bread.
Remove dependency on the *"known"*; Presuppositions that *"I already know this"* (e.g., Kittel usage).
• *Of intercessory prayer through discipline.*
Renew holy habits of systematic coverage; Reawaken prophetic insight as I pray; our body, our city, our world.
Remove laziness of soul; Misplaced value of time.
• *Of loving gratitude for Your call to me.*
Renew sense of ministry—availability, shepherd duty—*love* for sheep; lay down life. Remove weariness in well-doing.

❋   ❋   ❋   ❋

(A primary point of daily accountability before God is in His presence on the day(s) following. While waiting on Him, I was strongly corrected for the way I had expressed myself at a lunch appointment the day before. Being "accountable" to God, I felt I needed to write my sense of failure and put it in the form of a letter to the persons I had spoken to; not because they were likely to expect it, but because I knew I was "accountable" to do it.)

May 11

Dear (❋❋❋):

It was such a beautiful time at lunch with you...as Anna and I said, we always enjoy being with you. I'm so glad for the gift of our friendship—from Him, and from both of you. I was, of course, greatly rejoiced to see the steadfast increase of grace bringing about the Holy Spirit's recovery processes in each of you according to your specific need.

However, this letter is to express *my* need—and I've just placed this uncolorful piece of stationery into my typewriter to inscribe my words of repentance. My sense of failure is more before God than before man, but nonetheless I felt it needful to express what follows to you—for two reasons: (1) you were there when I believe I grieved the Spirit of God, and (2) you are people to whom I would hold myself accountable.

When I walked from The Peppermill yesterday, I was smitten in my spirit. The Lord showed me how my having experienced the angry remarks of people (for my having joined those who breakfasted with the public official they objected to) was begetting a mirroring anger in me—an anger that virtually exploded in unworthy words.

When I spoke as I did, I don't believe the issue before God was as much my word choice as it was the spirit in which I spoke. As you probably detected, I was miming those who feign care for our nation's needs while showing something approaching hatred for our city, state or nation's leaders.

I could elaborate my feelings about how blind and hypocritical I believe this order of "moral-posturing-while-violating-Christian-love" is, but that would only seem (or become) self-justifying. God is dealing with MY "moral-posturing-while-violating-Christian-love." He showed me an anger in myself that is no better than the unloving anger in those I have judged neglectful of appropriate Christian spiritual responsiveness.

As for the words themselves, I believe the wrongness of the spirit to which I unwittingly submitted lent a force—an "evil anointing" if you will—that changed my speech from a "miming" to a "mucking" of the air. Whatever note you two may or may not have made of my "dramatization," I know I need to ask your forgiveness just as surely as I have asked God's (as well as Anna's, of course). I think you understand why I request this of humans as well as The Father: the principle of "release," to my understanding, requires a "loosing on earth" as well as "in heaven."

So, please forgive me for learning something about myself at your expense. If it's not inconvenient, I would appreciate a call to indicate you've received this confession/ contrition/repentance. I'm not asking this for the sake of receiving what I know would be your acknowledgment of gentle understanding—and forgiveness which I know you would automatically give. Rather, I would like your confirmation that you understand/accept my *need* to take this action before our Father. And further, I would welcome any further observation or counsel you might have to give me; i.e., anything you saw or see that I didn't or don't yet.

With this writing, then, I put my words and action under the redeeming covenant of the Blood of Jesus—inviting complete cleansing in my tainted spirit, as well as full release from the spiritually entangling power of my words.

> "Father, in Jesus' Name, please forgive:
> my having given place to a self-righteous spirit of anger;
> my having spoken unadvisedly with my lips, and
> my having violated the presence of Your pure Spirit—
> not only in Your sight, but in the souls of my brothers and sisters.

> "And may the words of my mouth and the meditation of my heart continually be acceptable in Your sight, O Lord, my Strength and my Redeemer."

Thank you, dear friends. Welcome to part of the price of being a friend with a soul whose sanctification is still in process.

In Jesus' life and love,
Jack

PS: Incidentally, for the record—though they don't know who Anna and I were with, as a part of my accountability to our pastoral staff, I've confessed this to them as well. Thought you should know.

(I realize that relating this incident invites criticism; that this order of sensitivity of exaggerated action may constitute a kind of "parading" of pretended righteousness. However, I believe many more will not only trust my motives, but may also be assisted in processing "accountability" in ways to which I believe New Testament life calls us.)

I conclude the offering of these few expressions of my interaction with God's Spirit as He confronts and corrects me. NOT included are a set of recurrent, repetitious rededications to basic disciplines—to more prayer, to sound diet and nutrition, to fastings neglected, to exercise and physical care and so on. Also NOT included are what seem like a thousand inscribed cases of self-discovering in the wake of or in the face of normal daily events—at church, in the family, in ordinary conversations and so on.

These items related from my journal, however, are sufficient to answer any inquiry, "Jack, how do you go about 'being accountable'?" For me, the answer involves "the ropes"—the *four forces* or *influences* that factor in; all of which are built on and rooted in the fourth—my interactive, journalized tabulations of God's correction and instruction. That is the point of accountability that, if lacking, increases the likelihood of an eventual delusion of a leader.

It is also the point of "accounting" that, joined to a daily walk with God, sets up a spiritual sensitivity that will make a *positive* increase—an increased discernment and dynamic in the spiritual struggle.

A thief is trying to steal your promise.

Following a time of self-assessment upon approaching a new year, I shared from the following outline with our men. I introduced my remarks, themed, "Staying True to Your Call," using Paul's *"This one thing I do"* commitment to priorities in Philippians 3:12-21 as a text. In the light of the apostle's model—

- Always be open to growth and expansion in Christ (v. 12);
- Never bound to a "plateau" mind-set (v. 13);
- Be dominated by goals established "in Christ" (v. 14);
- Be steadfast to the lessons learned in Him (v. 15);
- Be warned by failures where integrity is compromised (vv. 16-21)—in "walking accountably," I noted.

NINE THINGS THAT CAN "REMOVE MY EDGE"
(THAT IS, DULL MY SENSITIVITY TO GOD'S "HIGH CALL" ON MY LIFE)

I. DIVERSIONS—Things that distract from your purpose.

A. Opportunities: Need to distinguish between the good and the best; between the divinely ordered and the humanly opportune.

B. Interests: Need to distinguish between the legitimately acceptable and the completely profitable. Examples: exercise, reading, entertainment.

C. Voices of others: Need to distinguish between the opinion of the world mind and the counsel of the godly. Examples: proliferation of management resources; self-help resources.

II. TRIALS—Things that test your patience in pursuit.

A. Difficulties: Relational (wife, boss); Financial reversals.

B. Stress: Schedule (invasive, intrusive); environment (noise, circumstances).

C. Assault: Personal attack (people reject, judge, criticize); physical attack (sickness); spiritual attack.

III. TEMPTATIONS—Things that seek to destroy your purity.

A. "The lust of the eye" (carnal attractions); e.g., evaluate media input and personal entertainment and recreation habits.

B. "The lust of the flesh" (fleshly indulgence); e.g., food, being controlled by any dimension of sensuality, etc.

C. "The pride of life" (motivated by appearances); e.g., who you are with (societal) or how you look (style).

THREE THINGS THAT WILL HELP ME "KEEP MY EDGE"

I. MAINTAIN DEFINITION—(re: problems and priorities).

A. Regular journalizing in God's presence.

B. Honesty with the Holy Spirit's dealings.

C. Regular sharing, submission of your present "focus" with wife and brothers. Always keep this before others.

II. GAIN THE INVINCIBLE GROUND—
(when facing battle).

A. Need for partnership: "If any two of you shall agree."

B. Need for honesty: "Put on the whole armor of God...girding your waist with truth."

III. SUSTAIN ESSENTIAL STRENGTH—
(through constant inflow).

A. The Word of God, through daily feeding (see Matt. 4:4).

B. The joy of the Lord, through daily praise (see Neh. 8:10).

C. The health of Christ, through corporate worship (see Heb. 10:25).

D. The purifying gained through transparent fellowship (see 1 John 1:7).

REFLECTION QUESTIONS

1. How do you relate to the four influences recommended for shaping "accountability": relationship with your wife, your friendship with brothers, your stewardship with money and your interaction with the Lord?

2. How have you used writing in a journal? Do you ever focus on your shortcomings? Your strengths?

3. What steps of response do you think can help a leader "Stay True to Your Call"? (Use Paul's "*This one thing I do*" commitment [Phil. 3:12-21] as a text for measuring your answer.)

4. Have you found any of the writings, letters or prayers in this chapter helpful to your thinking?

5. Review the "Nine Things That Can 'Remove My Edge'" and the "Three Things That Will Help Me 'Keep My Edge.'" Are any of your experiences similar? Do you identify with any of these "things"?

CHAPTER TEN HIGHLIGHTS:
....

- "Flights-of-not-so-fancy" abound around the soul of quality leadership. There is a "Thief" who seeks to break in—to argue against your *promise*.
- Satan has one tripartite mission: to steal, to kill and to destroy. He is the enemy of your soul and your ministry.
- There are tactical weapons for resisting the thief.
- We set forth 10 points of promise for the pastor-leader.

And the God of peace will crush
Satan under your feet shortly.
ROMANS 16:20

WHEN THE THIEF TRIES TO STEAL THE PROMISE

An entire gallery of memories is located along the corridors of my mind—memories of moments when weakness, discouragement or despair seemed dominant. I can easily rewind my mental videotape and summon up those ghosts of seasons past, especially those times when I did not discern that my struggle was *indeed* with ghouls of hell more than the frailties of my flesh.

- I remember being taunted by a recurring mental image of a respected peer in pastoral work. My esteem for his excellence and effectiveness seemed to require my acceptance of the "judgment" I felt was passed on me every time I thought of him: *Shallow! Insubstantial! Superficial!* I was not "hearing voices," I was only drawing what I thought was an "esteem others better than yourself" comparison—but it was defeating me.
- I remember lying in bed for the better part of a month, weakened and weary with a painful and embarrassing affliction. The intertesticular infection, requiring groinal ice packs for hours each day, was not only awkward to report to whoever asked about my condition, but it also seemed to hold a symbolic message. Again, no "voices"—but rampant thoughts were ceaseless

in their suggestions: *Barren! This depicts your future ministry: Unproductive from now on!* I feared my physical condition was something of an omen—an argument shouting down the spirits of a man just turned 50 years old. It might sound like a bad joke, but amid the pain and at such a milestone in life, it is amazing what even an emotionally healthy person can be tempted to believe (or to doubt) about himself.

THE PARADOX OF PROMISE

It would not be hard to provide a sizable library of similar experiences, all of varying intensity in terms of their "discouragement" factor. The two mentioned, however, scored perfect 10s—lambasting my soul with wilting blasts I received as though they were something deserved.

But they were not deserved!

No child of God's promised purpose deserves to live through a sustained time of internal wrenching, tolerating doubts that present themselves as logical propositions when given the "facts" of our limitations! Yet, it is still a paradox of the life of a believer—and, I believe,  YOU SUCCESSFULLY FIGHT BACK THE TEMPTATION TO BE JEALOUS BECAUSE YOU HAVE NOT BEEN INVITED TO SPEAK, BUT YOUR MIND IS BUSY—*YOU'RE PASSÉ. A DINOSAUR!*
even more of a pastoral leader—that our "promise" seems to be constantly berated by shouting doubts and whispered suggestions of failure.

- An elder's "tactful inquiry" regarding a program you are launching in the interest of evangelism and growth becomes a pinprick that explodes a balloon of hope about to lift you and the church upward. Because you seek to walk purely before God, your mind accepts the proposition that your motive to growth is only *"Pride!"* The residue of uncertainty born from miles of afterthought following that one moment's remark cripple your confidence and weaken your resolve to lead with boldness.
- The newsletter from your regional denominational office arrives, containing information about an upcoming conference. The announced agenda of speakers includes a workshop to be presented by a man a dozen years your junior, but whose congregation has suddenly burgeoned. "Paradigms for Spiritual

Renewal" looks more to you like an accusation of your own ineffectiveness rather than holding the possibility for insights that might refresh your own soul and thereby your congregation. You successfully fight back the temptation to be jealous because you have not been invited to speak, but your mind is busy—*You're passé. A dinosaur!*

FLIGHTS OF "NOT-SO-FANCY"

I note these kinds of "flights of not-so-fancy" because they abound around the soul of quality leadership. Sometimes, their source unidentified, they can sink us to dark seasons of the soul. Their common denominator is that, given time to argue their case, they consistently propose our removal from the ministry. Resignation would be *a giant leap forward for* both *of you—the Church and yourself!* However, I want to make a clear designation of the source of these struggles; one, that I hope might once and for all destroy his efficiency. *Brother, this kind of tripe and all similar mental manipulations that present circumstances as a convincing case against your **promise**, are mental break-ins of none other than the thief!*

Jesus not only taught us clearly about Satan's tactical objectives—"The thief comes to steal, to kill and to destroy,"—but He also taught this in a pastoral context. John 10:10 is set in the Good Shepherd photograph the Savior presents of Himself, and biblical warnings against the devil's enterprise needs to be reviewed with increased frequency and intensity in our time.

So the great dragon was cast out, that serpent of old, called the Devil and Satan, who deceives the whole world;...Woe....For the devil has come down to you, having great wrath, because he knows that he has a short time (Rev. 12:9,12).

We are not only engaged in a wrestling match with hell's powers (see Eph. 6:10-18), but we have also answered God's call at an hour in history when the struggle is more intense than it has ever been. Our Lord's prophetic teaching in Matthew 24 and 25 is often paraded with the Bible in one hand and a newspaper in the other—stirring excitement about the fact that "Jesus Is Coming!" I do not doubt those prophecies, and I have no quarrel with preachers who get excited about them. It appears to me, though, that many leaders themselves fail to catch the tone of one solemn note Jesus sounded: "Because lawlessness will abound, the love of many will grow cold" (Matt. 24:12).

I have not always been as wise as I might have been to see how those words were directed toward the devil's efforts at chilling the fire of my passion for ministry. I more readily and exclusively could only see his deluding the spiritual fervor of others—the general populace like those I led.

FEAR OF "SUPERSTITION"

I had been in the ministry for nearly 10 years before I was introduced to any real dimension of discernment in the arena of spiritual conflict. I recognized the existence of "spiritual warfare" as a concept because of my professional studies, as well as from rare encounters with demonic situations in public settings. But I was almost completely oblivious to the slithering, serpentlike tactic of the thief, to "break-into-the-mind" with such stealth that he could convince me his reasonings were my own.

I had not yet realized how commonly we as spiritual leaders have become seduced by the materialism of our time. To my observation, this starts with a subtle bent toward intellectualized anti-supernaturalism during our college or seminary studies. Hearing stories of a few instances of fanatical preoccupation with the demonic, we are prodded toward a fear of *becoming* superstitious, producing a hesitancy to even suspect a satanic source to our own struggles.

As a consequence, a blindness to the devil's operations develops, so that when he attacks *us*, we easily fall prey to attempting explanations at a naturalistic level. "Mental" answers are preferred to "spiritual" ones, so that rather than expecting to receive Holy Spirit-enabled discernment, and learning to exercise spiritual authority over the works and lies of Satan, a cool but incompetent rationalism tends to dominate our ministry mind-set. True spiritual perception becomes foggy and circumstances succumb to human rather than holy resources.

Given time, we come to situations in which the agony of our own sense of weakness and ineffectiveness, or the struggle with people or circumstance, begins to erode confidence in our call—our *promise* as pastors. Worst of all, when these times of discouragement gain momentum, the drift inevitably moves toward self-blame, and to a self-defeating condemnation that argues against even trying to continue—*seeing I'm the center of the problem anyway*!

What a masterstroke of hell:
  to sow doubt or fear, fan it to flame,
  to begin to burn out hope,
  to argue against the wisdom of having hope in the first
    place,
  to convince of the good sense of doubt,
  to take glee over the inner soul-struggle going on
    throughout all this,

to level blame at you for the entire circumstance,
and THEN suggest YOU are superstitious to even think hell
would EVER be the source of something like this!

SHATTER THAT ILLUSION!

Fellow servant, I would like to shatter that illusion! If it is needed, hear me! *Exit* that dreamworld of accepting nightmares as possible precursors of truth!

Make no mistake, Satan is a totally merciless adversary. There is not one day of your life or moment of your ministry that he is not perched in a vulturelike pose, awaiting your collapse. Peter used another metaphor:

> *Be sober, be vigilant; because your adversary the devil walks about*
> *like a roaring lion, seeking whom he may devour. Resist him, stead-*
> *fast in the faith, knowing that the same sufferings are experienced*
> *by your brotherhood in the world* (1 Pet. 5:8,9).

There is possibly no more important issue in this book.

As deeply as I feel the significance of everything I have discussed with you, the issue of *detecting the thief* is ultimately pivotal. Please be patient with my passion about this point, but I am sorely troubled by the number of faithful, biblically-oriented, devoted pastor-servants I meet who are passive about this point. They have either been warned against "exaggerated emphases" to the point they underestimate the underworld, or their deception is wrapped in the garb of a proposed "theological error," which says, "If you make too much of the devil's abilities today, you are demeaning the triumph of Christ's cross."

Paul apparently was unaware of this danger. No one was more focused than he was to "glory in the Cross," and yet not anyone more aware and advising than he was about spiritual warfare. Not only does his classic Ephesians 6 passage declare the reality of the relentless struggle in which we are engaged. In the same text Paul calls us all to become "armed and dangerous" against the adversary. This is no isolated concept, but appears throughout his writings.

To another church, Paul warns "lest Satan should take advantage of us" (2 Cor. 2:11). Strikingly, his next words affirm something Paul could say for those he had taught, but not always true of us today. With the materialistic milieu of contemporary church leadership, can it be said of us, "We are not ignorant of his [Satan's] devices"? I am not so sure we're not: I could cite a dozen cases of my own "slow-to-discern" history as evidence.

For example, I didn't gain the victory over the debilitating effect of the haunting vision I described in opening this chapter, until Anna made a remark that yanked me into the realm of spiritual realism.

"Honey," she said, when I described my feelings to her (after weeks of saying nothing, only struggling within myself), "that's an *'imagination'!*"

She was referring to a text I had taught many times, but now I was obviously blinded from seeing how it applied to me. Too often "spiritual warfare" is only defined as a struggle of philosophies—a "battle for the minds of men." But Paul in this passage is describing his own struggle—not merely lecturing to others or making broad cultural observations, when he writes:

> *For though we walk in the flesh, we do not war according to the flesh. For the weapons of our warfare are not carnal but mighty in God for pulling down strongholds, casting down arguments* ["imaginations," KJV] *and every high thing that exalts itself against the knowledge of God, bringing every thought into captivity to the obedience of Christ* (2 Cor. 10:3-5).

The larger context reveals the apostle's soul-wrenching relational struggle with the Corinthian church, and here he is unhesitant to assert, "This thing is from the pit." Similarly, I was shaken awake. By God's grace, through my wife's word of wisdom, I was ignited with a fiery illumination of what had been going on. The "imagination" of the haunting specter that was relentlessly sitting in judgment on my ministry had, unwitting to me, become an idol which my soul was bowing before in defeat. What I thought was intellectual honesty with my own limitations had turned into a self-defeating surrender to "reason" instead of "revelation." But God's Word had now spoken about the subject, and my faith and conviction rose to "cast down" that lying image.

I was instantly released! Identifying my *true* adversary changed everything!

The story is too long to relate in its entirety, but focused prayer and warring praise became pivotal to my freedom. I have brought my message "Casting Down Imaginations" to tens of thousands of pastors to relay how *alive* the reality of Jesus' victory over every demon, and Satan's hatred of every shepherd of souls became to me. The gist of it is this: None of the dynamic of confronting the works of darkness will ever come into play until you and I, as shepherds, recognize two things:

1. The glory of our call to pastoral promise is a visible reality that surrounds us, and it provokes the thief's fiercest hatred.
2. There are no limits to the lengths of subtlety or cruelty to which he will go in sowing doubt or breeding despair.

The very mention of those two facts, I have learned, often seems to strike fear rather than stir bold faith in some pastors' hearts. I have heard good men express the fallacious notion that if they dare become assertive in identifying or confronting the adversary, they will only create trouble for themselves. They sincerely entertain the idea that in regard to "spiritual warfare," it is presumably best to keep a low profile—to "let sleeping dogs lie." But what may become a fatal flaw exists in that strategy: The enemy of our souls and your ministry is no sleeping dog. Satan is a deadly serpent who has one tripartite mission:

WHEN OUR "PROMISE" IS BEING STOLEN—*A DAY OR A CIRCUM-STANCE AT A TIME!*—THERE IS A MIGHTY POINT OF RESORT: THE CROSS OF CHRIST!

- *To steal*—to deprive you of peace, drain off your joy and undercut your confidence;
- *To kill*—to smother hope, suffocate expectation and abort faith in God's promises to you; and
- *To destroy*—to render inoperative the might and majesty inherent in God's call and purpose in you as a spiritual leader.

No, dear fellow warrior, to suppose passivity on your or my part will charm that serpent or tame that lion is to be lulled asleep by the prince of darkness. Though a calculated détente may not be your conscious plan, you may have—as I had—become hypnotized by a situation that develops with such apparent "naturalness" that your discernment is dulled. If that is the case, the Holy Spirit has a wonderful way of breaking the spell, as He did through my wife's sensitivity and assertion.

When our "promise" is being stolen—*a day or a circumstance at a time!*—there is a mighty point of resort: **The cross of Christ!**

We have more than the *right* to rise up and boldly denounce the devil—we have the *light! In the light of calvary's triumph over all the works of the devil, we have been qualified to resist him and to cast down his stratagems.*

> *He has...nailed it to the cross, having disarmed principalities and powers, He made a public spectacle of them, triumphing over them in it* (Col. 2:14,15).

Remember, none of us are beyond or beneath such struggles with hell's counsels. Paul is forthright in admitting an occasion of long-term struggle that brought him to distress: "A messenger of Satan to buffet me,...And He [Jesus] said to me, 'My grace is sufficient for you, for My strength is made perfect in weakness'"(2 Cor. 12:7,9).

Let us once and for all be done with the apathy-producing approach often applied to this strategic passage. This text provides no argument for a passive surrender to satanic attack, "so that greater grace may be acquired." Rather, here is a discerning account of how the works of hell seek to weary and break the servant of God. It is also a triumphant statement of how God's grace—*which has been manifested in the Cross alone, and which only flows where it is appropriated*—can be applied to our struggles!

That moment Anna's insight brought the light of truth's dawning to the night of my struggle, there came a holy eruption in my soul. The Spirit of God helped me draw on the arsenal of almightiness that is available because of the eternally pivotal moment that was established when Jesus' blood was shed to end the dominion of darkness.

- I began to praise the Lord for the Holy Spirit's revelation to my soul, letting the wellsprings of hope's joy refill again (see Eph. 5:18,19).
- I staked my claim against the devil, denouncing each component of the complex lie he had gradually fabricated in my mind. I neutralized each facet of my fear, each detail of my depression, with the *truth* of God's Word of promise (see John 8:32).
- Because my mind was the staging ground for the battle, I literally reached up (as in praise), and saw myself receiving armor from the hand of my Captain, Jesus.
- I put on *"the helmet of salvation"* (Eph. 6:17)—declaring: "I hereby take the blood of the cross of Jesus Christ, which purchased salvation for every part of my life and being, and both cover my mind with its authority and purge my thoughts of intimidation with its power!"
- I put on the shoes of *"the preparation of the gospel of peace"* (Eph. 6:15), being reminded that *my* feet are "beautiful" in their commission (*and so are yours, fellow preacher*—see Isa. 52:7!).
- Wearing those "shoes," I took my stand, knowing *"the preparation of the gospel"* is the full and finished triumph of Christ over all the power of sin, death and hell. That is why, alone where I was pacing the room in animated prayer and praise, I lifted each foot and stamped downward (as though smashing some foul, creeping thing beneath them), and spoke the words:*The God of peace will crush Satan under your feet shortly!*

This was no pious parade for a fanatical flailing the air. I was confronting the same enemy Paul fought as he possessed the promise of God's purpose in his ministry. When he describes the sufficiency of God's grace, we are not hearing the wimpish words of a man saying, "I couldn't seem to get an answer to my prayer, so I decided to endure my problem as a life-long weakness." Instead,

LOOK TO THE CROSS, AND ASK THE HOLY SPIRIT TO HELP YOU ADMINISTRATE ITS VICTORY AT YOUR SOUL'S ADDRESS.

Paul is saying, "No victory comes easily—and it's often a long time in coming. But I've learned this: the victory is sure, and the grace Jesus gives is adequate to sustain you until the battle is over and unto the full triumph of your resting in His faith!"

Any other approach is not in keeping with the tone of the apostle's behavior *anywhere in the New Testament*. He indicates *peace* amid the conflict, but never *pacifism*. The man is a warrior—expecting victory:

- *"Thanks be to God who always leads us in triumph in Christ"* (2 Cor. 2:14).
- *"In all these things we are more than conquerors through Him who loved us"* (Rom. 8:37).
- *"I want you to be wise in what is good* [i.e., to understand ALL that God's good grace and calvary's victory supply], *and simple concerning evil"* [like a child, readily accepting the reality of the devil's heinous ways, and unsophisticated in the ways of rationalizing away the supernatural realm]. The verse, in that light, is the context of his declaration I repeated: *"And the God of peace will crush Satan under your feet shortly"* (Rom. 16:20).

Those are the steps to take in blocking the thief's success. Through the years, I have learned to be a little wiser in discerning Satan's craftiness, but never so wise as to have mastered his tactics—at first. The Holy Spirit is a faithful war advisor, however, and even if I am slow to perceive, I have determined to be quick to respond when He blows the fog from my view and helps me see any ways the wicked one is maneuvering a new assault.

Here is promise, pastor! There is victory for you, too, at whatever point you may be experiencing the draining or devastating enterprise of darkness. The light of the Word, and the Holy Spirit's strategy for your application of it, may come about differently than my testimony describes. I have experienced victories in spiritual warfare in dozens of ways, so I have not proposed these steps as a formula. However, there is promise! Look to the Cross, and ask the Holy Spirit to help you administrate its victory at your soul's address.

TWO UNFORGETTABLES

I am drawing toward the conclusion of these pages and words with you now. As I do, I feel a deep longing—somehow to again affirm an absolute assurance: *God will work in your ministry all that He has intended for your ministry.* Settle that by making a permanent registration of two grand and unforgettable realities in your mind and in your heart.

Contrary to the lies of the thief—whose one pursuit is to creep into your mind with lies, cripple your will with discouragement and crumple your vision into a wad of despair—*Jesus Christ has His hand on your life and ministry. You are a better shepherd than you think!* So whoever or whatever may argue to the contrary, please remember—always:

First, heaven has no "second thoughts" about choosing you.

Your placement has come from the hand of the Highest. God's Word settles the source of your appointment and the sufficiency of your gifting— you are *given* by Christ and *graced* by His hand (see Eph. 4:7-11).

> The mind of Christ selected you,
> The hand of Christ directed, too;
> So whatever is unperfected, you,
> Take heart—He's not defected. True!
> (J.W.H.)

Paul said, "I thank Christ Jesus our Lord...because *He* counted me faithful, putting me into the ministry" (1 Tim. 1:12, emphasis added). So when a critic's sneer or your own "bad hair day" self-assessment feeds your doubts about God's leader-selection or placement process, look in the mirror again, and repeat: Jesus says you're a leader! Stop second-guessing heaven's choice!

Second, hell has no kind thoughts about you—ever!

Never minimize the enemy's efforts at undercutting your sense of significance. He wants you *out of the way!* Your existence is a redemptive presence: At your weakest, you are still an annoyance to his councils.

Never surrender to the sophistry that doubts the source of doubt. Our adversary's style excels at infusing minds with deterring thoughts. His hatred for all that belongs to God is reason enough for his assault. Seeing the Hand that placed you in leadership, Satan's motivation is further fueled to cultivate your belief in his denigration of your role and call.

Believe it! You are a better leader than you think—just by "being there." Turn your back on the bad-breath whispers of hell: they have never argued for truth, and they won't start with you. So, fellow-warrior, take your place under the authority of Jesus' cross and denounce the devil. As heaven's choice, refuse to become hell's chump. It is *that* fact of God's calling you that occasions *the* fact that *any* facts are ever posed to the contrary.

On the grounds of the eternal Word, let us stake our claim:

> *I know whom I have believed and am persuaded that He is able to keep what I have committed to Him until that Day* (2 Tim. 1:12).
> *He who calls you is faithful, who also will do it* (1 Thess. 5:24).
> *Being confident of this very thing, that He who has begun a good work in you will complete it until the day of Jesus Christ;...for it is God who works in you both to will and to do for His good pleasure* (Phil. 1:6; 2:13).

Let us stand together in our promise as pastors: *"My beloved brethren, be steadfast, immovable, always abounding in the work of the Lord, knowing that your labor is not in vain in the Lord"* and all the while remembering, *"God is not unjust to forget your work and labor of love which you have shown toward His name, in that you have ministered to the saints, and do minister"* (1 Cor. 15:58; Heb. 6:10).

LET US ANNOUNCE AGAIN

On those solid grounds of His Word of promise, let us announce again:

1. I am **called** by God my Creator, to *minister with promise* in declaring the gospel of my Lord Jesus Christ.
2. I am given my Father's *promise* of unshakable faithfulness, and my Savior's *promise* of *fruitfulness.*
3. As a son of the Father, I am a *bearer of the promise* that His grace shall **reproduce "sons"** through me.
4. As a husband of one wife, I am a *keeper of my promise* to **love her** as Christ loves the Church.
5. As a child born of God and filled with His Spirit, I am *promised growth* in Christ's character as I guard my **heart with integrity.**
6. As a spiritual leader, I am *promised spiritual authority* as I joyfully choose to live an ordered *life of submission.*
7. As a man of God, I welcome the *Holy Spirit's promised power,*

flowing daily from my *personal communion* with Jesus.

8. As a servant of the Most High, I hold the *promise of an increasing stewardship* as I **live accountably** before God and man.

9. As a warrior of the King, *His promised presence* and victory assure my **conquest over the adversary's** lies and tactics.

10. As a *pastor of promise* I live in the hope of **God's fulfilled purpose** in me, the men I lead and those we influence together. **Amen and Amen!**

Let that declaration ring with confidence, my brother! Let us join our arms as brother-shepherds as we receive God's promised touch upon us and Christ's fruitfulness through us.

And let us join our hands with other men...to see His promise fulfilled in them as well.

REFLECTION QUESTIONS

1. Have you experienced days like the ones mentioned in this chapter? Do jealousy or negativeness ever seek to creep into your soul?

2. Such days are not deserved, but have you been tempted to think they were?

3. Have the enemy's tactics bred a blindness in you due to any manipulation of circumstances?

4. Study Paul's concerns about the adversary. What can you see in Paul's struggle with adversity in his life, and how he handled it?

5. Repeat the 10 declarations at the end of this chapter. Which do you most need to take to heart as your given right from God the Father?

PART II

HIGHLIGHTS:
....

- Clarifying perspective about various approaches church programs use with men, and focusing on those that break through to the core of men and their needs—avoiding the threat of *spiritual sterility*.
- Assessing schedule possibilities, and reviewing proven patterns that can keep the church's ministry to men attractive, focused and vital—avoiding the numbing effects of *program predictability*.
- Analyzing 10 essential concepts that can frame the grid for a pastor's formation of a curricular structure to guide his teaching and exhortation with his men—avoiding *spiritualized redundancy*.
- Providing summary thoughts and message resources that elaborate the 10 curricular concepts proposed above—seeking to assist the pastor-leader toward his own *anointed creativity*.

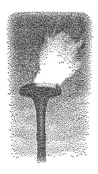

DYNAMIC RESOURCES FOR ADVANCING A MEN'S MINISTRY

• CLARIFYING PERSPECTIVE ON THE CHURCH'S MINISTRY TO MEN

A men's awakening has been launched by the sovereign work of God in our day, and every alert pastor has begun already. Your sensitivity to *men's ministries* has doubtless begun providing opportunities for your congregation's men to respond through some program possibilities.

Even prior to the explosion of attention that stadium events around the nation has brought, many denominational programs were in place and operating with varying degrees of success—from vital action to program apathy.

When I first answered the stirring of the Holy Spirit, calling me to "begin gathering men," it was not as though churches I had attended or witnessed were without any men's program at all. Many had "something" going, and besides the variety of offerings I could observe in other congregations, such parachurch groups as the Christian Business Men's Committee, or the Full Gospel Business Men's Fellowship were succeeding with men's breakfasts, fellowships and retreats.

Considering my call to "pastor," and seeking to answer what the Holy Spirit was wanting to do with the men He had given me to shepherd, I began to think through the focus and fruit of various existing churches' approaches to meet men's needs. Not until I had conducted my earliest gatherings did my perspective about "what actually happens in most men's ministries" become distilled and framed. The following is what I perceived.

I NEEDED A DISTINCTIVE FOCUS

I could see four basic approaches already being used with men: (1) para-church gatherings, (2) denominational service organizations, (3) athletic and action programs and (4) Bible study and discipleship groups. Each served an unmistakable value, but none of them answered to what I believed our men needed.

Parachurch Men's Organizations

First, the breakfast/lunch/dinner events sponsored for men by local or area parachurch groups were serving a definite value. Relatively few men I pastored were involved, but those who were found profit in the fellowship, and the events also provided opportunities for evangelism—through inviting guys they worked with to come and hear another businessman talk about his faith in Christ.

Denominational/Church Action Programs

What parachurch groups offered was being answered to by some denominations whose programs provided similar options for their men. Whether it was inviting men to support national goals (such as Missions), providing regional retreats, or a locally evolved focus on "men's projects" of service to the congregation or community, there was no challenging their value. Guys gained unquestionable personal satisfaction for having employed their time and talent in service, and sporadic retreats brought refreshment to those who attended.

Athletic Programs

Softball or basketball teams or action programs (centered on areas of special interest or hobbies, or helping with boys) certainly attracted some men and served yet another value. However, whatever in evangelism, service or action any of these approaches served, I felt they all fell short of coming to terms with a believing man's need for real spiritual input and growth.

Bible Study and Discipleship Programs

To my view, Navigator resource plans, or men's Bible study or prayer groups came a lot closer to meeting men's needs. They were certainly geared to focus on building the man's spiritual life, and had an eye toward influencing his practical, daily walk. Even with these approaches, however, I had long since come to recognize how easily they result in either (1) failing to attract a large percentage of the congregation's men, or (2) playing to a subtle "pride factor," as some guys inevitably seemed to end up vying for apparent spiritual superiority. (For example, through the vainglory of his achievement, by proven "faithfulness" at a weekly early morning prayer meeting, or through intellectual or spiritual "insightfulness" at the regular men's Bible studies, a man can do his "man thing" and still fail to come into a face-to-face confrontation with God.)

THE MEN'S GROWTH SEMINAR

In the wake of my analysis, and shortly after beginning to meet with men, I framed the focus of what I began calling "Men's Growth Seminar." I framed up the definition, schedule and objectives—and wrote a personal letter to all the men in our congregation.

> Dear (first name, typed to each one personally):
> I'm writing you because I believe you care! I'm thankful for men like you who have made a clear choice to receive Jesus as your Savior. It means a lot to me—both the privilege and the responsibility—that God and you allow me to be called "Pastor" by you.
> You've heard me talk about "Men's Gatherings" lately, and know how important I feel they are on the Lord's agenda for us both. Now, approaching the fall season, I feel a sharpened focus is in view for these gatherings; one I believe you'll care about.
> Take a few minutes, would you please?
> Look over the enclosed sheet, and notice the way I've described a *new and ongoing resource* I want to provide for the guys in our Body. I'm calling it the MEN'S GROWTH SEMINAR—because I honestly believe men like you want that—*to grow* as a man!
> As the schedule shows, it'll cost a time investment—but only eight times a year. That's something I think we can do together, and I sincerely hope your schedule will allow it.

I went on to give the date and time, then I followed up with a public mention on Sunday that "My Letter" was coming to each man that week. The remarks were reinforced by a brief article I wrote in the church bulletin, not *promoting* an event, but *conceptualizing* the significance of men in God's program for His people. The enclosed sheet to which I referred in the letter included the following:

Agenda of the Men's Growth Seminar

Definition:

A *monthly* (eight months per year), about two hours (7:00-9:15 P.M.) *seminar* (with worship, power prayer, "men's stuff" teaching in God's Word, and practical real-life application).

Objective: Men's Growth

1. To *establish* and increase the Father's purpose in the life of the man who has made up his mind to let God make him all he can become.
2. To *enlarge* a man's understanding of himself, his responsibilities as a man, a husband, a friend and as a servant of Jesus Christ.
3. To *expel* from men's minds the false concepts of masculinity, which hinder the freedom of the individual to function in true spiritual confidence and authority.
4. To *engage* men at a spiritual commitment level, which will release each one's individual capacity for genuine transparency and fruitful relationship.

BROTHERLY CONFRONTATION

The actual events were upbeat and positive, but they were also downright confrontive. I believe that a men's gathering is incomplete unless the three monsters—*pride, fear and doubt*—are confronted. My strategy was to be totally "brotherly"—openly relating as a man who wrestles with challenges the same as any man, but at the same time leading with conviction at three points:

- In *WORSHIP*...convinced that being drawn to forthright, expressive praise, and thoughtful, humility-invoking confrontation with biblical requirements of worship, can break the back of carnal pride;
- In *PRAYER*...convinced that bringing men to *pray together*, to openly share personal needs with face-to-face candor (as I show the way to do this), can *erode barricades of fear* that separate men; and,
- In *TEACHING*...convinced that the presentation of cut-to-the-gut subject matter (focusing on tough issues guys struggle

with), while calling for their interactive participation along the way, can *demolish doubt and grow men of vital, practical faith.*

The general schedule of our gatherings went something like this:

30 minutes *prior* to the meeting: Guys begin gathering, refreshments and fruit are made available, especially for those who come directly from work.

30 minutes of praise and worship: Bright opening songs, then I help the worship team lead the men in "turning the corner" to worship—more pensive, deeper.

10 minutes of "set-up" for prayer: I take time to describe an aspect of our masculine reticence to relate to one another. I give an example of biblical male transparency, and use some personal example (my own or a testimony) of God-in-action when men pray.

10 minutes of small group prayer: Having led the men into groups of three to five guys each, I direct them to (1) share personal concerns of their own, then (2) take turns praying aloud for each other. (Music "pad," playing quietly during this time, seems to help free communication.)

10 minutes of "regroup" and "business": Singing together brings a regrouping from the prayer circles and makes a bold expression of faith. I conclude with a prayer of praise-in-advance for answered prayer. Men are called to "greet each other with a holy, manly embrace," then announcements are made while an offering is received. (This is made very positive and usually has a ministry/missions focus.)

About an hour featuring teaching, interaction and concluding prayer: I provide a printed outline, often with discussion points. I move into subject matter "in depth," and call the guys to talk about what I am saying—reinforcing the truth by *repeating* to other guys what they have heard, and then later *praying* together (again with the guys they shared with earlier) asking the Lord to help them apply the seminar's teaching.

These are the essential means I have taken to clarify my own perspective on our men's ministry. The defined focus, approach and schedule have proven both the value and effectiveness of this perspective, and breakthrough has been realized. "Sterile" is the last thing any man would ever say about our local Men's Growth Seminars. They confront a man's pride, fears and doubts, and crowd him in toward God and man—to meet God, in worship, prayer and the Word; and to do that in conjunction with other like-minded guys.

PROVEN PATTERNS AND POSSIBILITIES

While clarifying our perspective, the outlined schedule I provided and have used with our men for most of the years is not the only approach we have used. Our experience has been that a pattern will maintain vitality for about three years, and unless it is adjusted, the predictability of the program breeds a passivity toward it. For example, on two occasions—for about a full year each time—we have conducted our men's gathering at a restaurant site on Saturday mornings.

The "Men's Breakfast" (titling can't get any less creative than that!) not only provided a fresh "feel" and a different venue, but also the day and the idea of "breakfast" garnered some new participants. Some guys find it easier to imagine themselves at the men's meeting if the "props" of a table and a meal are on his side. Whatever "tweaking" of the time, place or pattern, however, we maintain as inviolable the fundamentals I outlined in the preceding paragraphs.

Any variety introduced in the schedule or setting, as a creative means of attracting or maintaining interest, must never be at the expense of a clear-eyed vision of the program *content*. The *container* (the schedule, setting, program structure) can be varied—and perhaps ought to be to avoid a numbing sameness—but the content dare not be diluted.

For example, when we used a breakfast setting, (1) our worship time was abbreviated to four or five songs following breakfast; (2) I introduced a brief interview time, by having one of the men share (a personal discovery, an answer to prayer, a transforming encounter); and (3) our prayer format centered on the whole table as the "prayer circle." The teaching time, however, was still constant—pointed straight and hard at the stuff men struggle with, and how God's Word speaks to it all.

Various times and settings do, however, affect an element of trading one benefit for another. Some men could not budget the breakfast every month, although we encouraged guys to help each other (inviting buddies as guests), and also provided some unannounced "free" tickets for men we knew were facing a temporary financial crunch. We gained some men on Saturday morning that could not attend Friday night, but such a change of day or circumstance swings both directions—some gained, some lost.

EXPLORING SCHEDULE OPTIONS

The factor of "which day is best" has led us on two occasions (each lasting four months) to offer *both*, Friday night and Saturday morning sessions, duplicated at the church to serve the convenience or availability of the men. Our efforts at this plan have proven unsatisfactory, both times (there being about 10 years between the experiments). Although men seem at first to appreciate the offer of options, soon virtually everyone recognizes the loss in unity, spontaneity and energy. Although we have had multiple Sunday morning church services for years, *without* any loss of those values, something about the "men needing to be together" value has shown the "dual meeting" efforts to be counterproductive to our goals.

Seeking to involve men whose schedules almost never allow their regular participation has verified the value of *weekend retreats*. Every pastor knows the awesome potential of *two days* and a *retreat site* removed from the mundane daily setting of life, to provide the time and the atmosphere for a soul's renewal. A well-planned, much-prayed-over, wisely programmed and effectively executed men's retreat is probably needed at least every two or three years. (If an ongoing local program is not in place, more frequent retreats may work, but our experience is that an annual retreat is not effective—it becomes a substitute to achieving primary goals—if the month-to-month program is working.)

The strength of the retreat is the sustained dynamism of a 36-to-48-hour span of availability to the presence of God, without distractions and with a clear theme-focus. "Theme-focus" is very important to a men's retreat because few men are going to set aside a weekend simply to "go away." We work hard on the subject and the titling of the weekend, making it clear that something of substance will be offered, and will contain something of a practical "carry-back" value the man can expect when it is over. Further, the choice of a speaker is pivotal. He does not need to be "known," if there is credibility in the announcement of what he has to offer to the men. (And presuming the planning team knows for certain that the speaker will indeed be able to "stand and deliver").

A potential weakness is present in the retreat format if the event becomes so "separated" from the local church thrust that its values are not seen as (1) *born* in the climate of the *church's care for its men*, and as (2) *blessing* the guys with *something to take home*. Further, as powerfully as a guest speaker may minister, and as thoroughly as he may fulfill the planned goals, he still is not the *pastor*. Only you and I, the local shepherds, know the "rams" of the flock and, after the wonder of a weekend is over, we have longer-termed goals we will want to see served. So at some point during the weekend, the local pastor himself needs to lead in ways that "integrate" everything that is happening. The target needs to *always* be kept in view: we are *"growing"* men for *living where they do every day*, not just *"exciting"* guys with *a spiritual "quick-fix" for a weekend*.

This pastoral role can be fulfilled any number of ways.

1 A solid, salty and sensitively pointed over-the-breakfast-table devotional, about 12 to 14 minutes each morning of the retreat, can establish focus and assure a sense of expected "follow-through with what God's doing while we're 'up here.'"

2. The pastor can be the emcee (and, or, worship leader), providing a happy, warmly paced flow to the weekend (including humor); keeping generously unconfining to the guest speaker, but summarizing "focus toward home" when the weekend turns toward its conclusion.

3. The last morning, the pastor might lead in a communion service as a climax to the weekend. The speaker's last session could perhaps be scheduled at 9 o'clock, with a brief break before all the men come together "to meet Jesus as we conclude our days with Him and with each other." I have found that around the Lord's Table with my men, an excellent opportunity is afforded for shepherdly exhortation with faith-building encouragement and application.

A DYNAMIC NEW DISCOVERY

During the past two years—as I am seeking to transfer part of my mantle of "leading the men" to younger leadership in our church—God brought me to a dynamic discovery. I knew I still needed to keep a high priority on the men, and that I therefore—as senior pastor—needed to maintain a high profile in that arena of ministry. I also felt the need for younger men to spearhead the month-to-month gatherings.

I am blessed with outstanding guys who have been shaped through our men's ministry, and who not only have the truth-grasp and the speaking ability, but who are "received and trusted" by our men as well. So I was prayerfully seeking God for an approach that would integrate the continuing "monthly Men's Growth" meeting (led by men other than myself), and yet still provide times of focus where I would meet the men for special events.

During this quest, I one day came across Deuteronomy 16:16: "Three times a year **all your males** shall appear before the Lord your God in the place which He chooses: at the Feast of Unleavened Bread, at the Feast of Weeks, and at the Feast of Tabernacles; and they shall not appear before the Lord empty-handed" (emphasis mine). I was struck with these thoughts:

• For some reason, God liked the idea of a THREE-TIMES-A-

YEAR pattern for meeting ALL THE MEN (see also Exod. 34:23).

- He issued a call that was intended to bring them all together at the center of the people's worship life (Jerusalem, for them).
- He set the times in relationship to seasons that focused His redemptive activity, which also related to their work setting (the second two feasts being agriculturally oriented).
- He expected their coming to "cost something," (not only in their making the trip to Jerusalem, but also in bringing a gift).

I believe there was something of a spiritual principle here, which I have not stretched to abstraction, but which we have found *mightily* effective this past year—the first year of our applying it. It has been simple:

September (as the Church Year begins);
January (as the Calendar Year begins); and
May (as the season of Pentecost climaxes).

I have called the men to all come together at the church, "presenting *yourself* as an offering to the Lord" for one full evening.

The results have been dramatic, and the blessing felt in our midst has been wonderfully confirming! As the schedule reveals, I obviously have not attempted to stretch the application of the "three-times-yearly-all-the-males" principle to an exact observation of the "Feast" dates. Yet, though I have made the focus (each of the three events, in sequence) similar to the feast-theme that Passover, Pentecost and Tabernacles featured, I have not belabored this point.

The format of these evenings is similar to most of our men's gatherings, but the distinctive is that it gives me—at this time of my pastoral leadership—a solid three strong times a year with the men.

My purpose for including this innovation we have begun here is that I think it might be a "starting place" for some pastors who feel that a month-to-month program may be too hard to launch or sustain with their men. (Remember, however, the "month-to-month" I recommend is only *eight* months of the year—launching in September, skipping December and ending in May.)

These several considerations are offered as a means to assist a pastor and his men's planning team in assessing various schedule possibilities for programming the men's ministries in the church. I hope this brief review of proven possibilities might help you frame an ongoing attractive, focused and vital approach that avoids the numbing effects of when even the best program becomes "deadly" in its predictability.

FRAMING A CURRICULAR STRUCTURE

From the inception of our men's gatherings, we treated the content of the sessions as vastly more than "challenges," or "inspirational/motivational" talks or messages. When I wrote, inviting that first group of men to my first gathering with them, I told them I wanted to share how the Holy Spirit had impressed me to "begin meeting with men." I also announced that my teaching would be an interactive time of studying the demanding subject of how the Holy Spirit "leads," how God "speaks" to people and how we can wisely and biblically respond with discernment and good sense.

I did not present a fiery exhortation about "The Need for Men Today," or some other true-but-trite proposition that may have garnered a few hearty "Amens!" but not registered substance a man could build upon. Rather, from that first meeting, I have approached my Men's Growth Seminar teaching times with three guidelines governing my material.

THREE GUIDELINES IN PREPARING

- *First, there has to be a principle a man can bite into; something on which he can imagine himself taking action.* For example, that first session I did not simply give "rules" and "warnings" about the danger of subjectivism in "hearing the voice of God." I gave examples of times I have *known* God's direction, *searched* His Word to verify He underwrote what I sensed, and *sought* confirmation from mature eldership within my circle of acquaintances. I encouraged the guys to talk together in circles of interaction, expressing questions, feelings or lessons they had or have gained, then responded to feedback as time allowed.
- *Second, I seek to tie into Bible events —both to provide an expository base, and to unfold action-examples of God at work.* Again, in focusing on "God's voice to us" as an example, I have developed passages in the book of Acts where the Holy Spirit has manifestly spoken by dreams, visions, prophetic promptings and circumstances, as well as other Scriptures. I have also used Galatians (especially noting Paul's voluntary submission of his perspective of Gentile believers to the Jerusalem elders for their counsel —Gal. 2:1,2). I have also used 1 Corinthians 14 to emphasize ways the Holy Spirit moves upon people with "words" of encouragement for others — prioritizing an expectancy toward "ministering to others," rather than being preoccupied with one's own personal interests.
- *Third, I look for ways to teach from my own learning process, from my struggles as a man, then my triumph as a growing disciple.* Through the

years, I have come to believe that one very pragmatic facet of the biblical idea of "fellowship" has been overlooked by many of us who lead. In his first Epistle, John speaks from his experience ("what we have seen and heard") in laying the groundwork for his announced goal, ("that you may also have fellowship with us"). John is not "prooftexting" a practice, but simply describing a way of life that characterized the Early Church. Sharing my experience as a fellow-learner is an authentic means of teaching.

EVOLVING THE "CURRICULAR" CONCEPTS

Several years after cultivating our Men's Growth Seminars, I framed the concepts in the format that follows. Although I worked diligently to keep our Seminar content relevant to men and broad in scope, I had not formulated a formal grid of concepts to build on. What I *had* done was to structure a list of 24 themes I saw as essential to building New Testament Church life, and in my preaching and teaching to the whole congregation, I made an effort to provide not only substance, but also dimension with balance. But as my special focus on men evolved, the habit of seeking to enlarge each man's life and growth—particularly being sensitive to matters I found men need for input—my list of "Tapes for Men," catalogued by our tape ministry, increased to a rather remarkable number. One day as I was preparing to speak to a group of pastors about church ministry to men, I looked through the now-lengthy list and began to categorize the broader topics into which they all fell. Thus, the "curricular" list of 10 concepts evolved.

I mention this frankly, wanting to avoid any notion that we were "so together" from the start! For that matter, I am not ready to propose that the following curricular categories exhaust what every pastor would wish or what men fully need. However, the list that follows contains what I consider "essential areas of curricular coverage." By "curricular," I do not mean I propose a schedule for either the relative frequency of a theme's focus, or its priority in comparison with the others. The sequence here is perhaps somewhat revealing of a progression in development I would follow, but for the most part I am simply offering "a list."

The following is a summary statement of each of the 10 basic ideas that constitute our "curricular structure." Before I elaborate each one, let me state the "concepts"—the 10 "areas for growth," and what we try to achieve in each one.

1. **Resisting False Manhood**
   Answering man's challenge to resist the world-mind's false definition of manhood, and assist him in withstanding social pressures and spiritual forces that erode and emasculate true manliness.

2. Addressing Guilt
Addressing the relentless problems of guilt and condemnation that constantly cripple the confidence of a believing man and effectively remove his ability to serve his true ministry potential.

3. True Male Sexuality
Focusing on and defining true male sexuality, affirming its divine intent and proper place, describing the strategy behind the world's tactics that pollute it, and charting the pathway to nonprudish purity.

4. Concepts for True Manhood
Enunciating biblical concepts for true manhood, developing the picture of genuine humanity revealed in the way Jesus Himself manifested and modeled it—and by His life within us will enable it again.

5. Daily Christian Discipline
Presenting men with patterns of daily Christian discipline so that each one may learn to grow in his use of the Word of God, his walk with Him in prayer and his faithfulness in giving, service and witness.

6. Qualifications for Spiritual Leadership
Detailing the scriptural qualifications for men who are growing toward spiritual leadership, showing how every man leads in someone's eyes; be it his peers, his wife, his family, his church or work associates.

7. A Man's Responsibility
Leading each man—married or unmarried—to a maximum grasp of the concepts of husbandly responsibility and love, fatherly understanding and authority, and how to fulfill these two roles.

8. A Man of Integrity
Calling men toward building a circle of personal accountability, helping each one learn to live in transparent fellowship and biblically based commitment to integrity and trustworthiness in all relationships.

9. A Man's Perspective
Developing each man's perspective of himself as a viable agent of the kingdom of God; teaching how to receive and minister the fullness of the Holy Spirit, and how to move in intercessory power and spiritual warfare.

10. A Gifted Man
Teaching each man the value of his gifting and vocation, and the significance of his role in the workplace as a man born of God and appointed to penetrate his world with the life and love of Christ.

Curricular Structure of the Ten Concepts

1. Resisting False Manhood

Answering man's challenge to resist the world-mind's false definition of manhood, and assist him in withstanding social pressures and spiritual forces that erode and emasculate true manliness.

The following outline is from a message about the world's constant revision of the image in which we were created. This is an important subject in working with men; it will help them come to grips with the facts:

- Man's sin caused him to forfeit the original place of authority God had intended.
- Although we were created in the image of God, the world image is imposed on man from many directions—from all directions.
- Resistance to this false image can lead us to regain the proper areas of dominion intended for us by the Father.

Men Resisting the World Image

I. The dominion God gave man, man forfeited.

In Genesis 1:26,27, God has given man dominion of the earth. Following, in Genesis 3, we read the account of man's loss of dominion, entry of sin into the race and his beginning of hiding both from God and other people, even his wife.

Genesis 5 shows us a sad comparison:

> v. 1—God created man, He made him in the *likeness of God*.
> v. 3—And Adam...begot a son in *his own likeness* after *his image*.

What had begun in the image of God is now being reproduced in the sinful image of man.

II. The process of returning to the "image of God."

"Present your bodies a living sacrifice,...transformed by the renewing of your mind" (Rom. 12:1,2).

"Where the Spirit of the Lord is, there is liberty" (2 Cor. 3:17). This refers to freedom from being shaped by the forces that would make us less than "God-countenanced" men, people whose image is like His.

Second Corinthians 3:18—4:6—Seeing His face, it begins to mirror in mine. That mirroring results in the recovery of the lost image of God—the image I reproduced in my children, and that was produced in me by my father, and so on.

"Not redeemed with corruptible things" (1 Pet. 1:18). We have been redeemed by the blood of the Lamb from vain or empty character we received by the tradition of our fathers. As man continues to be made in *man's* likeness, from generation to generation the *image of God* is spoiled.

III. The Lord has fashioned for us a pattern of life.

"All things work together for good...be conformed to the image of His Son" (Rom. 8:28,29).

Thus, all things are designed to bring about the shaping of the image of Jesus Christ in us, so we will be conformed to His likeness.

A recovery process is occurring:

1. The Spirit of the Lord is bringing liberty.
2. We can learn to renounce the hidden things of dishonesty.

James 1:23—25 equates the one who hears the Word without acting on it with a person who observes himself in a mirror and immediately forgets what he looked like.

We let the Word shape us. As we look into it, we decide we will let that image shape us rather than turn and forget how we looked by comparison with what we saw.

The importance of this shaping process is seen in that all ministry flows from *who we are*, not from *what we do*. All the ministry, all the love, all the power, all the understanding, all the wisdom that will come from our lives will be something of Jesus' image and likeness being reproduced in us. The image of the Lord Jesus Christ is something that is *imprinted/sealed* on us. The Lord puts the melting wax of the Holy Spirit on us, puts the seal on it and says: "There. Now there's the image, that's the message." You go and take it, and that working of the Lord in our lives is what makes any kind of ministry possible.

For ministry to flow at increasing dimensions in the life of the congregation, a rise of men will need to occur. It does not happen through one fountainhead who stands in the front of the church and talks for an hour on Sunday. If so, we are in trouble.

The Lord will prepare us for ministry. The ministry will flow from people in whom the image of Jesus is being fashioned and shaped.

IV. The world's system is set against the Lord's image in our lives.

"That He might deliver us from this present evil age" (Gal. 1:4).

A system is set against the image of the Lord being shaped in our lives; it is the system of this present evil world. The image of the world will lift its head against you, saying: *No, you cannot minister, this world belongs to me, the god of this age.* That god wants to blind the minds of those who do not believe, lest the light of the glorious gospel of Christ who is the image of God should shine on them.

V. The world image is being set up in our path.

Daniel 3:1-18 is the narrative of "set up" of Nebuchadnezzar's image.

- vv. 1-4—We see the world image being pressed on some men.
  In verse 4 the herald cries: *"To you it is commanded."* That is the world talking. It says you *have* to do this, you have no choice.
- v. 5—What you are to do—"fall down and worship."
  In doing this, you are swearing allegiance to this "thing." Why fall down? So the stamp can be put on you—the image. As you bow, you come under its dominion and shaping influence.
- vv. 6-13—Here Nebuchadnezzar is a picture of Satan, roaring in rage and fury when his system is balked at.
- vv. 14-18—These men believed they would be saved, but even if they were not, they were determined *not* to worship Nebuchadnezzar.

SIDE NOTE: 3:1—The image—"he set it up." Notice verses 2, 3, 5 and 7. All contain the phrase "set up." That is what we run into daily, "setups"; things that are set up to put you down, or set up to shape you in the image of the world. We live in the face of a whole system of setups.

VI. A few patterns that are set up to put you down.

You can be delivered from them, too. Just as these men were.

1. Patterns from our past make memories that influence us.
2. Experiences from our past have so shaped us that as we move into different situations we are limited to say: *That's the way I am and always have been.* The Lord wants to heal and "reprogram."

3. Gilgal/Circumcision (see Josh. 5). The Lord put His mark on them and "rolled away the reproach of Egypt from them." They were now marked for the Lord.
4. The Lord will change past patterns as we listen to Him calling us to a higher level of obedience and purity. As He calls, we must respond and put that part of our past behind us—put it under His lordship.
5. The Lord wants to shape our habits. The Lord continues to ask us to bring things to Him for shaping. As the Lord begins to change us, He shapes us into people that are full of His love, life and strength of purpose.
6. Our job situation. Many times our jobs can be pattern situations in which we have cultivated a set of learned responses to coworkers. This inhibits the flow of the life of Christ through us. Let the Lord bring new patterns of relationships and conduct in your response to situations at work.
7. Patterns in your marriage. For example, how you speak or respond to one another.
8. Patterns in your schedule. For example, church may be a "negotiable" because it has not been made a priority in your schedule, or perhaps "negotiable" simply based on your feelings

Conclusion:

When old patterns are identified, do not try to do the paring job yourself. Let the Lord work on you, and just respond to what He says. You will please Him if you just stay available to Him. He is ready to release you from past influences that even today set their stamp upon you and your responses to the people and situations you encounter daily.

The Lord wants us to be *conformed* again to *His image*, and receive the stamp of *His Holy Spirit's anointing* for living in *His image* instead of in the world's.

(The reader may reference tape 295 from Living Way Ministries if desiring to receive this message in its entirety.)

2. ADDRESSING GUILT

Addressing the relentless problems of guilt and condemnation that constantly cripple the confidence of a believing man and effectively remove his ability to serve his true ministry potential.

The devil makes concerted assaults on the personalities of each of us who seek to follow God. Who of us does not struggle with thoughts of inadequacy resulting from our past failures? It manifests itself not only in our relationships with other believers, but also in our relationship with the One who has ultimately delivered us from those sins.

This message focuses on how to experience release through a cleansed conscience. It addresses vital points that plague believers and limit spiritual progress in their lives. It deals with the following facts:

- One sacrifice paid the price for our sins—we are now new creations in Christ.
- Once we are forgiven, our sins are forgotten—we are now cleansed and can walk with full assurance of our faith.
- Open, honest relationships are key in our lives—we are now able to have fellowship with Jesus and with one another.

RELEASED THROUGH A CLEANSED CONSCIENCE
HEBREWS 10:10—25

Introduction:

The Word of God is the guideline by which we measure all things. It is the plumb line for everything in our lives. As the Word becomes flesh and ministers in us and to us, we also will receive the Word being made alive in people around us when we have healthy fellowship.

I. One sacrifice for sin makes way for relationship.
A. Jesus made one sacrifice.
Look at these statements:

- "Jesus Christ *once for all*" (v. 10).
- "This Man,...offered *one sacrifice for sins*" (v. 12).
- "For *by one offering* He has perfected [them] forever" (v. 14).

Sacrifice is something Jesus did once. He laid Himself down to pay for our sins and by that one offering He makes two things possible:

1. Our acceptance before God;
2. Our becoming accepting of one another.

B. Jesus offers forgiveness with compassion.
The Pharisees were preoccupied with keeping the Sabbath, multiplied washing of hands, the letter of the law, the fulfillment of everything of an

entire human system extending well beyond anything the Lord said in His Word. Sadly, their laws were absolutely inconsiderate of people. A classic example is when they threw the woman taken in adultery down before the Lord Jesus. He chose to do what was reflective of the heart of God, saying not only, "Thy sins be forgiven thee," but also, "Go and sin no more."

C. Jesus establishes vertical and horizontal relationship.

A new dimension of relationship toward people was established when Jesus summarized the whole law saying, *"'You shall love the Lord your God with all your heart, with all your soul, with all your strength, and with all your mind,' and 'your neighbor as yourself'"* (Luke 10:27). This new dimension is the *vertical and horizontal relationship*—relating to God and relating to each other.

The Lord shows us the pathway to this new dimension of relationship through Jesus' one-time sacrifice for sins—"one offering, once for all accomplished." This was the final execution of God's judgment on sin. As a result:

- Our sins are forgiven and forgotten (Heb. 10:17).
- I can come into the holy of holies before God (vv. 18,19).
- Our High Priest established a "new way" for us. Jesus went in and once for all made this one-time sacrifice complete. His presence before the Father is the ongoing guarantee that everything He established at the cross is continually available for us (vv. 20,21).
- Having a High Priest then we can be assured of our purified hearts and cleansed consciences before the Father (vv. 22,23).

II. Restored relationship with the Father and with each other.

We have begun with the sound doctrine that Jesus is the ultimate and final sacrifice. His unique provision through saving grace brings us total acceptance with God the Father. We receive this announcement that our sins and iniquities He "will remember no more" (v. 17).

Many men's relationships with the Lord are hindered, and that in turn hinders our relationships with each another. This limits the freedom of our interaction and fellowship.

True fellowship has nothing to do with that which the world depends on to establish some level of relationship. Human skills of maneuvering through a conversation are not enough. The Lord calls on us to develop relationships of personal openness and the ability to simply communicate with one another. These flow from the current status of our relationship with the Lord.

We need to do two things:

1. See Bible's directive about how to build a solid foundation of relationship with God.
2. Build a relationship with one another on that foundation.

III. First forgiven, then forgotten.

"Their sins and lawless deeds will I remember no more.' Now where there is remission of these, there is no longer an offering for sin" (vv. 17,18).

A. How can God forget sin? Follow this series of thoughts:

- We have all been raised to think that forgetting is a weakness.
- But the foolishness of God is wiser than men.
- If you could forget the thing that most shames you from your past, if you had the capacity to selectively reach into your mind and pull out any given episode of your life and permanently destroy it, you would say that is a powerful exercise of a mind.

God has the power to selectively remove sin, not only from the records of heaven, but also from the record of universal history. The Bible says, "If anyone is in Christ, he is a new creation" (2 Cor. 5:17). As post-salvation sins are committed, the Bible tells us in 1 John 1:9 to confess them and—"He is faithful and just to forgive us our sins and to cleanse us from all unrighteousness."

B. Hebrews 10:22 shows two steps for living this way:

1. We can come to a place where we have the assurance that our hearts and consciences have been purged.
2. We can have a sense of actual physical cleanness. Think about the deeds your body and hands have performed; words spoken by your lips; images viewed and received into your eyes; and sounds listened to with your ears. The Lord is saying, "I want to purge your mind and your heart. The record of your sins I will hold no longer." We have been cleansed by the blood of Jesus.

IV. Our application.

Verse 22 says, "Let us draw near," and is not just talking about our relationship with God. We continue to verses 24 and 25 where we are told to "consider one another in order to stir up love and good works, not forsaking the assembling of ourselves together,...but exhorting one another." It becomes clear we are also to draw near to each other.

In light of this, we are told to do the following three things:

1. **Draw near to God.** "Let us draw near...[and] hold fast the confession of our hope." We are to first consider our relationship with Him.
2. **Consider one another.** "Let us consider one another...to stir up love and good works, not forsaking the assembling of ourselves together." Relate to one another in such a way that the other person does not even have to think about whether he is responding in love and good works. It becomes an automatic involuntary response.
3. **Build one another up.** "Exhort one another." Let your conversation build each other up and be an encouragement to love and to good works. The word "exhort" is a "Holy Spirit" word; directly related to the word for "Comforter." To "exhort" one another is to come together to help one another, to stand beside.

Let the involuntary response bring about good works and an expression of love. Learn to relate to one another in that way.

V. Relationship built through open communication.
After your sin is forgiven and forgotten through the blood of Jesus, be open to share with a brother all that God has done for you. Relate to a brother with "love and good works" and come together to exhort one another.

The following prompting questions will help you cultivate a real and open communication with another man on a deeper level. These questions may also challenge you as you give thought to each one.

1. What Scripture is especially meaningful to you?
2. What is your most recent point of fulfillment?
3. What is the Lord currently doing in your life?
4. What area makes you feel most inadequate?
5. What has most contributed to your liberty in Jesus?

- Was there a turning point? Water baptism? Holy Spirit baptism? A milestone decision for Jesus?
- A discipline?
- A point of understanding that came? "I heard this tape, read that book, the Lord spoke, etc."

6. What do you most fear?
7. Where do you hurt?

8. What most hinders the fulfillment of your expectations of yourself as a spiritual man? (Possibly circumstances in your job,
with your associates, in your home or in your heart.)

Remember as you talk about these things to "hold fast the confession of
your faith." Do not compromise the truth of the Word. Be assertive toward
gaining victory instead of letting doubt and apathy rule your situation.

Conclusion:

Our recognition that our sins have not only been forgiven by Jesus, but forgotten as well, is a key to the release of a clear conscience. Guilt is a tool of our
adversary, the devil, to keep us from experiencing all God has for us in life—
not only what we can become, but also the short-circuiting of relationships that
could develop. Meaningful fellowship and open accountability with another
brother are tools Jesus will use to build us into the men He desires us to be.

*(Living Way Ministries tape 1038 contains this message in its
entirety. The theme is also developed in Pastor Hayford's book* A
Man's Confidence.*)*

3. TRUE MALE SEXUALITY

*Focusing on and defining true male sexuality, affirming its divine intent and
proper place, describing the strategy behind the world's tactics that pollute it,
and charting the pathway to nonprudish purity.*

The following is a message I presented to a small group of men shortly after the tragic announcement of Magic Johnson falling victim to the
HIV virus. I have two important reasons for including this message:

First, it is a good study of the world's pollution of true male sexuality
as God originally intended.

Second, this is an example of how I will handle tragic information that
comes to us through the media. I refer to jumping on a "stone-throwing"
bandwagon, making accusations at the expense of having compassion or
seeking a deeper understanding through biblical examination of the subject.

WHEN THE MAGIC FAILS
JAMES 1:21-25

Introduction:

Few things have impacted the emotional psyche of this nation in recent
years like the announcement that Magic Johnson, beloved hero of the Los

Angeles Lakers professional basketball team, has been diagnosed with the HIV virus (human immunodeficiency virus).

The fact that he does not presently have the AIDS disease does not alleviate much pain for anyone. The sense of identification with this remarkable athlete is incredible in its scope, reaching well beyond sport fans to encompass the majority of the general public.

I do NOT want to appear either opportunistic or seeking to capitalize on the overwhelming emotion of the moment. This is no time for sensationalism.

But abundant lessons can be recognized, to be perceived and responded to by thoughtful souls everywhere. This has already been enunciated by the press. At least two lessons are repeated with parrotlike regularity, and Magic Johnson's announcement forces into full view:

1. The vulnerability of *every* person to the AIDS virus; and
2. The importance of carefulness in observing only "safe sex."

These are society's "lessons to learn," and I repeat them *not* as a mocking gesture, but to contrast their shallowness with far deeper issues that ought to be understood.

I want to establish perspective about my remarks:

First:

I admire Magic Johnson.

His skill, his achievements;

His manliness and upbeat way in handling this situation.

I am happy for the good things.

That he is NOT an AIDS patient as of the present;

That his wife is NOT infected;

That the child in her womb is expected to be free of the virus.

I commend Magic for his commitment.

The way he showed that toward his friends through his resignation;

The plans he has to be a spokesman for the HIV/AIDS crisis.

I want in no way to be perceived as speaking against him, or to appear to be accusatory toward victims of this or any other venereal disease.

When Magic came to the Los Angeles Lakers 12 years ago, I acted just as quickly to appreciate the qualities of his PERSON, quite beyond his TALENT—and that has not changed. I feel sorry for his sickness, and I will pray for him. I CARE about Magic Johnson.

Second:

My remarks are intended for people who have a basic understanding of God and His Word. I am not addressing people outside Christ. Nor am I rising to assert the obvious, *"Your sins will find you out."* That is true. But that is not my primary goal.

My primary goal is to come to terms with larger lessons we need to be certain we understand; to see, in the wake of this man's tragedy, lessons that can help us avoid (1) our own disasters, and (2) the subtle, delusive mind-set of a culture that cultivates such disasters.

I have titled these observations "When the Magic Fails," because of the disposition of our culture to see life as a kind of phantom reality; something you can manipulate and cause to work out however you want.

Somewhat like a magician "does it with mirrors," as the saying goes, the idea is that you can cast any image you want—holding the mirror up to reveal whatever "trick" you want life to perform, hoping the magic will work.

But the Bible says something else:
James 1:21-25

- v. 21—a call to purity and discipline (meekness) compares discipline with indulgence.
- v. 22—a call to the WORD.
- v. 23—a warning about spectatorism as opposed to spiritual wisdom.
- vv. 24,25—a pointer to (perfect law of liberty); a pointer to the way of blessing (life, fullness, satisfaction, salvation)

Two segments to this message are:

1. The unannounced lessons inherent in this tragedy;
2. The biblical call to wisdom in response.

1. The unannounced lessons we need to be hearing.

A. There is certainty of sin's triumph when we dabble with its danger. *"Can a man take fire to his bosom, and his clothes not be burned?"* (Prov. 6:27).

POINT: Magic was as aware as anyone of this plague prior to his indulgences. He knew of the potential consequences.

Society's submergence of its spread—there have been 200,000 AIDS cases nationally and 126,000 deaths.

This is not a matter of "I told you so." This is simply a lesson about the emptiness of the supposition, "It won't make any difference this time."

B. The tragedy of sin's impact on our whole race.
"The wages of sin is death" (Rom. 6:23a).

NEWS REPORT: The reporter stated that he does not understand why God lets these things happen. He enforced the view of life as "chance," God as "fate" and judgment as "vendetta."

POINT: Magic Johnson's sickness is not an act of God; it is an act of man. We need to understand the difference between "judgment" and "wages."

"Weighed in the balances, and found wanting" (Dan. 5:27).

Life flies "loose" because it is not anchored in substance; weight of sin instead of weight of glory; SINKS instead of RISES.

But, *"the gift of God is eternal life"* (Rom. 6:23b).

I want to pray for Magic Johnson's salvation.

C. The irony of human persistence on known pathways of destruction.

"You shall not follow a crowd to do evil" (Exod. 23:2). The "everybody's doing it" syndrome.

NEWS REPORT: "Perhaps this will occasion allowing condoms to be advertised on TV." Magic Johnson: "I want young people to realize they can practice safe sex."

Contrast: I lament the talk of "safe sex." It is dishonest with reality. I have never heard of "safe Russian roulette." Men ever learning and never able to come to the KNOWLEDGE of the truth. (Called to *know* truth, not *learn* truth.)

D. The difficulty of acknowledging sin as "sin" because of relativism.

"How long will you falter [halt] between two opinions?" (1 Kings 18:21).

CULTURE: The relativism governing our mind-set.

"The need to lie"—deception.

"Feel good about yourself"—self-justification.

POINT: There is a crippling effect of refusing to call sin "SIN."

More and more you will hear the statements: You're "missing the mark" or "off target"; or "You're not measuring up."

Do not whitewash sin by saying: "I'm having a struggle"; "I'm 'growing through'"; or "I need to improve."

Look in the mirror and tell God and yourself what you see. Let Him wash your face and clean your hands instead of comparing them with others.

WE FORGET...and give place to BONDAGE.

2. Our biblical call to a wise response to one man's tragic sickness. Identification is easy; we see ourselves in Magic.

A. *To repent* for any self-righteousness, spitefulness or bigotry of soul. Luke 13:3—Do I harbor self-righteousness toward anyone?

B. *To let compassion* find a new dimension in our life and living. Matthew 9:36—"When He saw the multitudes." We must direct compassion toward others.

C. *To pray* for miracles as a divine visitation of God's mercy. Matthew 10:8—Leprosy today: "cleanse the lepers."

D. *To believe* for breakthrough in the research process for a cure. Romans 5:20—Call for *grace*: "Where sin abounds."

E. *To understand* God's Word and will and to obey it. Jude 17-25.

F. *To be ready* to give a reason for the "hope" that is in us. 1 Peter 3:15.

G. *To serve* this house of need with sanity and sensitivity.
   1. Discern the subtleties.
   2. Note: Pat Riley's The Lord's Prayer, New York Madison Square Garden.
      • gracious
      • giving
      • godly

Conclusion:
When the magic fails...use the only real mirror—
No *TRICK*...Just *TRUTH*.

(This message in its entirety is found on tape 3515 from Living Way Ministries. You may also note Pastor Hayford's book A Man's Image and Identity.*)*

4. CONCEPTS FOR TRUE MANHOOD

Enunciating biblical concepts for true manhood, developing the picture of genuine humanity revealed in the way Jesus Himself manifested and modeled it—and by His life within will enable it again.

The concepts of true manhood are daily diluted in the deluge of worldly human ideas that are constantly imposed on all of us. The truth becomes twisted to serve the purpose of our enemy when true manhood is distorted and viewed as chauvinistic, counterfeited and entitled "macho," or de-emphasized, ultimately emasculating man from his intended role.

The following message is a good example of how to address this topic. This message focuses on two major issues:

First, it helps us to understand man's role and purpose—what God has called us to be and His intent for true manhood.

Second, it describes many of the obstacles we must overcome to fully accept our roles.

We must learn to think like Jesus—being like-minded with Him and putting off the thinking patterns of the world.

LEARNING TO THINK LIKE JESUS
1 PETER 2:1-17

Introduction:

Peter tells us in this passage that we are a chosen generation and a royal priesthood. That means we are people ordained to lead other people to know God (that is the meaning of "priesthood").

God's intent in redeeming Israel was to make them priests to the world (see Exod. 19:6), bringing the world into a worship relationship with Him. We know from Scripture that only one segment of Israel accepted this responsibility, but the rest went their own way.

We as men have been called as priests to the world (see 1 Pet. 2:5,9); not only to see our own lives supervised under the will of God, but also to become men who lead homes, businesses and people in the way of the Most High God. This knowledge is essentially established and developed through worship.

As priests, we need to readjust our thinking to come in line with the way Jesus thinks. We need to be people who learn to think like Jesus. The following five steps can help us.

I. We are a penetrating force.
"Beloved, I beg you as sojourners and pilgrims" (v. 11).

A. Sojourners and pilgrims.

The word "sojourners" means "foreigners." The focus is on this world. We are actually a foreign element to this world. When the Scriptures speak of us as "foreign," it is recognizing that we are foreign to the world's system, its mentality, its methods of control and to its values.

Pilgrims are "in motion"—on a journey. Our journey is here—in the middle of a world system and lifestyle that is alien to what the Lord is wanting to bring us into. Yet He leaves us here.

B. Who's the threat?

Many, raised in the church, may view the topic of being separate from "the world" with a defensive attitude. Some may actually be afraid of "the world." The instruction of Scripture is not for us to be afraid of being sucked under by the world, but instead to see ourselves as people who are *different from* the world; the ones who are the threat *to its* control, rather than it being a controlling threat to us.

C. Salt and light.

Jesus uses two illustrations in Scripture that break down any defensiveness we may feel. He tells us we are salt and light.

- Salt is not threatened by anything around it, rather it invades and pervades. Salt flavors. It may itself disappear, but in its disappearing it totally penetrates all that it contacts.
- Light is never intimidated by darkness—it, too, is penetrating. The darkness must always yield to the light.

From these two pictures, we see the intended influence we can have in the world. We are distinctly different from both, the darkness and the blandness of this world.

Sojourners and pilgrims may be foreigners to this world, but they are definitely an invading, penetrating force.

II. We have a renewed mind.

"And do not be conformed to this world, but be transformed by the renewing of your mind" (Rom. 12:2).

The believer's strength can be found when keeping his thought patterns established in the "system" of the heavenly Father. This builds a "certain mindedness"—a confidence that comes only to those who have an understanding that comes from above.

The only thing that can keep us unintimidated in this "world system" is the security of knowing that though we do not talk the same as the world, and we do not function in its value systems, and we sometimes do not understand why it operates the way it does, we are equipped to operate on a higher level—with a renewed mind.

Problems come to the believing man whenever he tries to mix these two systems of thinking. There are two minds—"the mind of Christ" and the "world mind."

Romans 12:2 says a development is taking place—a remodeling process in our mentality. This renovation causes a shift in our minds from being controlled by the thought and value systems of this world to being brought into the thinking patterns of Jesus.

III. We experience a changed pattern.

"Abstain from fleshly lusts which war against the soul" (1 Pet. 2:11).

A. What is the soul?

The soul is the command center of the personality. It is essentially made up of the *intellect, emotions* and *will*. Intellect is how you think and emotion is how you feel: our feelings and our thoughts that determine what we do; thus the *will* comes into play.

B. Where is the attack?

First Peter 2:11 talks about carnal lust patterns that attack the mind and the emotions and produce decisions that govern behavior. We are to abstain from those carnal forces that control behavior and battle against our "own mindedness"—how we think, feel and act.

Inevitably, once the word "lust" is heard, we instantly think *sex*; immorality, impurity, etc. come to mind. It is one of the most recurring points of attack and temptation men face.

We do not have to search far to have such a "war" begin. Just walking down the street, we see the newsstands, billboards and signs scream at us. This verse, however, is talking about a lot more than just the basest drives of sexual impurity of thought or activity. It relates to our conquest of *anything* that seeks to control our behavior.

C. How do we conquer?

Start praising the Lord first instead of saying, "Oh no, Lord, You've got to help me!" When our minds are set upon Him, rather than what the world system is hurling at us, it's hard for the enemy to dominate our minds.

Do not be intimated by your foreign status as you move through this world and its systems. Conquer it by learning to live with the mind of Christ as a part of a royal priesthood.

IV. We live in a regained control.

"For all that is in the world—the lust of the flesh, the lust of the eyes, and the pride of life—is not of the Father but is of the world" (1 John 2:16).

Here is a categorical outline of the entire attack that comes on the believer from the forces of this world: lust of the flesh, lust of the eyes and the pride of life. Two-thirds of this fall under the category of lust.

The whole idea of lust has to do with control. Lust *is* the "quest for control"—of the mind, heart and behavior. It wars against the thoughts and emotions of the believer; against our thinking processes and emotional responses and thus the decisions born out of them. We are called to "abstain" from whatever introduces the world's control patterns. The Word says, *"flee also youthful lusts"* (2 Tim. 2:22)—and then we will regain control. Thought patterns established within us during the years of our youth, as we see, hear and are surrounded by the world in our daily living, socialize and acclimate us. God can break these "control points" evolved in our youth.

V. We think with a like-mindedness.

"Therefore if there is any consolation in Christ, if any comfort of love, if any fellowship of the Spirit" (Phil. 2:1).

A. Sorting through two minds.

How do you learn the like-mindedness that is according to the Lord's mind? How do you sort through what is world-mindedness and what is Christ-mindedness?

"Only let your conduct be worthy of the gospel of Christ, so that whether I come and see you or am absent, I may hear of your affairs, that you stand fast in one spirit, with one mind" (1:27).

The idea of "one mind" causes us to turn toward Jesus. We are to check our thoughts and actions to see how they align with the gospel, and live our lives in the power of the Holy Spirit.

B. Living in humility.

"Let nothing be done through selfish ambition or conceit, but in lowliness of mind let each esteem others better than himself. Let each of you look out not only for his own interests, but also for the interests of others" (2:3,4).

We are told to esteem others better than ourselves. This is humility; allowing us to accept the fact that others may excel in areas in which we do not.

Next, we see the concept of consideration—looking out for the interests of others.

Humility is the ability to be comfortable with the good things God has given us and the ability to receive from the giftings or graces we see in others around us.

C. Produces like-mindedness.

"Let this mind be in you which was also in Christ Jesus" (v. 5).

We are moving toward a like-mindedness with Christ. Because humility and consideration are both attributes that cause us to look outward, we need see other people's situations through the eyes of Jesus. If we think like Him, we will see like Him; that's how "like-mindedness" comes.

Conclusion:

Accepting priestly responsibilities in our life situations requires a refocusing of our thinking, and a shift in our actions. Effective priests, however, are those who have consideration for the people they are serving. To see this role violated in biblical episodes teaches the tragic results possible (e.g., 1 Sam. 2:12-36).

We are a penetrating force in the world—called to be agents of transformation who live under a completely new mind-set. We experience changed patterns of living, and have regained control in areas where the world has none. We are called to be "priests," and Jesus equips us for the task by teaching us to think as He does.

THE CONCEPT OF SUBMISSION

The outline on the theme of submission is offered here to assist you in a future examination of the subject. I have used it in many pastors' seminars and have found strong, positive response.

I. The semantics of submission, Matthew 8:5-10.

A. Jesus' "I have not found such great faith" commends the man's recognition of Jesus' authority as born of a person's being "set under authority." The New Testament word *hupotasso*, essentially a military term denoting "order," "place" or "rank," occurs 44 times and in 14 books.

B. *English terms* answering to this idea include "yielded" and "obedient." Our expression "surrender to God's will" describes submission at its entry point; "walking in the Spirit" conveys the idea of submission as a life pattern.

C. *The term "covering"* is heard much today. It is also related to the idea of order and therefore to submission. (Example: Ezekiel 28:14 uses the term denoting Satan's rank *before* his transgression.) "Covering" implies protection by virtue of one's yielding to or acceptance of an overseeing and loving authority. Thus, some say "through faith we become 'covered with the blood of Jesus'"; a figure that alludes to the original Passover concept, and that affirms we have *submitted* ourselves to the protection Christ's blood provides from judgment on our sins.

II. The significance of submission, Hebrews 2.

A. *All sin* is the resultant outflow of the rejection of one's place in God's order of things. First, Lucifer's "I will ascend," and second, Adam's seeking of knowledge not intended for him (see Isa. 14:14; Gen. 3:5,6).

B. *All redemption* is the resultant outflow of the submission of the Son of God to the Father's will: (1) *to incarnation,* Hebrews 5:5-7; (2) *to identification* with man, Matthew 3:13-17; (3) *to suffering in life,* Hebrews 5:8; 12:3; Matthew 26:52-54; and (4) *to death,* Philippians 2:8; Hebrews 2:9.

C. *The highest of human destiny* in God's redemptive program through His Son is *restoring man to his intended place of authority as ruler.* Hebrews 2 shows man removed from being "subject to bondage" (v. 15) and recovering "all [things] in subjection" under him; an achievement gained through Jesus' pathway of submission by His unquestioning life of trustful obedience to the Father (vv. 8-10).

III. The specifics of submission, 1 Peter 5.

Seven basic arenas of life relatedness call for learned submission on the part of mankind. (Each bears far more Scripture support than the brief list of references given here, but the following is a framework for further study.)

A. Submission to *God the Father,* Hebrews 12:5-9; James 4:6,7.

B. Submission to *the truth,* Romans 10:3. (Receiving God's provision of righteousness through Christ alone, without works.)

C. Submission to the *Body of Christ.* This refers to all three: (1) Jesus as the Head, Ephesians 1:20-23; Colossians 2:18,19; (2) local eldership,

Hebrews 13:17; 1 Corinthians 16:16, and church government; (3) individuals of the membership, Ephesians 5:21; 1 Peter 5:5.

D. Submission to *parents*, Luke 2:51; Ephesians 6:1-3; Colossians 3:20.

E. Submission to *civil authority*, 1 Peter 2:13-23; Romans 13:1-7.

F. Submission to *employers*, Colossians 3:22, Ephesians 6:5-7.

G. Submission to roles as *husband and wife*, Ephesians 5:22-33; Colossians 3:18,19.

IV. The spirit of submission, Psalm 37.

Any truth can be stretched over the rack of cold, literalistic application and made into a dried hide of demanding duty. New Testament life, however, is not centered in legal demands, but focused on grace; *filling* man with new possibilities for living in God's love by the overflow of the Holy Spirit (see Rom. 5:5). Presumption can make the principle of submission destructive, ruling people by fear. The biblical order, though, ministered in love, will generate trust and understanding in doubt, in presumption and in love. Finally,

A. *The Spirit of submission is not cowardly*, 2 Timothy 1:7. He will not produce passive saints who bow to anything in undiscerning, supposed "submission." We are *not* to submit to: (1) Satan—1 Peter 5:8,9. Example: sin/sickness are resisted; (2) flesh—1 Corinthians 9:24-27. We are to make no provision for it; or (3) Legalism—Galatians 2:4,5. It is *always* in opposition to the gospel.

B. *The Spirit of submission is not confused*, Acts 4:15-21; 5:26-42. This text focuses on the question: How does one submit to conflicting authorities? The apostles satisfy *both* God and rulers—submitting unto both. They do *not* submit to demands of silence, but they do submit to scourging with joy.

C. *The Spirit of submission is not contentious*, 1 Corinthians 11:16.

D. *The Spirit of submission is not comparatively competitive.* Second Corinthians 1:12 warns against the ugliness of a carnal spirit of competition; Proverbs 27:17 reveals the best aspects of "sharpening" one another by interactive activity.

Conclusion: New Testament believers want to be effective in ministry, and Christ has modeled how the flow of *His* kind and quality of ministry comes from His kind and quality of submissiveness (see Phil. 2:1-10).

(Tape 950 from Living Way Ministries contains the message from which this outline was derived. Also note Pastor Hayford's book A Man's Starting Place.*)*

5. DAILY CHRISTIAN DISCIPLINE

Presenting men with patterns of daily Christian discipline so that each one may learn to grow in his use of the Word of God, his walk with Him in prayer and his faithfulness in giving, service and witness.

There are few areas Christian men struggle more than the area of Christian discipline. Daily time in the Word and a regular pattern of prayer become difficult obstacles for us to overcome. The release that takes place as we move in the power of these disciplines, though, is well worth the cost of our commitment.

The following message outlines our call to become men who pray. It shows us the results of the labor of men who have decided to pray. Through biblical examples of men who prayed with passion, we see:

- Both physical and spiritual deliverance;
- Men called into deeper dimensions of discipleship; and
- Release of personal understanding of call and purpose.

The principles in this message will show us the importance of how to think about the effects of Christian disciplines on our everyday lives, as well as the lives of those with whom we come in contact.

MEN WHO PRAY WITH A PASSION

Introduction:

The power in prayer is not in our human energy, but in God's divine commitment to answer if and when we will pray. The *condition* of prayer is underscored here.

All of God's dynamics—His power, the possibilities for our own personal lives, His purpose in our lives—are all contingent upon *our* response. People often confuse the place of our response as though *it* were what generates results with God—but it is not.

We have to respond to the principles that make room for Him to do the things He wants to do, and is delighted to do, in our lives. As we begin to see and acknowledge these things, our growth begins.

I. Jesus' passionate praying.

A. His Agony—Luke 22:39-46.

In this passage Jesus is saying, if there is any way out of this, let it be. What you are hearing is the true humanity of Jesus crying out—humanity that would prefer to live, but is willing to die. The willingness to die, however, comes at a great price. It will cost Him His life, but even before His lifeblood is taken from Him by the nails, spear and the crown of thorns, He will, by His own earnestness and agony, give of blood.

Hebrews 5:7—9 refers to this time in Jesus' life so preciously. More is happening than Jesus wishing the cross would go away. We are not encountering either a coward or a confused man. We are meeting a man possessed—who has a sense of purpose; who is sinless and totally conscious and committed in the face of the situation.

This passage reflects our opportunity to become men who are the exact opposite of the kind of man pressing circumstances would dictate.

B. Begetting seed—Isaiah 53:10-12.

This passage reveals what is happening to Jesus in Gethsemane, leading to and culminating in calvary. This is "travail unto birth."

"He shall see His seed" (v. 10)—He is begetting a seed.

"He shall see the labor of His soul" (v. 11)—compare with a "labor" unto natural birth; but His soul's "birthing process" is unto spiritual life for us.

C. Running the race—Hebrews 12:1-4.

See this text in the light of Jesus' passionate prayer.

"Run with endurance the race that is set before us" (v. 1)—Run at an even pace with a set pattern, not in spurts. This is not an arbitrary course; it is a set race.

"Consider Him who endured such hostility" (v. 3)—He saw His joy, which was His seed. Let us, in prayer, do the same and not become weary or discouraged.

Putting it all together.

We get a picture of Jesus' agony during this time of intercession. Jesus was in a struggle for our salvation, and everything of human sin and failure was being brought upon and against Him.

In the Garden, Jesus is locked in a time of passionate, agonizing prayer. The Bible tells us that He is giving birth to a new breed of people. His "labor" was endured so He could see His offspring; a labor seen and accentuated in as passionate a kind of praying as can be imagined.

There is a direct relationship between "passion" and "life bearing." The obvious parallel is in the passion of married love and the resultant offspring of that love. Similarly in the spiritual realm, passionate prayer makes life possible because of that praying. How passionate a "pray-er" are we open to becoming?

It is a special thing when men begin to recognize that part of renouncing the world image is to do away with the ideas that:

- Passionate praying is something that is reserved for a special few;
- Passionate praying is fanaticism;
- Passionate praying is something departing slightly from reality;
- Passionate praying will put you on the borderline edge of some emotional ridiculousness.

It is important to recognize that passionate praying is the only way life breaks through in any situation. The things that make life flow are not the things that man thinks; it happens with people who pray!

II. Four biblical men of prayer.

A. Elijah: James 5:16-18.

Elijah was afraid at times, worried, got mad and was uptight. He was a human being, and yet *"he prayed...and it did not rain on the land for three years and six months. And he prayed again, and the heaven gave rain."* The man seeking God, earnest in travail, was birthing a breakthrough—but we are encouraged to note he was a man "just as we are."

B. Paul: Galatians 4:19.

It cost Paul greatly to see the Church of Jesus established in Galatia— a place that had nothing but idol worship and indulgence of every kind. Paul said, *"My little children, for whom I labor in birth...until Christ is formed in you."*

Paul had a passion in praying for these people—for breakthrough and stability in their lives with Christ. His passion to see them mature in Jesus was in prayer "unto birth."

What is released on earth is dependent upon men who touch heaven in prayer. The question is not, Is God able? The question is, are there people who will pray with a passion?

C. Daniel: Daniel 9:3; 10:2,3.

"Sackcloth, and ashes" expresses manifest repentance; someone who actually puts on the garments of repentance and seeks the Lord. (Daniel 10:2,3 is another instance of fasting along with prayer.)

To study the entire book of Daniel is to see an entire nation freed from Babylonian captivity. Daniel prayed and a nation was loosed from bondage.

Passionate praying is the kind of prayer that makes men not look neat (compare with "sackcloth"). It costs us to overcome our own self-indulgence (fasting), and it takes time to seek God earnestly.

D. Jacob: Genesis 32:24-28.

Jacob's name means "one who wins by the might of his own cunning" (i.e., by the strength of his own intelligence).

Jacob's all night of wrestling is a picture of the passion with which a person enters into a committed relationship with God. What is birthed is not Elijah's breakthrough in the physical realm; or Paul's breakthrough in people's lives; or Daniel's release of a nation. In Jacob's case, we see a breakthrough of an entirely new identity in his own life.

During times of passionate prayer God changes our view of ourselves. The main thing that hinders the release of any of us to become what God wants us to be is how we view ourselves. Our own view of our strengths, weaknesses, skills, style and how to act will shape how we expect God to use us.

Conclusion:

When Jesus prayed in agony, an entire new race was born. When Daniel prayed, a nation was delivered. When Elijah prayed, the world around him was affected in the physical realm. When Paul prayed, people found a release in new dimensions of what Jesus wanted them to be. When Jacob prayed, he found out who he was.

They all had a common denominator; they were men who **prayed with a passion.**

The summons to passionate praying is a call for men who will recognize that they can shape history, change lives and discover the person they are meant to be.

"The effective, fervent [passionate] prayer of a righteous man avails much" (Jas. 5:16).

(Tape 1956 from Living Way Ministries contains this message in its entirety. Also note Pastor Hayford's book A Man's Walk with God.*)*

6. QUALIFICATIONS FOR SPIRITUAL LEADERSHIP

Detailing the scriptural qualifications for men who are growing toward spiritual leadership, showing how every man leads in someone's eyes; be it his peers, his wife, his family, his church or work associates.

First Timothy 3 and Titus 1 have a great deal to say about leadership. Both chapters delineate certain qualifications and clarify the expectations of how leaders in the Body of Christ are to live. The question is: Who is a leader? The definitions in these books are intended for the terms "elders" and "deacons," and, quite frankly, most men tend to disqualify themselves from leadership based upon their supposed understanding of what these two words actually mean.

However, though a man may not pastor a church by vocation, or become an elder in his local congregation, we are all "spiritual leaders" in some arena of our lives. Every man operates in some sphere of authority in his life—whether that is a local church, a Sunday School class, the lunchtime Bible study at the office or his own family—every man has some area of responsibility for spiritual leadership, whether acknowledged or not.

The following are my study notes of Greek words focusing on leaders from these two chapters. Use these word studies as you prepare to equip men to rise to excellence in whatever level of spiritual leadership they have, and help them see that God has called them to a specific place so they can positively and spiritually affect that place.

1 TIMOTHY 3
ELDERS

1. *anepilempton*—irreproachable in conduct; "blameless" (v. 2); without reproach. (*einai*—to be, present infinitive). Not to be a source of disgrace or shame; not to justify an action of censure; not a cause of blame coming upon.

   See also section on Titus 1 word number 1 from Titus 1:6.
2. "Husband of one wife" (v. 2).
3. *nephalion*—temperate in the use of wine; "temperate" (vigilant). Marked by moderation, self-controlled, avoiding excess. In view of number 8 (*paroinos*), seems to be emphasizing moderation rather than specifically temperance concerning drink.
4. *sophrona*—prudent, thoughtful, self-controlled (of women: chaste, decent, modest); "sober"; sensible. Marked by wisdom or judiciousness.

   - Proverbs 16:21—"The wise in heart will be called prudent."
   - Discretionate in the management of business affairs. (*Not to be confused* with "*prudish*"—straight-laced; snobbish/fearful about sexual matters.)

5. *kosmion*—respectable, honorable, "of good behavior"; orderly (of women: in modest apparel).

   - Ecclesiastes 12:9—"Because the Preacher was *wise*"; *kosmion*. Decent in behavior or character; *exhibiting a respect for the appropriate;* worthy of note.
   - Interesting: One meaning or aspect of "respectable" is "moderately good," "pleasing but not exceptional." This is encouraging because the emphasis is on the fact you do not have to be excellent, but neither should you cause shame.
   - "Respectable" seems to also carry the idea that a person "has *respect toward*" matters of *social grace and taste.* Something of carelessness often travels under the heading of "freedom," and is actually *dis*respectable.

6. *philoxenon*—hospitable; "given to hospitality."

   - Given to generous or cordial entertainment and reception of guests.
   - Offering a pleasant and sustaining environment; not hostile.
     See also Titus 1:8 and 1 Peter 4:9.

7. *didaktikon*—skillful in teaching; "an apt teacher" *(NRSV)*. (*Didaktos* means "teachable, taught," so *didaktikon* transmits that which "teachableness" received.)
   See also 2 Timothy 2:2,24.

8. *me paroinon*—not drunken; not addicted to wine; not an excessive drinker; "not given to wine."

9. *me plektes*—not pugnacious, not a bully; "no striker" *(KJV)*.

   - Pugnacious: having a quarrelsome or belligerent nature; *thriving on a challenge,* in the sense of a proof of masculinity.
   - Herman Melville wrote of "pugnacious spirits...who lamented because there was so little prospect of an exhilarating disturbance." This is the trait of *plektes*—the challenge is one of upsetting peace, unity.

10. *epieke*—preceded by *alla*...strong adversative, which places it in direct contrast to *plektes*. "It is NOT *plektes*, BUT *epieike*."

    Definition: yielding, gentle, kind; "patient"; forbearing; slow to *press*...the idea is "forbearing"—which means "to delay in enforcing debts" (forgiveness), or to delay in enforcing rights of action, rights or privileges (i.e., patience).

11. *amachon*—peaceable; "not a brawler" *(KJV)*; uncontentious.

    - Marked by freedom from war, strife, hostilities.
    - Lacking noisiness or restlessness.
      Element of communicating peace present in personality. "Peace I leave with you, My peace I give to you" (John 14:27).

12. *aphilaguron*—not loving money; not greedy; "not greedy of filthy lucre" *(KJV)*.

    - In one ancient writer's usage, he records this as a quality desirable in *midwives* and *generals*. Interesting, considering the life-bearing and leadership qualities required of an elder.

13. *me neophuton*—literally: "newly planted"; "not a novice."

    - Used of new converts, *but* ought to refer in such a mobile society as ours to a mature believer newly placed by the hand of Jesus Christ in another place of the Body. Needs time to take root.

- This is similar to the idea of organ transplants. They must accommodate to the new body or they will be rejected. Transplants as opposed to amputations, or "floating livers." THE DANGER, otherwise—"puffed up with pride," and thus, fall into the *judgment* (punishment) of the devil.

14. *kalen marturian*—"a good report," notably, of those that are "without" *(KJV)* a good witness. The world sees him as consistent in demonstrating in its arena the traits believers declare. THE DANGER, otherwise—"fall into reproach [disgrace]"; thus, fall into the "*snare* [trap, bondage] of the devil" *(KJV)*.

15. FAMILY REQUIREMENTS: *proistnmi*—lead, rule, manage, be concerned for, care for, give aid, busy oneself with, engage in.

- Leading "his own household well" (v. 4).
- Having his children in order with all *semnotntos*—reverence, dignity, seriousness, respect.
Compare with Titus 1:6: believing *(pistos)*; not accused of profligacy, incorrigibility *(asotias)* or not accused of undisciplined, disobedient, rebellious *(anupotakta)*. (These latter qualities describe the attitude of the children toward their father.)
- "Having," "keep, preserve" (1 Tim. 3:4). To hold in your grip (have grasp on); to have something in one's hand.

DEACONS

Readiness to accept development in: (see boldfaced word in numbers 1—5).

1. *semnous*—worthy of respect, noble, dignified, serious; **Temperament.**
2. *me dilogous*—"double-tongued" (insincere, in that they keep repeating themselves...multiple-tongued, might carry the idea); unclear confession: not "yea, yea; nay, nay"; **Character.**
3. *me oino pollo prosechontas*—not caring for or giving attention "to much wine" (extensive drinking); **Conduct.**
4. *me aischrokerdeis*—"Not fond of base gain." The idea: "He isn't scrambling for a buck!" **Charity.**
See also Titus 1 word number 6.
5. *exontas to mustnrion tns pisteos en kathara suneidnsei*—holding the mystery of the faith in a pure conscience; **Conscience.**

Warning: 1 Timothy 1:19,20.
Goal of the law: 1 Timothy 1:5

Good conscience: Not unresponsive to those things the Holy Spirit tells you are wrong, or what you are to do. The monitor of the soul, now quickened by the love of God and the light of His Word. Shipwreck is what happens when a man supposes that his knowledge of the truth exempts him from being sensitive to the correction, the instruction and the direction the Holy Spirit gives him continually. He makes the conscience *alive* and *alert*. (*Contrast:* 1 Timothy 4:1,2.)

Proving period:

6. They are to experience a proving time (3:10).
7. *anegklntoi*—irreproachable (proven to be).
   See also Titus 1, word number 1.
8. Family requirements:
   Husband of one wife (v. 12);
   proistimi–lead, rule, manage well their own children and their own households (v. 12).
   See also 1 Timothy 3, word number 15.

TITUS 1
ELDERS

1. *anengklntos*—irreproachable, blameless.
2. *me authadn*—not self-willed, stubborn, arrogant.
3. *me orgilon*—not quick-tempered, inclined to anger.
4. *paroinon (me)*—See Elders, word number 8 from 1 Timothy 3.
5. *me plekten*—See Elders, word number 9 from 1 Timothy 3.
6. *me aischrokerdn*–not fond of dishonest gain. See also Deacons, word number 4 from 1 Timothy 3.
7. *philoxenon*—See Elders, word number 6 from 1 Timothy 3.
8. *philagathon*—loving what is good (people, things); Philippians 4:7,8 is the idea.
9. *sophrona*—See Elders, word number 4 from 1 Timothy 3.
10. *dikaion*—upright, just, righteous; living according to the laws of God and man and conforming to them.
11. *hosion*—devout, pleasing to God.
12. *egkrate*—self-controlled, disciplined.
13. *antechomenon*—holding to *the teaching* (this is what he learned) of the faithful word (faith-word or word of faith).

So that:

- By the *teaching exhort the healthy in faith* (this is what he gives);
- By the *teaching*...Convince the Contradicting.

14. Family requirements:
Husband of one wife, v. 6—i.e., totally committed to the one woman in his life;
Have faithful children *(pistos)* believing (v. 6);
Not accused of incorrigibility *(asotias)* or undisciplined *(anupotakta)*.

7. A MAN'S RESPONSIBILITY

Leading each man—married or unmarried—to a maximum grasp of the concepts of husbandly responsibility and love, fatherly understanding and authority, and how to fulfill these two roles.

The many strained marriage relationships in our world today is the tragic realization of two facts:

First, our adversary, the devil, hates wholesome, healthy marriages.
Second, many do not fully understand what the Word has to say about the establishment of a quality marriage relationship.

No matter what a man's current marital status, it is crucial that he realize the truth the Bible has to offer about the subject of marriage.

The following outline derives from a message that illustrates the strong parallelism drawn between Jesus' relationship with the Church, and our relationships with our spouses.

HOW TO CREATE A LOVABLE WOMAN
EPHESIANS 5:22—33

Introduction:

This is a message for men about how to relate to women; essentially, *the* woman in our lives. There are three different kinds of men—each has different reasons why this message is important:

- Those who are married—we need to hear this teaching to enrich our husbandly skills.

- Those who *have* been married but have gone through the pain and disappointment of separation or divorce. It is necessary to understand principles that will assist you when the Lord redemptively works new possibilities for you in terms of marriage.
- And those who have never been married—these are vital principles to learn now.

I. A word about divine order.

Take a minute and look at the introduction of divine order into an imperfect world. Although this has to be lived out in the context of imperfect people, we have to decide whether we are willing to trust the overruling grace of God working through His system of government. This spans the spectrum from world governments to governing our homes and relationships: God has an ordained order. Now, in this one area of government— the husband/wife relationship—let us look at God's design.

II. The difficulty of submission (v. 22).
A. Submit to whom?

The Bible says women are to submit to their *own* husbands. We need to understand that women are not automatically, generically submitted to men. Men have no inherent authority over any woman other than in terms of their marriages. Illustration: While I have a role of authority over women who work on our church staff, this is not because of gender; rather, it is because I am the senior in authority of the church staff.

- If you recognize where the arena of authority lies, then you will understand it has nothing to do with gender. In terms of husband/wife relationships, a woman only has an inherent responsibility to submit to one man: her own husband.

B. Study of Greek word for "submission."
Hupotasso —meaning "to set in order." The concept of this order is for everybody to win.

1. It is a military word. It assures the troops go out in a right order. They are ranked and structured in such a way that everybody knows what to do to protect one another, so no lives are lost, and the enemy is defeated.
2. Another easily understood picture is football. If each player

goes where he is supposed to and does what he is supposed to do, then the team will win. That's *hupotasso*—submission.

Submission is when things are arranged so one person calls the shots, as in the quarterback or commanding officer, so we move together and everybody wins. Submission has to do with *everybody* winning.

III. Authority and headship (vv. 23,24).

The concept of authority and responsibility relates to headship.

1. Prepare to accept authority and responsibility in your home. You must first decide that you want to be a complete man, and then concentrate on any areas that may need development.
2. How you relate to your wife also relates to the release of your own ministry. It affects authority and responsibility—authority in your life, in your home and the authority released through you in ministry.
3. Jesus models headship for us. It is directly related to His Saviorhood. "He is Savior of the body." Thus, laying down life gives the authority for headship. Our authority is to be derived from our loving care for our wives.

He is in charge. But the way Jesus won lordship in my life was not by demanding, but in loving and dying for me He invited and won my trust and submission.

Submitted to Jesus we receive the following things; things we are to model toward our wives:

- **Release and forgiveness.** He releases and sets free. He does not hold responsible for what has been done or said in the past. He lets it go. No past record—unconditional acceptance. Husbands: do this with your wife.
- **Understanding and provision.** He gives us the time to grow, and provides for us in the meantime. Model this, men. Also revealing Jesus' creativity and ministry as He develops His beloved into the maximum possible of their personhood.

Wives have every right to expect the same thing from their husbands: release and forgiveness, understanding and provision, creativity and ministry. Every way you relate to her helps to develop these things in her, but it flows through you through the power of Jesus working in you.

IV. The power in self-giving (v. 25).
A. Self-giving is the key.
"Love your wives" is a present imperative; a continuous command. It says to keep on loving your wife the way Christ loves the Church.

The terminology "Creating a lovable woman" is appropriate because *that* is what Jesus has done. He is the Creator of this new creation called the Church, His Bride. He is building that Church into a beautiful, lovable people unto Himself.

B. Relationship has a cost.
Jesus says, "If you will learn to relate to your wife the way I relate to the Church, you can create a lovable woman the same way I have." But it costs us just as it cost Jesus. Scripture makes clear that we will never become mature men until we learn to relate from a self-giving perspective.

This is why the Bible makes it clear that if a man does not rule his home correctly, he cannot qualify for significant leadership or influence in the Body of Christ.

V. Self-giving leads to sanctification (v. 26).
A. How self-giving works.
Self-giving is a purging, beautifying process. This is the concept of sanctification. Sanctification develops "beautiful people"; it sets them apart for a special purpose, establishing "the beauty of holiness" in their lives.

It is important to recognize that God's holiness is *therapeutic* in its goal. Holiness is not just an ethical standard; it is healing. By His inward working of holiness, Jesus is bringing us toward perfection; developing a liberty in us where we learn how to live under His authority—unto His releasing. If your wife truly is being brought unto perfection by the way you relate to her, more beauty and "release" of personhood will be happening in her all the time.

B. Sanctification through the washing of water by the Word.
Jesus sanctifies and cleanses us "with the washing of water by the Word." This relates to the *action* of the Word of God.

Applied to our marriages, we put this into action by how we talk with and respond to our wives, as well as by tone of voice. If the purifying and beautifying process of Jesus in our lives comes through His application of the Word to us, the parallel applies in relationship to our wives.

Look at Jesus' use of timing. He never "jumps down anyone's throat." He speaks when the time is best suited for maximum effect: sometimes immediately, but without harshness; other times later, after the situation had taken place. He was always straightforward and uncompromising, but compassionate and understanding. We can learn from this modeling He gives in the way He treats *His* bride.

VI. Present a glorious Church (v. 27).

1. Jesus is the One doing the work. He does not *command* a glorious Church, but instead, *presents* it to Himself by the things He does to that Church. He does take authority and speak assertively toward us, even to the issue of commands. But His commands are all issued within the context of His readiness to die in order to release us to live in obedience to those commands.
2. The Greek word for "spot" is *spilon*. The word "spill" derives from it. Another fascinating word is *rutida*, the word for "wrinkle." It is something that has become drawn together or taut.

In presenting our wives as not having "spot or wrinkle," consider for a moment the actual facial appearance of a woman. A woman whose face appears rather drawn and taut may not be merely the product of age. It may be a result of unhappiness, or not being loved the way she needs to be loved. Nothing is wrong with wrinkles. We have all seen women who are just aglow, and wrinkles seem to give another point of reflection for the radiance. *Rutida,* however, describes a tautness that comes not from wrinkles themselves, but as a product of inconsideration and thoughtlessness.

VII. Nourishing and cherishing (vv. 28-30).
The word "nourish" means "feed," and "cherish" means "to care for tenderly." We would certainly not neglect our own bodies. These verses tell us to feed our wives (affection) and care for them tenderly (consideration).

One thing that feeds women, that most men are not sensitive to, is doing nice little things. The old song says "little things mean a lot." It is true, little treats, little times, cards, notes, an occasional flower—this is feeding and caring. Each of us thrive on something. Find out what your wife thrives on, then "nourish and cherish" her.

VIII. Establishing a new order (v. 31).

1. This text is more than a simple observation concerning marriage's physical union. That is a part, but is not the primary point. This verse applies to the idea of the immersion of two lives together completely at every human level—emotionally, mentally, attitudinally.
2. A new order and a new family is being established (leave par-

ents). This is saying: let no constrictions impose on your marriage's possibilities, regardless of previous family examples or relational experiences. This is not to spurn family or former relationships, but says: whatever limitations we inherit from past relationships are to now establish a new order.

Just as we were once of Adam's race, but Jesus established a new order when He came into our lives, so this verse points to leaving what is past to see a new order established in our marriages. There is the promise of a breaking of anything that has flowed into you; you are establishing a new home. Come to a total identification with each other—both yielding to this call. That is what "one flesh" means—my total identification with her—in total commitment, which will attract her response in kind.

IX. The mystery revealed (vv. 32,33).

Under a touch of the Holy Ghost, Paul says that this is a great mystery. A "mystery" is a great truth now open to be understood. Here is the gospel bringing light to the subject of marriage.

Every relationship is brought under review in the light of the gospel of Jesus. The same truth that gives us freedom from sin also gives us freedom in our marriage relationships.

Conclusion:

Such a relationship with our wives is possible. Because of Jesus' work and example toward the Church, His Bride, we learn how to relate properly to our spouses.

(Tape 1402 from Living Way Ministries is the message from which this outline was derived.)

8. A MAN OF INTEGRITY

Calling men toward building a circle of personal accountability, helping each one learn to live in transparent fellowship and biblically based commitment to integrity and trustworthiness in all relationships.

Integrity has all but fallen by the wayside as an issue in much of our culture. The attitude of "relativity" toward most action, and the erosion of personal and professional honesty in the marketplace have caused more than social decay—it has contributed to widespread decay of soul in men everywhere. Few topics are more worthy of our attention than how to become a man with an integrity of heart.

This outline focuses the subject of a man's integrity, showing:

- Stark biblical contrasts between those who have walked with integrity and those who have not.
- The importance of honesty in all areas of our human dealings.
- The dangers of "pet sins" that will eventually cause destruction in the heart of man unless a man allows them to be destroyed.

THE LEADER'S INTEGRITY: INTEGRITY OF HEART
GENESIS 20:1-6

Introduction:

A. What is the essence of "the power of a man or woman of God"?

Various qualities might be presumed as essential: Creative skills, leadership style, personal dynamism, intellectual grasp, prophetic vision, spiritual zeal, managerial ability, magnetic personality and supernatural gifts.

I want to discuss what I believe to be the most important.

B. What is the secret to success in leadership ministry?

Example: The supposition that "hours" totaled in Scripture and prayer may be the key. Of course, these are important, but I am persuaded that nothing exceeds the importance of cultivating "a heart of integrity."

C. This text introduces us to a reoccurring Old Testament idea.

The first occurrence is in this passage.

Abraham compromised because of fear. It is a curious fact that we are taught "integrity" in a setting where a man of faith has violated honesty.

I. The foundational insight.

The interpretive principle: "Law of First Usage." The first occurrence in the Bible of a concept usually established the idea in a way that consistently follows throughout the Scriptures.

A. God's confrontation with Abimelech and his response (v. 5).

B. The Lord's reply, and the principle this reveals (v. 6).

God is patiently understanding where our ignorance produces innocent failure or Lack of wisdom.

GOD SAID: "The reason I'm here to stop you is because I know you are acting without knowledge or without compromise of your own understanding."

C. The inverse/opposite is also contained within this concept.

God holds us responsible to walk in the light of understanding/revelation we have.

When integrity has been violated from the outset, God will not intervene until judgment eventually accrues. GOD ONLY WARNS/INSTRUCTS/CORRECTS where His intervention is allowed by reason of the honest quest of the individual to walk in His way.

This story makes it dramatically clear that possibly no more essential trait or value is to be sought and maintained in a leader's life than "integrity of heart."

II. A dynamic word.

A word study of "INTEGRITY" unfolds ideas that can help us recognize HOW "integrity" is to be maintained.

A. Old Testament: "thom"—idea of "completeness/whole."

In mathematics, we speak of "whole numbers" as contrasted with "fractions," where one number is divided by another. Integrity of heart describes that attitude of heart that disallows "dividing" FULL HONESTY WITH GOD OR WITH ONESELF, through supposedly "minor" deviations.

This is done through:

Rationalizing—providing an excuse to myself for compromise.

Self-justification—arguing that "my case is an exception," or "God doesn't take this seriously," or "He accepts my compromise."

B. A practical example.

We have an inner correcting mechanism in the Holy Spirit. *"And do not grieve the Holy Spirit"* (Eph. 4:30).

Ephesians 4:17-32:

- Full range of verbal purity, attitudinal constancy;
- Refusal to "flavor" the truth;
- Refusal of sexual indulgences of any kind;
- Refusal to give place to anger, unforgiveness.
  "Nor give place to the devil" (v. 27).

III. Dynamic obedience to principle.

A. David, a man after God's heart—an example of integrity.

Listen to David's words:

1. *"Teach me Your way, O Lord; I will walk in Your truth; UNITE MY HEART to fear Your name"* (Ps. 86:11; emphasis mine). NOTE two steps:

- I WILL be teachable.
- I WILL be committed to WALK in what you show me. THE RESULT: THUS, LORD, You can "keep my heart in one piece."
2. *"Keep my soul, and deliver me; let me not be ashamed [embarrassed], for I put my trust in You. LET INTEGRITY AND UPRIGHTNESS PRESERVE ME, for I wait for You [i.e., listen for your voice]"* (Ps. 25:20,21; emphasis mine).

Under David's leadership, the boundaries of Israel were extended to their widest limits. Incapable to patrol boundaries, the question rises, "How can I PRESERVE my kingdom?"

He prays: *"YOU, LORD must preserve me."*

IV. Tragedy following disobedience to principle.
A. Solomon's pathway to solve problems on his own.

Solomon faces the same problem David did in defending boundaries. His choice of diplomatic solutions through **alliances** is a stark contrast to how David handled his dilemma.

With each treaty comes a new princess to seal the political bond. Jerusalem becomes filled with the idols brought by these "treaties" designed to assure personal/professional security.

B. Remember Solomon's original prayer:

"Therefore, Lord God of Israel, now keep what You promised Your servant David my father" (1 Kings 8:25).

God's response: *"I have heard your prayer...I have consecrated this house which you have built to put My name there forever, and My eyes and My heart will be there PERPETUALLY. NOW if you walk before Me as your father David walked, IN INTEGRITY OF HEART and in UPRIGHTNESS,...then I will establish the throne of your kingdom"* (1 Kings 9:3-5; emphasis mine).

Concept: All of us are "house builders"—We are building FAMILIES, CONGREGATIONS, MINISTRIES.

The key to a HOME, a CHURCH, a MINISTRY that LASTS (i.e., "that God will perpetuate") is wrapped up in a will to perpetually sustain **a heart of integrity.**

HOW?

V. The pathway to obedience.
A. The plural form of "integrity" (thom)—THUMMIM.

God has given the picture for our maintaining a heart of integrity.

The high priest's breastplate: urim and thummim.

No one knows exactly what it was made of, but we know how and when the urim and thummim was "consulted."

"And you shall put in the breastplate of judgment [i.e., decision making unto a divinely guided verdict], the Urim and the Thummim, and they shall be over Aaron's HEART" (Exod. 28:30).

Example: In a quest for a pure priesthood, God's people were instructed to wait *"till a priest could consult with the Urim and the Thummim"* (Neh. 7:65; Ezra 2:63).

Rabbinical literature suggests how this was actually done. By using the Urim (lights) and the Thummim (wholeness), could this be a combined "manifestation" joined to an "inner witness"?

Whatever the case, a clear picture is given to us of the importance of a leader's maintenance of a heart of integrity.

B. The New Testament word: "peace."

Not only "ceasing hostilities," "private solitude" or "emotional relief," BUT:

1. Inner confirmation of the Holy Spirit, uncluttered by any quest for self-justification or rationalization.
2. Private confidence pursuant upon laying bear the heart before God.
3. "Nothing between my soul and the Savior."

Warning: Solomon's demise teaches us:

1. By seeking conventional wisdom as the means for securing his boundaries, he filled Jerusalem with pagan ways.
2. He did not set out to have 1,000 wives. We all have the capacity for gradually accumulating carnal tolerances, such as unforgiveness and concessions to flesh.

Conclusion:

Men will often give themselves areas of indulgence where they knowingly violate integrity—but only on what they would consider the smallest scale. These are "pet sins" that are very real, though a man may feel that their danger is restrained. They are similar to keeping a small snake in a cage on a shelf and occasionally taking it out to play with and stroke it, but then returning it to its hidden location and thinking all is under control. The truth of the matter is that though the snake may be able to be tamed, the serpent (that sin) cannot.

"Their poison is like the poison of a serpent; they are like the deaf cobra that stops its ear, which will not heed the voice of the charmers, charming ever so skillfully" (Ps. 58:4,5).

There is no way to charm the serpent; he will deceive, and our hearts are uniquely deceivable.

"The heart is deceitful above all things, and desperately wicked; who can know it?" (Jer. 17:9).

THE ANSWER:

"Search me, O God, and know my heart; try me, and know my anxieties [troubled thoughts]; and see if there is any wicked way in me, and lead me in the way everlasting" (Ps. 139:23,24).

(For more information about this resource, order Living Way Ministries JWH album "Honest to God," and Pastor Hayford's book A Man's Integrity.)

9. A MAN'S PERSPECTIVE

Developing each man's perspective of himself as a viable agent of the kingdom of God; teaching how to receive and minister the fullness of the Holy Spirit, and how to move in intercessory power and spiritual warfare.

When we have a clouded perspective, we limit our "becoming" what God intends for us. If we view ourselves as holding our *primary* citizenship in *this* physical world, rather than perceiving our primary citizenship as spiritual—in the heavenlies—we lose the ability to move with real power and clarity regarding life issues.

The following brief outline is an example of how to grasp this concept by addressing the topic of true spirituality. It helps to bring into proper perspective the reality of the spiritual world and the frailty of the physical world. It is important to understand:

- The twist in popular thinking;
- And the power of God's living Word.

Clear perspective develops the appropriate mind-set to grasp the concepts of true spirituality, and enables us to see our viable role in the kingdom of God.

TRUE SPIRITUALITY
EPHESIANS 1:15-23

Introduction:

The concept of "true spirituality" is not a trite saying or a self-righteous judgment. It is a pursuit for reality and dimension in our spiritual walk. We need to examine the basic factors that constitute the strength of believers so we will be more than merely plastic ornaments in a stained-glassed sanctuary. We must not only exhibit the beauty of true spirituality, but experience its quality and depth as well. Jesus Christ is developing true people. He is the author of "Humanity II"—those who are being born into real life by His resurrection power.

We, as believers, can live apart from the bondage under which mankind presently exists. There is a possibility of our living NOW in the dimensions of His triumph—this is Kingdom living. It is important to remember that His triumph is in life, not in death. His victory was at calvary—He slew sin and defeated Satan (see Col. 2:14), but His **triumph** is manifested in His resurrection.

The objective of this message is to point out the basic principle that makes it possible to live in the **physical world a life of spiritual achievement.**

I. The most real world in the world.
The basic frustration that limits every man in his quest for fulfillment is the

result of his trying to start from a premise that the real world is the physical one. If by real we mean the "ultimate," the "original" or the "primary," logic tells us that the physical world is not the real world. Although some adjust to this premise with varying degrees of success, the evidence argues for acknowledging a spiritual basis to everything around us. God tells us how to start:

A. The Word.

1. John 1:1-3 tells us the Word was in existence prior to everything else. Genesis 1 states God speaks everything into being. Hebrews 11:1,3 declares His Word as the foundation to the universe, and Colossians 1:17 and Hebrews 1:3 tell us that the Word is all that sustains the whole Creation in its present state. Second Peter 3:7-14 describes the end of this present order of things in the world we call "real," and Revelation 21 and 22 give a glimpse of the *true* world that shall appear.

2. To help man from the dilemma of his frustration, the "Word" took on human form (see John 1:14) to accomplish two things:

- To provide a present relief from mere existence (see John 10:10);
- And to lead into the **true** world that shall rise beyond the ashes of this one (see John 7:39,40,44,47,53).

B. The warp.

This is the twist in our thinking. Contrary to the Word, we try to figure out our own way to solve the problems that are created by the vacuum inside us. But the Word spoke to us about that: Luke 12:13-32 makes clear that spiritual beings cannot be satisfied, EVER, with material attempts at an answer. Consider this:

1. The living dead trying to come alive with the application of death (see Jude 19; Jas. 3:15). These are those who operate only on the level of the knowledge of this world. They are "sensual"—coping with situations only with the five senses of this world. Being completely spiritually blind, they open themselves up to the spiritual work of darkness in their lives.

2. The newly alive trying to sustain life drawing on death's resources (see 1 Cor. 3:1-3; Gal. 3:3). Though they are redeemed, they continue to handle situations based upon the knowledge they have of the world.

3. The fully alive who learn to live in the resource of the Word (see Rom. 12:1,2; John 7:30-39). When life is truly transformed, it changes both thoughts and actions.

II. The most real life in the world:

1. Is born by the Word—John 3:3,5; 1 Peter 1:23. Faith is conceived by the Word (see Rom. 10:17), and the statement of its truth brings life (vv. 9,10).
2. Is sustained by the Word—Matthew 4:4 is more than a recommendation to read the Bible; it is a statement about man's true life source and supply.
3. It walks in the pathway outlined by the Word—Psalm 19:7-10. It has learned that God's handbook is beneficial, not confining; enriching, not diminishing.
4. It speaks the Word—Matthew 17:20. Just as it was "spoken" into life by the Word, the most real life learns it has the capacity to speak in the authority of the life given by the "Word" (see John 1:12; Matt. 28:18-20).

Conclusion:
This is more than mere "witnessing." These are the ones who have been resurrected with the new life given by the King (who gives it because He is the Lord of resurrected living).
   They are learning:

- "The hope of His calling";
- "The riches of the glory of His inheritance";
- "The exceeding greatness of His power."

   True spiritual life is that life that has heard the Word...the written Word and the Living Word who—*"declared to be the Son of God with power...by the resurrection from the dead"* (Rom. 1:4).
   "Therefore lay aside all filthiness and overflow of wickedness, and receive with meekness the implanted word, which is able to save your souls" (Jas. 1:21). All **life begins** with the Word engrafted into your inner life. And all **life proceeds** through the dynamic of that life increasing in you.

   (More resources may obtained on tape series SC005 from Living Way Ministries.)

10. A GIFTED MAN

Teaching each man the value of his gifting and vocation, and the significance of his role in the workplace as a man born of God and appointed to penetrate his world with the life and love of Christ.
   Each of us, regardless of vocation, have areas of distinct gifting. We

must learn to be people who are open to allowing God's gifting to fully penetrate our hearts and lives, and then as a result be poured out on those around us.

This message points out an interesting similarity between the wise men and their encounters as they search for the new King, and us, as we gain understanding of how the Creator's gifts work in us. As we understand this we discover:

- We are given gifts for the purpose of delivering them, rather than retaining them exclusively for our own benefit.
- We will be changed as we become open and available to the working of the gifts within us.

A GIFTED MAN
ROMANS 12

Introduction:

God has created gifts, traits of design in each person. The gifts mentioned here are each resident in every person to some degree.

The world will try to maneuver and control the use of our gifts to its own deceitful purposes. We can learn to function in these gifts as we open ourselves to the Lord's purposes in us.

As a parallel to God's wanting us to function in our gifting, we will first observe perhaps the most famous "gift givers" in the Bible—the wise men.

I. The wise men, our example—Matthew 2:1-12.

Look at the parallel between the wise men and us. Four things stand out:

A. They were worshipers (vv. 1,2).

They came to worship. The star, mentioned in the book of Numbers, signaled the arrival of a world deliverer—King of the Jews. They believed God's Word and set out to worship.

We must recognize that the wise men had faith to believe a miracle was occurring. An important thing to understand about miracles is that after one has occurred it still requires faith on our part to believe. The wise men's faith brought them to a place of worship.

Worship is the foundation for the release of all we are made to be.

B. They encountered obstacles (vv. 3-8).

Immediately the world spirit, as seen in Herod, tried to manipulate and deceive to *its* advantage. Herod was not about to let a new king into his domain. He craftily tried to undo what the Spirit of God had set in motion, not only in the world, but also in the wise men. *All movement toward a man's "ministering" will be confronted by the adversary.*

C. They were gift givers (v. 11).

Their response indicates the wise men were moved upon more deeply than they had anticipated. They had *planned* a certain gift, but then were so greatly affected by the power of God's presence, "they...*opened their treasures*"—laying them before the Lord. The Holy Spirit wants to expand our gift-developing capacities.

D. They were changed (v. 12).

They were divinely visited and "they departed...another way." What a picture! May we depart *differently than we came*—man changed because of his encounter with Jesus.

II. The gifts—Romans 12:3-8.

Romans 12:3 is not a call to think too little of ourselves, but to think "soberly" (i.e., humbly and clear-mindedly). Humility is the forthright and full acknowledgment of what God has placed in us, born out of a spirit that is come into the security of life in Christ. Qualities and capabilities we have are gifts; they are not our identity. In contrast, a man gripped by pride, arrogance, presumption or conceit is a man who has made his gifting his identity. But God made us who we are; and faith-filled, grateful-for-His-gifts-in-me humility is the proper acknowledgment of these enablements.

Verses 6-8 list the gifts that are given by God the Father. Every person has gifts given by God's creative work in him. Further, gifts from the Son of God are distributed to those who open up to Him. The same is true with the gifts of the Holy Spirit. The Creator, however, in a unique display of His mercy and grace, has started by giving everyone "a measure of faith."

Faith means there is a capacity from out of the realm of the invisible for giftings to come from the Father, ready to function in lives that are willing to use them. God has given us a capacity to respond to His work in us; a capacity to respond to what we have not yet seen. We have the confidence that the living God who has created us has purpose, destiny, meaning, fulfillment and direction, and is going to work those things through us.

Most of the seven basic giftings in verses 6-8 are, to some degree, latent within each of us. Yet, our creative individuality reveals some giftings as more prominent, or manifested more frequently through one individual than is another. As we are open to that flow, each gifting will flow through us as the Lord's will.

A. Prophecy.

This occurs as men recognize it is within their capacity when they speak to others for God's Word to become alive through them.

Peter explained Joel's prophecy, saying when the Lord pours out His Spirit, all those who receive will prophesy (see Acts 2:14-17). Expect this!

In 1 Corinthians 14:3,4, Paul defines prophecy as words that comfort, that stir up, that build up, encourage and are from the Lord. Be available to this!

In 1 Peter 4:10,11, Peter calls us to recognize that we are God's mouthpieces. Talk like this—responsibly!

We have mystified so much of the ordinary workings of God's creative grace that we do not recognize the fruit when it is being born.

B. Ministry.

Ministering is an act of serving. This word used here is the source of the word "deacon"—someone called to serve. A key concept in ministry is actually taking what we have and applying it to a situation—making it usable and relevant, whether laymen or pastors.

All of us are capable of valuable abilities, but we too often minimize ours. As the wise men, let us come and open our treasure before Jesus and say, "Jesus, I want You to use this."

The world either tells us we have too little or too much; mocking God's gifts in us, or playing upon our talents—tempting us to pride and selfishness. Let us acknowledge the gifts God has placed within us and open them to *His purpose*.

C. Teaching.

Second Tim. 2:2 says, "And the things that you have heard from me among many witnesses." Four "generations" are mentioned here as truth is communicated—man to man—one spiritual generation to the next. We think of teaching in terms of a professor demanding the attention of a large group, but the practicality of a daddy teaching his child how to think about the world we live in is teaching just the same. But then, put value on the fact *you* have something to teach.

D. Exhortation.

This literally means "encouraging" (see Heb. 12:12). "Therefore strengthen the hands which hang down." This refers to strengthening people—especially the Body of Christ—the Lord's people. How we need the sensitivity of people to lift others up—to stand by them and encourage when tough times come. It can be as practical as praying for someone, taking a moment to listen to someone who is hurting, making a phone call to a guy God brings to mind. Do it!

E. Giving.

The idea of giving relates to more than just giving things. As givers, let's associate ourselves with the gift—and with the recipient of that gift. With each gift let us give something of ourselves—transmitting or imparting *life* as well as helping and caring.

This act of giving a gift is made "spiritual" as we call upon God's resources and abundance to enable this fuller dimension of giving.

F. Leading.

Literally means "standing in front." This refers to more than the pas-

tor. There is a practical application to us all. Leading refers to the person
who steps away from the crowd and moves forward. He is the first to
respond when there is need for somebody to say something; the first to
offer himself when something needs to be done; the first person available
when there is a need for care or assistance. These people are servants—yet
they are leaders. "Leading" is being quick to move in when you see a need.

G. Mercy.

Let it be with cheerfulness. Be glad and ready to show mercy.

Two important ideas:

- A person who shows mercy is a person who is more concerned
  with people's recovery than he is with their correctness. In other
  words, people need somebody to help them out of what they are
  experiencing, rather than somebody saying, "shape up."
- Mercy is more concerned with helping than with its own status.
  Avoid the Pharisee attitude that distances itself from those who
  don't meet our higher expectations. We need to reach, love and lift.

Conclusion:

Prayer: God make us to be "wise men"; men who open our treasures, invite Your help and employ Your wisdom in dispersing
and transmitting the gifts you want us to see given to those with
whom we come into contact daily. Help us to remember gifts are
not so much things we **have** as things we **deliver**—like the wise
men. Gifts are not to hold on to, but to distribute—to transmit to
others. You have given the gifts—present and ready to be used.
Now we invite You to direct our "gift giving" as ones whose lives
have been forever changed through our encounter with You.

*(This outline is derived from tapes 2098, 2116 and 2134, obtain-
able from Living Way Ministries. Note also Pastor Hayford's book
A Man's Worship and Witness.)*

More Ways for Men to Worship His Majesty

The Power-to-Become Book Series for Men

This series covers practical, life-transforming topics geared to men–yet gladly read by women as well. Each book in the series includes a dynamic, practical study of biblical truth; guidelines for personal or group study and application; and pointers for walking with God day-to-day.

Six Book Paperback Box Set · ISBN 07852.7798G

A Man's Starting Place

A Man's Confidence

A Man's Walk with God

A Man's Image and Identity

A Man's Integrity

A Man's Worship and Witness

Men in Worship

Men in Worship is a live, fully participatory worship experience. Listen and join in as over 1,500 men sing out and lift the name of Jesus. Led by Pastor Hayford, these men will wake you to the power of worship and affirm your identity as a man of God.

Cassette · SPCN 00768.00664
CD · SPCN 00768.00662

Ask for these resources at your local Christian bookseller.

Fan the Flame with These Resources from Jack Hayford

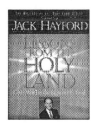
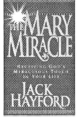

Resources for Cutting Edge Leaders

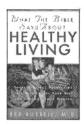

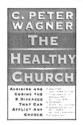

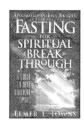

Setting Your Church Free

Neil T. Anderson and Charles Mylander

Spiritual battles can affect entire churches as well as individuals. *Setting Your Church Free* shows pastors and church leaders how they can apply the powerful principles from *Victory Over the Darkness* to lead their churches to freedom.

Hardcover • ISBN 08307.16556

What the Bible Says About Healthy Living

Rex Russell, M.D.

Learn three biblical principles that will help you improve your physical— and spiritual—health. This book gives you practical, workable steps to improve your health and overall quality of life.

Paperback • ISBN 08307.18583

The Healthy Church

C. Peter Wagner

When striving for health and growth of a church, we often overlook things that are killing us. If we can detect and counteract these diseases we can grow a healthy, Christ-directed church.

Hardcover • ISBN 08307.18346

Fasting for Spiritual Breakthrough

Elmer L. Towns

This book gives you the biblical reasons for fasting, and introduces you to nine biblical fasts— each designed for a specific physical and spiritual outcome.

Paperback • ISBN 08307.18397

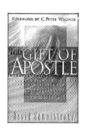

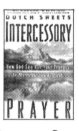

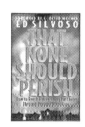

Intercessory Prayer

Dutch Sheets

Find inspiration to reach new levels of prayer, the courage to pray for the "impossible" and the persistence to see your prayers through to completion.

"Of all the books on prayer I have read, none compares to Intercessory Prayer!" –C. Peter Wagner

Hardcover • ISBN 08307.18885

That None Should Perish

Ed Silvoso

Ed Silvoso shows that dramatic things happen when we pray for people. Learn the powerful principles of "prayer evangelism" and how to bring the gospel to your community, reaching your entire city for Christ.

Paperback • ISBN 08307.16904

The Voice of God

Cindy Jacobs

Cut through confusion and see how prophecy can be used in any church. You'll get a clear picture of biblical prophecy and how an individual can exercise this spiritual gift to edify the church.

Paperback • ISBN 08307.17730

The Gift of Apostle

David Cannistraci

Find out why God has given the Church apostles—leaders with a clear mission to mobilize and unify the church—and see what the Bible says about the apostolic gift for today's church.

Hardcover • ISBN 08307.18451

Ask for these resources at your local Christian bookstore.

Regal
A Division of Gospel Light

Continuing Education for Church Leaders

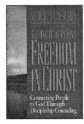

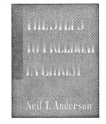

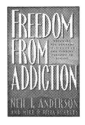

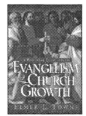

Helping Others Find Freedom in Christ

Neil T. Anderson

Help people become better connected to God with "discipleship counseling." Neil Anderson gives you clear guidelines for leading others through the steps outlined in his previous books, *Victory Over the Darkness* and *The Bondage Breaker.*

Paperback • ISBN 08307.17862

Video Training Program
• SPCN 85116.00949

The Steps to Freedom in Christ

Neil T. Anderson

This spiritual and personal inventory allows a person to help others or themselves break free from addictive and debilitating habits and beliefs.

The Steps to Freedom in Christ Guidebook • ISBN 08307.18508

Freedom from Addiction

Neil T. Anderson and Mike and Julia Quarles

Here's a Christ-centered model for recovery that has already helped thousands of people break free from alcoholism, drug addiction and other addictive behaviors.

Hardcover • ISBN 08307.17579

Evangelism and Church Growth

Elmer L. Towns

In one volume you get everything from Sunday School lesson plans to suggestions for launching a capital fund drive. Dr. Elmer Towns pulls together the most up to date, definitive work on evangelism and church growth available today.

Hardcover • ISBN 08307.18575

Turning Vision into Action

George Barna

George Barna lays out powerful how-to action steps to implement the vision that God has for your ministry—and how you can bring it to life both in your church and at home.

Hardcover • ISBN 08307.18524

Evangelism that Works

George Barna

Get an up-to-the-minute view of the unchurched in America, and about successful efforts to reach them. Through interviews and surveys, Barna provides feedback on methods of soul-winning that are working.

Paperback • ISBN 08307.17765

Resurrecting Hope

John Perkins with Jo Kadlecek

A dramatic profile of 10 churches that are working positively and successfully in the city. These churches provide a powerful model of hope for any ministry.

Hardcover • ISBN 08307.17757

Healing America's Wounds

John Dawson

This reconciler's handbook provides a way to deal with sexual conflict, political polarization, divisive Christians, racial tension and more.

Paperback • ISBN 08307.16939

Ask for these resources at your local Christian bookstore.

Regal
A Division of Gospel Light